Blackstone's Guide to the

LAND REGISTRATION ACT 2002

Mark — For Charlotte and Emma

Robert — For Alexander Elliott Abbey

Blackstone's Guide to the

LAND REGISTRATION ACT 2002

Robert M. Abbey, BA, Solicitor

Legal Practice Course Director, University of Westminster
Consultant with Russell Jones and Walker Solicitors, London WC1

and

Mark B. Richards, LLB, Solicitor

Senior Lecturer in Law, University of Westminster

OXFORD
UNIVERSITY PRESS

OXFORD

UNIVERSITY PRESS

Great Clarendon Street, Oxford OX2 6DP

Oxford University Press is a department of the University of Oxford.
It furthers the University's objective of excellence in research, scholarship,
and education by publishing worldwide in

Oxford New York

Auckland Bangkok Buenos Aires Cape Town Chennai
Dar es Salaam Delhi Hong Kong Istanbul Karachi Kolkata
Kuala Lumpur Madrid Melbourne Mexico City Mumbai Nairobi
São Paulo Shanghai Taipei Tokyo Toronto

Oxford is a registered trade mark of Oxford University Press
in the UK and in certain other countries

Published in the United States
by Oxford University Press Inc., New York

© Robert Abbey and Mark Richards 2002

The moral rights of the authors have been asserted

Database right Oxford University Press (maker)

First published 2002

Crown copyright material is reproduced with the permission
of the Controller of Her Majesty's Stationery Office

British Library Cataloguing in Publication Data

Data available

Library of Congress Cataloging in Publication Data

Data available

ISBN 0-19-925796-5

1 3 5 7 9 10 8 6 4 2

Typeset by Style Photosetting Ltd
Printed in Great Britain
on acid-free paper by
Antony Rowe Ltd, Chippenham

Contents — Summary

Contents

Table of Cases

Table of Statutes

Chapter 1

An Introduction to the Act and its Ancestry

1.1   AN INTRODUCTION

The preamble to the Land Registry Act 1862 states that '. . . it is expedient to give certainty to the title to real estates and to facilitate the proof thereof and also to render the dealing with land more simple and economical . . .'. More than one hundred and forty years later, it remains true that the aims of the system for the conveyancing of registered land should be reliability, simplicity and that the process be economic. These are the aims that underpin the drive for the complete registration of land throughout England and Wales. These are the reasons why the Law Commission and the Land Registry have called for reforms. They are also three of the main reasons for the passing of the Land Registration Act 2002 ('the Act'): certainty, simplicity and the ability to be economic. To that could be joined the need to create a framework for electronic conveyancing ('e-conveyancing') and the wish to reform the law of adverse possession as it relates to registered land. By s 122, the 1862 Act has been repealed and the registrar now has custody of records of title made under that original Act.

   The system of land law that exists in England and Wales is the result of an evolutionary process over many centuries. This has meant that the system of unregistered land law has developed in a piecemeal way with legislation being made when the need arose. As Fox LJ said in *Ashburn Anstalt v Arnold* [1989] Ch 1 at 26D, 'In matters relating to the title to land, certainty is of prime importance'.

Piecemeal development, however, creates uncertainty. As a result there was a clear need for reform as long ago as 1862. That need for reform has accelerated with the passage of time and it has been boosted by the demands of modern home ownership. In effect, this change in the nature of how our population has been housed has made new and complex demands of the system of land law. This clamour for reform has come to fruition with the passing of the Act. It has been the joint efforts of the Law Commission and the Land Registry that have made these reforms possible, however, and so a brief review of how the provisions of the Act were first considered and drafted is set out below.

1.2   THE 1998 LAW COMMISSION REPORT

The Act is the end product of six years' joint work by the Law Commission and HM Land Registry. In September 1998 the Law Commission, with the assistance of the Land Registry, issued a consultative document entitled *Land Registration for the Twenty First Century* (Law Com No 254, 1998) ('the 1998 Report') in which it put forward a blueprint for conveyancing over the next two to three decades. This was done largely because of three growing pressures: first, the growth in demand for electronic conveyancing, secondly the fact that current legislation is unclear and complicated, and thirdly because at least 80 per cent of all property titles are now registered. The intention of the Law Commission was (and is) that future developments should grow from this reality rather than the historical position that existed in 1925 when, of course, the majority of titles were unregistered.

Among the main recommendations in the 1998 Report, the following remain of particular interest to conveyancing practitioners:

(a)   the methods of protecting rights over land such as easements and covenants should be simplified and the strength of the protection enhanced;

(b)   the number and scope of overriding interests should be reduced with a view to increasing the security of registered titles;

(c)   there should be a review of the status and definition of estates rights and interests and where necessary these should be clarified;

(d)   the introduction of a rule-making power that will enable a system of electronic conveyancing to be introduced.

This last element was perhaps the most far-reaching proposal. The suggestion was for the early adoption of an automated registration system of title to land, of a system of electronic transfer and creation of rights. Transfers would take effect only by registration and the electronic system would contemplate this being done automatically by electronic means and with all the immediacy of a computerized system, ie e-conveyancing. (This methodology has been tested in the Canadian province of Ontario. The authorities in Ontario created a framework for land transactions within a computerized system called 'Teranet', see 'Automated Registration of Title to Land' *Computers and Law* October/November 1998, p 34).

The computerization of title records is not limited just to one Canadian province. The Land Registry in England and Wales has been converting all its records from the original paper-based system to one that is computerized. As at January 2000 the Land Registry held records of 17,814,640 registered titles of which 17,199,482 were computerized title records. The number of computerized titles therefore represents 96.5 per cent of all the title details at the Land Registry. Indeed in the Land Registry Annual Report and Accounts for 1999–2000 it was stated that they dealt with 373,073 first registration applications, 79,616 first registrations of leases, 191,823 transfers of part and 2,851,082 dealings with the whole of titles of registered land. On these figures first registrations were up by over 15 per cent while dealings with the whole of titles was up 11 per cent over the previous report figures. The Land Registry annual report for 2001 states that 'the percentage of titles in the land register now capable of electronic delivery is 96.78 per cent against a target of 96 per cent. All title plans capable of electronic delivery have now been scanned and made available through Land Registry Direct. The target for scanned pages of filed deeds of 11 million was achieved with 14.3 million being scanned — only 75.7 million pages to go!' This clearly demonstrates how the work of the Land Registry is increasing as more of the country submits to compulsory first registration and in particular how most if not all the records will be fully computerized shortly. The registry now deals with approximately 400,000 transactions every month via their on-line service mentioned above and called Land Registry Direct.

1.3   THE 2001 LAW COMMISSION REPORT AND ACT

The Land Registration Act 2002 represents the outcome of several years' joint work by the Law Commission and the Land Registry. The 1998 Report gave rise to another joint report — *Land Registration for the Twenty-First Century — a Conveyancing Revolution* Law Com No 271, 2001 ('the 2001 Report'). The 2001 Report built upon the terms of the 1998 Report. It also contained a draft Bill ('the Bill') and a detailed commentary on its provisions. The Bill contains extensive reforming provisions to the system of registered land conveyancing. It is indeed so extensive that it is not an overestimate to call the effect of the Bill revolutionary. When you recall that a revolution can be defined as a sudden or momentous change in a situation, then the 2001 Report clearly heralded a genuine revolution.

In the 2001 Report the Law Commission explains the principal changes to the law which the Bill will make and then goes on to provide a detailed commentary on the Bill and explains how it is intended to work. The Bill published with the 2001 Report is in effect the Bill that was subsequently presented to Parliament. Indeed, with one or two limited amendments, the Act that was eventually passed is very much the same as the Law Commission Bill.

On Tuesday 3 July 2001 the Land Registration Bill was introduced in the House of Lords by the Lord Chancellor, Lord Irvine of Lairg, for its second reading. *Hansard* reports the Lord Chancellor as saying of the Bill:

The Bill will have a direct impact on the lives of the millions of people who buy and sell property in England and Wales each year. It represents the culmination of the long process through which land registration has become the primary means of recording and guaranteeing title to land in England and Wales. It also marks a new departure, providing a framework for electronic conveyancing which, through comparatively minor alterations in the law, will change the way in which conveyancing services are provided and make a major contribution to the Government's determination to improve the house buying process. The Bill will wholly replace the Land Registration Act 1925. It will lead to more land and more interests in land being protected by registration. Some valuable interests will for the first time be registrable voluntarily. The scope of compulsory registration will also be increased, in particular by bringing most leases, and therefore most commercial property transactions, within its reach. Commercial conveyancing must now use the cumbersome and complex unregistered law, and is excluded from the benefits and protections of registration, now and as they will be developed by the Bill. Extending registration will also enable the registry to improve the transparency of the property market . . .

For the first time, all land belonging to the Crown will become registrable, including land underlying territorial waters. What the register tells us about the land will be extended and improved, most notably by reducing the number and scope of interests that can impose burdens without appearing on the register. The benefits of the registered system will be extended. The procedures protecting the rights of third parties over land will be simplified and strengthened. The protection which registration offers to registered owners against squatters will be improved.

Lord Irvine concluded by saying:

. . . the Bill forms part of a comprehensive programme for the delivery of a thoroughgoing modernisation in registration law and in conveyancing services. It is the best kind of law reform: clarifying principles, reforming practices and making the law simpler and more accessible. But above all this is a practical Bill. It will make home buying and selling quicker, simpler and cheaper and will make a real difference to people's lives.

This is in effect the modern inheritance of the preamble to the Act of 1862, land registration that is simple, quick, and economic.

The Bill was taken to Parliament and passed through both Houses in a surprisingly swift manner, receiving the Royal Assent on 26 February 2002. The Act will be summarized in the following chapter. E-conveyancing, introduced by the Act, will also be summarized in chapter 2. However, in essence the fundamental aim of the Bill, and hence the Act, is focused closely upon making e-conveyancing a reality. The objective set out below is to enable an effective system of electronic dealing with land by ensuring the register is a completely accurate record of the state of the title of the land. This is so that it will be possible for conveyancing practitioners to investigate title to land on-line. The Land Registry's programme to develop and pilot a totally re-engineered system of conveyancing for England and Wales has been awarded over £1.5 million under the Government 'Invest to Save' Budget initiative, announced on 20 March 2002 by the Treasury. When announcing the award the Land Registry said that 'the aim of the electronic conveyancing programme is to introduce, over the next five to ten years, a radical overhaul of the systems for buying, selling and registering property in England and Wales. The opportunity which technology provides will be used to re-engineer the process.' The indication of a time scale is interesting. At best e-conveyancing will be with us in 2007 and at worst by 2012. Either way it seems it will be with us sooner or later. This special funding will be used to design, build, and introduce the proposed new system of conveyancing. The Land Registry intends to develop the framework, in consultation with others (who they describe as being key stakeholders in the process), with a view to its implementation nationally.

The 1925 legislation (as amended) covering registered land is said by the Law Commission to:

> . . . be both badly drafted and lacking in clarity. It is also very complicated. Not only are there the 148 sections of the Act, but there are also several hundred rules made under it. There is no clear division between what is in the Act and what is found in the rules. The land registration system has been made to work very effectively, but this has often been in spite of rather than because of its legislative structure. There is an obvious need for clear modern legislation.

The need has been addressed by the 2002 Act.

1.4 THE OBJECTIVE OF THE ACT

The fundamental objective of the 2002 Act is that, under the system of electronic dealing with land that it seeks to generate, the register should be a complete and accurate reflection of the state of the title of the land at any given time. The intention is that it should be possible to investigate title to land on-line, with the absolute minimum of additional searches, inspection, and enquiry. Thus, the Act generates an e-conveyancing framework that ensures instantaneous computerized updates of registered titles. By doing so, conveyancing practitioners will be able to check titles on screen without having to seek additional vital title information elsewhere. The objective is considered further in chapter 2.

In achieving this objective practitioners may care to note that the Act repeals the whole of the Land Registration Act 1925 (as well as the Registration Acts of 1862, 1936, 1971, and 1988). Other Registration Acts are repealed in part. Schedule 13 of the Act sets out full details of all the repeals made as a consequence of this new law.

1.5 EARLY CONCLUSIONS

The 2002 Act will challenge and alter the way conveyancers think and act. It will
do the same for all those who teach registered land law. Conveyancing practitioners are those who will be challenged the most, however. First, they will need
to change their mindset. They will need to relinquish their reliance upon paper.
Their working methodology will transmute into cyberspace and their expenditure
on information technology resources is also likely to rocket into the stratosphere.
They will need to be seen to be efficient and effective, failing which they might
fall foul of those at the Land Registry given the task of scrutinizing chains of
transactions. At worst, they may even run the risk of being disallowed from
carrying on in business as conveyancers of registered land. The Land Registry too
has an enormous task ahead of it — not the least being the drafting of the rules
required by the Act. There is much work to be done. Clearly many aspects of the
Act will be in place within 18 months. E-conveyancing will take longer. However,
how quickly the professions adjust to the revolutionary changes is another matter.

The Land Registry has created a website totally dedicated to the Land
Registration Act 2002. This can be accessed at < http://legislation.landreg.gov.
uk >. This contains links to both Law Commission reports mentioned above, as
well as the full text of the Act itself. (There is also a registry-created
e-conveyancing consultation website at < http://www.e-conveyancing.gov.uk/
default.asp >.) The site contains some guidance about the possible implementation
timetable. The registry say that this has not yet been settled but that it is anticipated
that the Act will come into force in the Autumn of 2003. The major activity to be
completed is the making of the many rules contemplated by the provisions of the
Act. The registry therefore says that the provisional timetable is likely to be as set
out below:

Month	Activity
July/August 2002	Publication of consultation paper on the rules.
Oct/Nov 2002	Review of consultation responses.
March 2003	Rule Committee approval of rules, regulations and orders.
Autumn 2003	Act brought into force.

There will be a consultation paper covering the content of draft rules that will
probably be published in July/August 2002. It will ask for customer views on the
subject matter of those draft rules. The draft consultation paper will be posted on
the above website. The registry has said that the consultation period will be 14
weeks. Interestingly they have also said that although the Act provides the
framework for electronic conveyancing, the rules to support electronic conveyancing will not be drafted at the same time. As a result they will not be included in
the consultation paper.

Will the changes contemplated by the Act work to the advantage of conveyancing practitioners? Various major reforms are highlighted in the following chapters

of this Guide. These reforms include an innovation, electronic conveyancing, which will eventually modernize registered conveyancing by establishing immediate registration contemporaneous with completion. The Act will make changes to the law relating to adverse possession that should make the law clearer in operation, if somewhat less favourable to potential claimants. However, it will also introduce extensive state control of conveyancing through the mechanisms of a 'network access agreement' whereby practitioners will (or possibly will not) conduct electronic conveyancing (see chapter 8). The Act could also revive sleeping ghosts from the past. In the *Law Society's Gazette* it was reported that 'E-conveyancing may open door to lenders' ((2002) 99 (22) LS Gaz 1). The article alludes to 'hints' made by the government that mortgage lenders could try to participate heavily in the market for e-conveyancing, possibly to the detriment of existing practitioners. The involvement of mortgage lenders could come about by the activation of the dormant authorized conveyancing practitioners (ACP) scheme contained in the Courts and Legal Services Act 1990. This was a scheme that would entitle mortgage lenders to offer conveyancing services. The entitlement would come about once certain presently undefined criteria were met. This part of the 1990 Act has not been brought into force but remains on the statute book ready to be put into force once there is sufficient pressure upon the government to do so. Presumably the big lenders might see the possibility of profit from combining e-conveyancing with their computerized lending arrangements. This would inevitably put further pressure upon conveyancing practitioners who will not be able to compete on the same scale.

As to what might happen, in the *Gazette* article there were two telling comments. First, 'Bernard Clarke, communications manager at the Council of Mortgage Lenders, said recent developments had re-ignited lenders' interest in the conveyancing market'. Secondly, 'Lord Chancellor's Department Minister Michael Willis said the government would keep its options open on ACPs if it benefited the consumer'. Whether the loss of the high street conveyancer, and as a result the consequent loss of high street law firms offering other vital legal services, was taken into account is not clear. However, the economic might of the mortgage lenders will no doubt be of some consequence in this future potential conflict of interests.

1.6 OUR APPROACH IN THIS BOOK

At the start of each chapter there is a list of contents for that particular chapter and the topics within it. This is to help the busy practitioner (or student) find the relevant area of interest as quickly as possible. We appreciate from our own experience of practice that there is nothing worse than spending hours of wasted time, fruitlessly searching through untitled sub-chapter sections trying to locate the desired subject.

Our approach in the book is to take the reader through the different sections of the 2002 Act, explaining and highlighting the important changes that will occur.

For ease of reference, the Act is set out in full at the back of the book together with the 13 schedules to the Act. To assist we start with a summary of the Act so that the overall structure and thrust of this important legislation can be seen and understood. We then move on to a detailed examination of the Act and schedules.

Within each chapter there is one further element designed to assist the busy reader. Where appropriate, we have included checklists at the end of each chapter to help the busy practitioner who may be seeking a quick overview of the important elements, or the reforms and changes, in any particular topic. Our overall aim is to provide a clear, useful and, in particular, practical approach to the Act that will help all those who use the book. In this way we hope to help readers to understand how the Act is going to affect all those who depend upon conveyancing for their livelihood or who intend to embark upon a career in conveyancing.

1.7   KEY POINTS FOR THE PRACTITIONER

- The three main reasons for the Land Registration Act 2002 are the desire to bring certainty, simplicity, and economy to the system of registered land law.
- The Land Registry annual report for 2001 states that 'the percentage of titles in the land register now capable of electronic delivery is 96.78 per cent'.
- The Bill was taken to Parliament in the summer of 2001 and passed through both Houses in a remarkably swift manner, receiving the Royal Assent on 26 February 2002.
- The aim of the Act is that, under the system of electronic dealing with land that it seeks to create, the register should be an accurate reflection of the state of any registered title at any given time.
- The Act generates an e-conveyancing framework that ensures instantaneous computerized updates of registered titles. Conveyancing practitioners will be able to check titles on screen without having to seek additional vital title information elsewhere.
- The Land Registry has created a website totally dedicated to the Land Registration Act 2002. This can be accessed at < http://legislation.landreg. gov.uk >. This contains links to both Law Commission reports mentioned above, as well as the full text of the Act itself.
- There is also a registry created e-conveyancing consultation website at < http:// www.e-conveyancing.gov.uk/default.asp >. This site includes information that will be of interest to all conveyancing practitioners.
- The time scale for the complete implementation of the Act suggested by the registry indicates that it should be brought into force by the Autumn of 2003 with e-conveyancing to start not before 2005/06.

1.8   AFTERWORD

As we were going to press it was announced that the Act will come into force on Monday 13 October 2003. Baroness Scotland from the Lord Chancellor's Department said:

This will allow sufficient time to consult on and make the necessary secondary legislation, to develop office procedures to accommodate the legislation and to carry out a thorough programme of education and training both within the Land Registry and across the wider conveyancing community.

We hope this Guide will assist in this process.

Chapter 2
A Summary of the Land Registration Act 2002

2.1 INTRODUCTION

The Royal Assent to the Land Registration Act was given on 26 February 2002, a little ahead of its intended time scale. This was perhaps a measure of the cross-party support that the Bill enjoyed in both Houses of Parliament. Of the Act at the time of its Royal Assent, Michael Wills, Parliamentary Secretary at the Lord Chancellor's Department, said:

> This piece of legislation marks an important step towards the fulfillment of the Government's commitment to develop a modern basis for land registration to make conveyancing faster and cheaper. Most importantly, it will make possible the development of an electronic conveyancing system, so that land and property transactions can be completed electronically. The Act will bring more information about rights over property onto the register. This will make the property transaction process more open, improving the efficiency of the property market.

By providing additional benefits for registered landowners, such as greater protection against squatters, the Act will encourage unregistered landowners to register their land, bringing more information about land into the public domain and increasing the transparency of the property market. I am pleased to say that there has been broad cross-party support for the Act in both Houses of Parliament. Credit for this is in large measure due to the excellent drafting and preparatory work of the Law Commission and the Land Registry, who undertook an immense project to deliver this reform. This was the single largest law reform project undertaken in the Law Commission since its foundation in 1965.

The Land Registry has indicated that over 80 per cent of all titles in England and Wales are now registered. Furthermore, the vast majority of the three million property dealings each year relate to registered property. However, the present legislation governing registration of title is said to be complex, confusing, and badly out-of-date. Certainly it was the subject of considerable criticism in both Law Commission reports referred to in chapter 1. This is because the Land Registration Act 1925 is largely based on an earlier Act of 1875 and also drafted on the assumption that conveyances of land will be paper based. This is of course perfectly understandable when the context of the 1925 Act is recalled, ie a paper-based legal and commercial infrastructure. To correct these perceived faults the 2002 Act will:

(a)   allow for the process of dealing with registered land to move from a paper-based system to an all-electronic system within a few years;
(b)   completely replace the existing legislation to allow land registration to be faster and simpler;
(c)   establish a register that will give buyers more certainty by giving fuller information about the rights and responsibilities of the registered proprietor;
(d)   improve the security of property rights in and over registered land by providing better means of protecting them;
(e)   provide better protection for the owners of registered land against claims of adverse possession.

By paving the way for electronic conveyancing, it is hoped that the Act will bring greater transparency to chains of transactions. While the new system will take some time to introduce, it should lead to quicker ways of buying and selling land as well as providing greater security of title. As a first step the Land Registry will be launching a full public consultation exercise about electronic conveyancing in late 2002 when draft Land Registry rules will be issued for discussion.

The main provisions of the Act are considered in summary form below. There are helpful explanatory notes available at < www.legislation.hmso.gov.uk/acts/en/2002en09.htm > and the following details and account necessarily rely heavily upon these notes prepared by the Lord Chancellor's Department.

2.2 OBJECTIVE OF THE ACT AND PRELIMINARY MATTERS

The objective is stated in the preamble to the 2002 Act in the baldest of terms, describing the Act as 'An Act to make provision about Land Registration; and for connected purposes'. A simpler statement probably could not be made. However, the fundamental objective of the Bill set out by the Law Commission is that:

(a)   under the system of electronic conveyancing of land and property that it seeks to create, the register should be a complete and accurate reflection of the state of the title of the land. Furthermore the register must be completely up to date and instantaneously altered whenever there is a dealing with the title. There must be no 'registration gap' between the completion of a dealing and the registration of that dealing.

(b)   Building upon the objective in (a) above, it will be possible to investigate title to land on-line, with the absolute minimum of additional enquiries, searches and inspections. More details about e-conveyancing are given in 2.9 below.

The first two sections of the Act are then set out in a preliminary section. They are both contained within Pt 1 of the Act. Section 1(1) states the obvious, being that 'there is to continue to be a register of title kept by the registrar'. Section 1(2) then adds an indication of where and how flesh will be added to this somewhat thin bone. It does so by providing that rules may make provision about how the register is to be kept. In particular rules will be made about the information that will appear in the register, and the form in which that information will be kept, as well as the arrangement of that information. There will necessarily be a lot of time and effort devoted to the drafting of the new rules required by the Act.

Section 2 states the scope for title registration. This requires the registration of unregistered legal estates made up of the following interests:

(a)   an estate in land (freehold and leasehold);

(b)   a rentcharge;

(c)   a franchise (a liberty or privilege). (At common law a franchise is a royal privilege in the form of a grant. Examples are the right to hold a market or maintain a ferry.);

(d)   a profit *à prendre* (rights of taking the produce or part of the soil from the land of another person, eg rights of pasture, etc); and

(e)   any other interest or charge that subsists for the benefit of or is a charge on an interest the title to which is registered.

These matters are covered by Pt 2 of the Act and specifically ch 2, see 2.3 below.

The Act also requires the registration of legal interests that arise from a disposition of an interest, the title to which is registered. These matters are covered by Pt 3 of the Act (see chapter 4).

Summary — Part 1: Preliminary
The purpose of this part is to continue provision for a register of title to estates in land, and explain what interests can be the subject of title registration.

2.3   REGISTRATION TRIGGERS

The intention of the 2002 Act is to extend the registration of land to as many legal estates as possible. Matters to do with first registration are covered within Pt 2, ch 1 and 2 of the Act. Chapter 1 deals specifically with first registration, covering ss 3–14 inclusive. The effect of this is to allow and extend voluntary first registration as well as to extend compulsory first registration triggers to include leases with more than seven years to run. (Indeed the clear intention is to reduce this period down to leases with more than three years to run and the Act contains a power to give effect to this intention.) Section 4 of the Act sets out the triggers to first registration and consolidates the position set out in the Land Registration Act 1997. Section 5 enables the Lord Chancellor to add new compulsory first registration trigger events by way of statutory instruments. Section 6 imposes a requirement upon the estate owner to register within two months of the date of the conveyance or transfer to the new estate owner. Should an estate owner fail to comply with s 6, s 7 provides that a transfer will become void. Should this occur then the transferor would hold the legal estate on a bare trust on behalf of the transferee. If the failure to register arises from the grant of a lease or mortgage they too will be void. They will, however, take effect as an agreement to grant the lease or mortgage.

The one major area of concern for practitioners must relate to the reduction in the length of leases inducing first registration. This is because until now, commercial leases in particular have been granted for terms usually between five and 21 years but typically ten to 15 years in length. They have not required registration but have operated as overriding interests. The Act changes the position by requiring all leases of more than seven years in duration to be subject to compulsory first registration. This could well lead to commercial leases being granted for terms of not more than seven years.

Part 2, ch 2 of the Act covers cautions against first registration. This form of caution allows an owner of an unregistered estate to be informed of an application for first registration that affects that land. If notice of an application is given the cautioner has a right to make an objection. The previously used process of warning the caution under the 1925 legislation has been abandoned. The registrar must keep a register of cautions against first registration.

Summary — Part 2: First registration of title
The purposes of this part are to:

- specify who is entitled to apply voluntarily for the first registration of a title;
- define when an application must be made, on whom the duty to make it lies and the consequences of failing to do so;

- define the titles in freehold and leasehold land which may be registered, and the effects of registration;
- provide for cautions against first registration.

2.4   DISPOSITIONS OF REGISTERED LAND

Part 3 of the 2002 Act spans ss 23–31 inclusive and deals with, for the first time, a definition of the powers of an owner of registered property. The contents of this part also cover the effect of limitations on the owner's powers. The right to exercise such powers will only be limited by any entry in the register or imposed by the Act. Section 27 sets out the dispositions that have to be registered, eg a transfer or a grant of a lease for more than seven years along with others listed in s 27(2) and (3). Finally ss 28–31 cover the effect of dispositions on priority.

Summary — Part 3: Dispositions of registered land
The purposes of this part are to:

- define the powers of an owner of registered land, and who can exercise them;
- make provision to define the effect of limits on the powers of an owner;
- define the dispositions of registered land which must be registered;
- set out regulations about the effect of dispositions on the priority of interests effecting registered land.

2.5   THIRD-PARTY RIGHTS AND PROTECTIVE ENTRIES

Protective entries are notices and restrictions and are dealt with in Pt 4 of the 2002 Act covering ss 32–47 inclusive. The Act reduces to just two the methods of protecting the interests of third parties over registered land. Cautions and inhibitions are effectively abolished while notices and restrictions are retained. Notices may be used to protect encumbrances affecting land that are intended to bind third parties. A typical example of the kind of encumbrance that could be protected by a notice would be restrictive covenants. Restrictions regulate the circumstances in which a transaction affecting a registered estate may be the subject of an entry in the register. For example a restriction might be used where any consents are required to a disposition. The restriction will give notice of the requirement that they be obtained. This will typically arise where a management company is involved and requires a new estate owner to enter into covenants with it before the transfer of the legal estate can be registered, with the prior approval of the company.

Either form of protective entry can be sought without the consent of the registered proprietor who must be notified and who will be able to apply for cancellation of the notice, or object to an application for a restriction. If a person or company applies for either form of protective entry, they are required by the Act to act reasonably when exercising rights granted by the statute. There is therefore a duty of reasonableness that is owed to any person who suffers damage as a consequence of a breach. No doubt damages will be awarded where an applicant has not acted reasonably.

Summary — Part 4: Notices and restrictions
The purpose of this part is to provide for the registration of third-party rights against registered titles by notices and restrictions.

2.6 CHARGES

Part 5 of the 2002 Act covers the topic of charges and extends from s 48 to s 57 inclusive. The first part covers priority and confirms the established position that priority is the order of registration in the register. Tacking and further advances are covered by s 49 while ss 51 and 52 cover the powers of a chargee. Practitioners should remember that by s 25 the Lord Chancellor can prescribe the form and content of any registrable disposition including a registered charge. This could in the future usher in a standard form of charge in registered land. (Practitioners should remember that mortgages by demise or sub-demise cannot be granted for registered land as s 23 limits the owner's powers by excluding this possibility. All future registered charges must be legal charges only.)

Summary — Part 5: Charges
The purpose of this part is to make provision about the relative priority of charges affecting registered land and about the powers and duties of lenders.

2.7 REGISTRATION: GENERAL

This is Pt 6 of the 2002 Act and covers a number of important topics contained within ss 58–78 inclusive. This is a bit of a pot-pourri of items but many are nevertheless of considerable importance and consequence. Registration is conclusive evidence of the vesting of the estate in the registered proprietor (s 58). Section 60 covers boundary matters, s 62 deals with title upgrades, eg from possessory to absolute. Alterations to the register are actually covered by sch 4 of the Act but s 65 enables the schedule to have effect. Section 66 makes the register open to inspection by the public while s 67 is a sort of successor to s 110 of the Land Registration Act 1925. This new section provides that office copies will be admissible in evidence to the same extent as the original. Section 69 gives the registrar the power to provide information about the history of a registered title while s 70 covers official searches by way of rule-making powers.

Section 71 deals with overriding interests. Under the Land Registration Act 1925, these included all the incumbrances, interests, rights and powers which were not entered on the register, but overrode registered dispositions under the 1925 Act. Such interests create a number of problems, since it is possible to buy a registered estate that is subject to adverse interests that are not apparent from the registers. In the 2002 Act, the categories of interests, which are not registrable and which exist as overriding interests, appear in two distinct lists. The first is relevant to first registration of title, the second to dealings with registered land. It is clear that the legislators want to limit the scope and effect of overriding interests. Consequently, in both lists the types of overriding interest will be reduced in scope. The range of particular categories will be lessened, with some categories being abolished altogether, while others will be phased out after ten years. The guiding principle here is that interests should be overriding only where it is unreasonable to expect them to be protected in the register.

In the report of 2001 the Law Commission helpfully summarized the likely extent of overriding interests that will be binding on a registered transferee of registered land ten years after the Act is brought into force and the ten-year transitional period has elapsed.

They are likely to comprise:—

- Most leases granted for three years or less;
- The interests of persons in actual occupation where (a) that actual occupation is apparent; and (b) the interest (i) is a beneficial interest under a trust; or (ii) arose informally (such as an equity arising by estoppel);
- Legal easements and *profits à prendre* that have arisen by implied grant or reservation or by prescription;
- Customary and public rights;
- Local land charges; and
- Certain mineral rights.

This is a much-reduced list of interests from that covered by s 70 of the 1925 Act and clearly there is an intention to ensure that the registers accurately portray the position as it may exist for any particular property with little or no regard for overriding interests.

Section 72 covers priority protection under land registry searches. Subsequent sections cover the right of persons to object to any application made to the registrar as well as the reference of unresolved disputes to the adjudicator (a new office).

Summary — Part 6: Registration: General
The purposes of this part are to:

- state the effects of registration of title;
- provide for alterations to the register;
- enable public access to the register;
- set out procedures for priority periods during which the rights of intending buyers can be protected;
- provide for a right to object to applications to the registrar; and
- enable the reference of disputes about applications to the adjudicator.

2.8   PART 7: SPECIAL CASES

This is another sweeping up part of the 2002 Act and covers various elements, one of which enables the Crown to voluntarily register demesne land. Demesne land is land in which no fee simple subsists and so belongs to the Crown absolutely. One other point of interest is that s 90 stops the registration of leases created for public-private partnerships relating to transport in London. It is curious that there should be this one area that appears to fly in the face of increasing registration.

2.9   PART 8: ELECTRONIC CONVEYANCING

One of the main purposes of the 2002 Act is to usher in electronic conveyancing within the next three to five years. The new legislation aims to create the necessary legal framework that will allow registered-land conveyancing to be conducted electronically. It is therefore worth repeating that the fundamental objective of the Act is focused closely upon making e-conveyancing a reality. This objective is to enable an effective system of electronic dealing with land as a result of the register being a complete and accurate reflection of the state of the title of the land at any given time. This is so that it is possible to investigate title to land on-line, with the absolute minimum of additional inquiries and inspections. From this fundamental objective flows the entire framework for e-conveyancing that has been constructed by the Act.

The Act constructs a framework in which it will be possible to generate and transfer estates and/or interests in registered land by electronic conveyancing. The statute does this by authorizing the execution of formal deeds and documents electronically. The Act also contemplates the formation of a secure electronic computer network within which to carry out e-conveyancing (this is dealt with in Sch 5 to the Act). It is envisaged that the execution of all such deeds and documents and their registration, will be simultaneous. To do this the process of registration will be initiated by conveyancing practitioners. However, there is state control. The permitting of access to the computer network is to be controlled by the Land Registry, which will also exercise control over the changes that can be made to the land register. The Act also provides for the Lord Chancellor to regulate by rules transactions that can be carried out electronically. Furthermore, the Act gives the Lord Chancellor power to make the use of e-conveyancing compulsory. Compulsory e-conveyancing will only arise after a period of consultation and after a transitional period when conveyancers will move from the existing paper-based system to an electronic system. There will therefore be a period of time during which the two systems co-exist.

As a result of Sch 5, para 1, substantial state control of the conveyancing process and those who conduct that process is ensured by this intended model of e-conveyancing. Only those solicitors or licensed conveyancers who have been authorized to do so will be permitted to conduct electronic conveyancing. The relationship with the Registry will be contractual, under a 'network access agreement', and the Registry will be obliged to contract with any solicitor or licensed conveyancer who meets specified criteria.

Summary — Part 8: Electronic conveyancing
The purposes of this part are to:

- enable dispositions of registered land to be made by means of deeds and documents in electronic form;
- enable title by registration so that electronic registration will give title to registered property;
- create an electronic network to effect land registration;
- provide for the circumstances in which conveyancers can use electronic means to complete and register transactions simultaneously.

2.10   ADVERSE POSSESSION

The stated aim of the 2002 Act is to ensure that registration, and nothing else, should guarantee title and ownership as well as all the details of matters affecting the title. The logical extension of this aim is the limitation of title claims by adverse possession. The Act reforms the law of registered land adverse possession. In effect there will be two methods by which a party can claim adverse possession. As to which method will apply to what property will depend upon whether or not the property is registered. The old law (the 12-year rule), will remain in place for all unregistered titles. For registered land the Act introduces a new scheme for protecting the interests of registered proprietors against the acquisition of title by persons in adverse possession. A person claiming adverse possession of registered land will be able to apply to be registered as proprietor after ten years' adverse possession. This, on the face of it, seems a liberalization of adverse possession. Nothing could be further from the reality of the reforms. This is because the registered proprietor will be notified of that application and will, in most cases, be able to object to it. Where the proprietor does object, the application will be rejected unless the 'squatter' can meet one of three limited exceptions. The whole basis of many successful claims for adverse possession will rest upon the lack of any need to notify the paper-title owner of the squatter's occupation. The new law for registered land changes all of that and will thereby dramatically reduce the number of successful claims.

The proprietor will then have to take steps to evict the squatter, or otherwise regularize the position within two years. Should the registered proprietor fail to do so and the squatter remains in adverse possession then, after two more years (making 12 in total) the squatter will be entitled to be registered as proprietor. It should be noted that the new law places the onus on the squatter to take the initiative. If the squatter wants to acquire the land, he or she must apply to be made the registered proprietor of the subject property. This is because the registered proprietor's title will not be barred by mere lapse of time; the ownership must be ousted by an act of registration.

Summary — Part 9: Adverse possession

The purpose of this part is to introduce a new system for dealing with adverse possession as it relates to registered land. The underlying purpose is to make the gaining of title by adverse possession of registered land much harder than is the case currently or is the case for unregistered land.

2.11 OTHER MATTERS

The 2002 Act makes other important changes. For example Charge Certificates are to be abolished and the role of the Land Certificate downgraded. Mortgages by demise will be abolished. The Act also makes one important management change applicable to land registration. It creates a new office, that of Adjudicator to the Land Registry. The adjudicator will be appointed by the Lord Chancellor and will be independent of the Land Registry. The adjudicator's duty will be to determine objections that are made to any application to the registrar that cannot be determined by agreement. Adjudication is contained within Pt 11 of the Act from s 107 to s 114 inclusive and is considered in chapter 11 of this book. Part 10 covers administrative provisions for the Land Registry dealing with such matters as their annual report, fee orders and indemnities.

2.12 SCHEDULES

Schedule 1 of the 2002 Act lists the unregistered interests that override first registration. These include a lease for seven years or less, a legal easement and a local land charge. Schedule 2 sets out registration requirements for registrable dispositions. Part 1 deals with registered estates while Part 2 covers registered charges. Much of this schedule is self-explanatory, eg para 2 states that in the case of a transfer the transferee must be entered in the register as the proprietor of the registered title. Schedule 3 lists the unregistered interests that override registered dealings. These include a lease for seven years or less, a legal easement and a local land charge. Of greatest interest to the practitioner is para 2 of this schedule, which introduces interests of persons in actual occupation. (This is in part the successor to s 70(1)(g) of the 1925 legislation.) Schedule 4 deals with alterations to the register and Sch 5 covers the land registry network required for e-conveyancing. Schedule 6 deals with the registration procedure required for an adverse possessor. Schedule 7 deals with internal Land Registry matters such as the remuneration of the Chief Land Registrar. Indemnities are covered by Sch 8 so that a person is entitled to be indemnified by the registrar if he or she suffers loss as a result of mistakes made in the registry such as a mistake in an official search. The detailed provisions relating to the work of the adjudicator are contained within Sch 9, while Sch 10 covers miscellaneous and general powers such as rule-making powers governing when a land certificate may be issued as well as the form and content of land certificates. Schedule 11 covers minor and consequential amendments to other statutes as a result of the Act, and Sch 13 lists the repeals caused by the Act including the Land Registration Acts of 1925, 1936, 1971, and 1988.

Schedule 12 contains transitional provisions. These flow from s 134 of the Act that allows the Lord Chancellor to make by order such transitional provisions 'as he thinks fit' in connection with the coming into force of any of the provisions of the Act. Thus, existing cautions against first registration shall remain in force even though s 56(3) of the Land Registration Act 1925 is revoked by the Act. There are similar transitional arrangements covering easements and former overriding interests as well as new cautions against first registration. The Act also makes detailed transitional arrangements for adverse possession matters, particularly because of the major alterations made to the law.

2.13   PRELIMINARY CONCLUSIONS

The 2002 Act is bringing about a revolution in registered land law and conveyancing. Practitioners must start to prepare now for the changes in the law and the consequential changes in practice that will follow. This is all the more important when it is anticipated that the Act could be fully operative by the end of 2003. The Act, once it is fully in force, will reverse the current emphasis of registered land law from registration of title, to title by registration. In essence, once e-conveyancing is effective the registration gap will be consigned to the rubbish bin of history. Section 27 stipulates that a disposition of a registered estate will not operate at law until the relevant registration requirements are met. With e-conveyancing, completion and registration will be simultaneous and as such title by registration will be fully effective.

There are many rules to be drafted and approved. A lot of the detail required to make the Act effective remains to be resolved. However, there are one or two points that are not clear. What will be done about auction contracts once e-conveyancing becomes compulsory? Bearing in mind that s 93 includes contracts for the sale and purchase of land within electronic conveyancing requiring the agreement to be made in electronic form, how will this accommodate auctions?

How safe are electronic signatures? This is clearly an area of great concern and will be mentioned further in chapter 8 on e-conveyancing. How will the management of chains of transactions be conducted and who will be the manager? This too will be considered in chapter 8. However, it is clear that these major concerns are not going to hold up the move to an electronic system. At the start of April 2002 the Chief Land Registrar wrote to all law firms and Legal Service Departments on its database of users, indicating that the Registry would shortly be launching an extensive consultation exercise about electronic conveyancing. The letter contained a request for persons to be identified as those interested in being a part of this consultation exercise. Plainly the process of change is advancing inexorably toward a digital future for all conveyancing practitioners. Practitioners need to be aware of these changes and of the need to structure their working environment so as to be ready to accommodate the information technology resources required to allow them to practice as e-conveyancers.

2.14   KEY POINTS FOR THE PRACTITIONER

- Section 2 states the scope of title registration. The 2002 Act extends compulsory first-registration triggers to include leases with more than seven years to run.
- Section 6 imposes a requirement upon the estate owner to register within two months of the date of the conveyance or transfer to the new estate owner.
- The Act reduces to just two the methods of protecting the interests of third parties over registered land. Cautions and inhibitions are effectively abolished while notices and restrictions are retained.
- Mortgages by demise or sub-demise cannot be granted over registered land as s 23 limits the owner's powers by excluding this possibility. All future registered charges must be legal charges only.
- The guiding principle for the law in the Act relating to overriding interests is that interests should be overriding only where it is unreasonable to expect them to be protected in the register. Thus the total of overriding interests has been reduced.
- The Act constructs a framework in which it will be possible to generate and transfer estates and/or interests in registered land by electronic conveyancing. The statute does this by authorizing the execution of formal deeds and documents electronically.
- The Act also contemplates the formation of a secure electronic computer network within which to carry out e-conveyancing. It is envisaged that the execution of all such deeds and documents together with their registration will be simultaneous.
- The permitting of access to the computer network is to be controlled by the Land Registry, which will also exercise control over the changes that can be made to the land register.
- A person claiming adverse possession of registered land will be able to apply to be registered as proprietor after ten years' adverse possession. The registered proprietor will, however, be notified of that application and will be able to object to it. Where the proprietor does object, the application will be rejected unless the 'squatter' can meet one of three limited exceptions.
- The proprietor will then have to take steps to evict the squatter, or otherwise regularize the position within two years. Should the registered proprietor fail to do so and the squatter remains in adverse possession then after two more years, making 12 in total, the squatter will be entitled to be registered as proprietor.

Chapter 3
First Registration

3.1   INTRODUCTION

Part 2 of the 2002 Act covers first registration of title. Part 2, ch 1 is entitled First Registration and deals with voluntary registration (s 3), compulsory registration (ss 4–8), classes of title (ss 9–10), the effect of first registration (ss 11–12) and miscellaneous rule-making powers (ss 13–14). Part 2, ch 2 deals with cautions against first registration (ss 15–22). These topics are all considered in this chapter but before embarking on a detailed examination of the provisions it may be useful to consider some background to them.

One of the main aims of the Act is to make the register of title as comprehensive as possible. In an ideal world, the remaining unregistered land in England and Wales would be phased out as quickly as possible so that all land would become registered. However in the 2001 Report the Law Commission stated there were three compelling reasons for not doing so at present:

(a)   First, a significant rise in voluntary first registrations is expected. This is because the Act offers extra benefits to those with registered titles (eg increased protection against acquisition of title by adverse possession, see chapter 9). Accordingly it was thought that the existing provisions should be given an opportunity to work before considering compulsory registration for all unregistered landowners. As an added incentive, the Land Registry fees payable on voluntary first registrations are lower than for compulsory first registrations. Even the Crown can now apply for voluntary registration.

(b)   Secondly, it was thought to be difficult to devise a system of compulsion other than the one that operates at present, namely on a disposition of land. The dangers of a more heavy-handed approach would also risk contravening the European Convention on Human Rights; any new means of compulsion would have to be proportionate to the desired ends.

(c)   Thirdly, as matters stand, the resources of the Land Registry and the conveyancing profession as a whole will be fully stretched by the substantial changes introduced by the Act. Adding further pressure at this stage was thought to be inadvisable for all concerned.

Nevertheless, the Law Commission's ultimate goal is still to achieve total registration for the whole of England and Wales in the comparatively near future. To this end, the Law Commission has declared that the ways in which this can be achieved are to be re-examined five years after the Act is brought into force. As it stands, the Act builds on the foundations laid by the Land Registration Act 1997 by extending the triggers for compulsory registration of unregistered land (see 3.3 below). Although the changes made by the Act relating to first registration are not as extensive as those made by the 1997 Act, four additional reforms are worth highlighting: leases (3.1.1), profits *à prendre* in gross and franchises (3.1.2), Crown land (3.1.3), and submarine land (3.1.4).

3.1.1   Leases

The length of leases that are subject to compulsory registration is reduced from more than 21 years to more than seven years (s 4(1)(c)). Similarly, the assignment of an unregistered lease which has more than seven years unexpired at the time of the assignment will have to be registered (s 4(1)(a), (2)(b)). Most business leases are granted for less than 21 years and therefore many will now become compulsorily registrable and subject ultimately to electronic conveyancing. The intention is to reduce the seven-year period to three.

3.1.2   Profits *à prendre* in gross and franchises

Profits *à prendre* in gross (eg fishing or shooting rights) and franchises (eg the right to hold a market) may now be voluntarily registered with their own titles. They must, however, be held for an interest equivalent to a fee simple or under a lease of which there are still seven years to run (s 3). Fishing rights, in particular, can be very valuable and so these may now be traded in registered titles. Previously these rights could only be noted on the register.

3.1.3   Crown land

The Crown may for the first time register land held in demesne, ie held in its capacity as ultimate feudal overlord. The Act enables the Crown to grant itself a freehold estate so that it can register it (s 79). This will assist the Crown in protecting its foreshore from the encroachment of adverse possessors (see chapter 9).

3.1.4   Submarine land

The territorial extent of land that can be registered is increased so that some submarine land will become registrable. As before, the Act applies to land covered by internal waters of the United Kingdom that are within England and Wales (s 130(a)). Additionally, however, s.130(b) includes land covered by internal waters *adjacent* to England and Wales which are specified for the purposes by order made by the Lord Chancellor. This would allow the Crown to register its submarine land out to the baselines which define the territorial limits of the United Kingdom (see Convention on the Territorial Sea of 1958, Art 4). This will protect such land from the encroachment of adverse possessors who might construct pipelines or other works within internal waters which are technically outside the body of a county (eg beyond the seaward limit of an estuary).

3.2   VOLUNTARY REGISTRATION (LEGAL ESTATES THAT MAY BE REGISTERED WITH THEIR OWN TITLES)

Section 3(1) of the 2002 Act lists the legal estates that are capable of being registered with their own titles. They are:

(a)   estates in land (ie fee simple absolute (freehold) or term of years absolute (leasehold));
(b)   rentcharges;
(c)   franchises; and
(d)   profits *à prendre* in gross.

The persons who may apply to be registered as first registered proprietors of a legal estate are the same as those permitted under the Land Registration Act 1925. They are either the legal owner of the legal estate or the person entitled to have the legal estate vested in him or her (s 3(2)). An example of the latter would be where the person is absolutely entitled as the sole beneficiary under a trust of land. Section 3(6) provides that a person may not apply to be registered if he or she has contracted to buy the land. This is because the contract will be completed by a conveyance which will be subject to the requirements of compulsory registration anyway (see 3.3 below).

The legal estates that may be registered with their own titles are now considered.

3.2.1   Estates in land

3.2.1.1   Freehold estate
In mirroring the Land Registration Act 1925, a fee simple absolute in possession may be registered with its own title (s 3(1)(a)).

3.2.1.2 Leasehold estate

Analogous to the previous law, not every leasehold estate is capable of being registered with its own title. However, the length of lease that is subject to compulsory registration is reduced from more than 21 years to more than seven years (s 4(1)(c)). Similarly, the assignment of an unregistered lease which has more than seven years unexpired at the time of the assignment will also have to be registered (s 4(1)(a), (2)(b)). There is power to reduce the period still further by statutory instrument after prior consultation (s 118(3)). Most business leases are granted for less than 21 years and so many will now become compulsorily registrable and subject ultimately to electronic conveyancing. Importantly, business leases granted for more than seven years the titles of which must be registered, will be open to public inspection, leading to more transparency in the commercial property market.

When electronic conveyancing is fully operative it is likely that the period for compulsory registration will be reduced still further to include all leases that have to be made by deed, ie those granted for more than three years (see Law of Property Act 1925, ss 52, 54(2)). To save the register being cluttered up with short leases that have expired, a mechanism will be needed in future to ensure that spent leases are removed from the register.

3.2.1.3 Reversionary leases

Another category of lease that is subject to compulsory registration is the reversionary lease, ie a right to possession under a lease that takes effect at a future date. A tenant sometimes holds under one lease but is granted another lease to take effect shortly after the first. A reversionary lease of any term granted to take effect in possession more than three months after the date of grant *must* be registered (s 4(1)(d)). Reversionary leases are quite common and may be difficult to discover (see 3.3.4 below for further commentary). Requiring them to be registered will assist one of the Law Commission's aims of promoting increased transparency in the property market.

In determining whether a reversionary lease *may* be registered, the new law mirrors the previous law contained in the Land Registration Rules 1925, r 47. Provided the reversionary lease is to take effect in possession on, or within one month of, the end of the lease in possession, the terms may be added together. If the two terms exceed seven years, the lease is capable of being registered (s 3(7)).

3.2.1.4 Discontinuous leases

A new provision is that discontinuous leases of any length may be voluntarily registered (s 3(4)). Discontinuous leases are very rare. They are sometimes used in time-share arrangements under which the tenant is entitled to occupy premises for a certain number of weeks annually for a specified number of years (see *Cottage Holiday Associates Ltd v Customs and Excise Comrs* [1983] QB 735). In computing the length of term, the discontinued periods are simply added together. Thus, such a lease would only become compulsorily registrable if the periods in possession in total exceeded seven years (at one month a year this would equate to 84 years' duration!). Compulsory registration of such leases will therefore be extremely rare.

Finally, in accordance with the previous law, where a mortgage has been created by a lease demise or sub-demise, the mortgage term is never registrable, provided there is a subsisting right of redemption (s 3(5)). These types of mortgage are in practice obsolete in any event.

3.2.2   Rentcharges

A rentcharge will be a legal estate if it is perpetual or granted for a term of years (Law of Property Act, s.1(2)(b)). The most important rentcharges are 'estate rentcharges'. These are created to enable positive covenants to be enforced and to secure the payment of service charges in a non-leasehold context. Under the Act it will continue to be possible to register a rentcharge voluntarily provided it is perpetual or granted for a term of years with more than seven years unexpired (s 3(1)(b), (3)).

3.2.3   Franchises

A franchise is an incorporeal hereditament and has been defined as 'a royal privilege or branch of the royal prerogative subsisting in the hands of a subject, by grant from the King' (Joseph Chitty, *A Treatise on the Law of the Prerogatives of the Crown* (1820), p 119). It may be acquired by royal grant or by prescription. The most common franchises today are those to hold a market or fair, or to take tolls (for a case concerning a market franchise see *Sevenoaks DC v Pattullo & Vinson Ltd* [1984] Ch 211). Under the previous law a franchise could only be protected against a registered estate by entering a notice or caution against the registered title. Under the Act, a franchise may now be registered with its own title if it is held for an interest equivalent to a fee simple absolute in possession or a term of years absolute with more than seven years unexpired (s 3(1)(c), (3)). So these often valuable rights can now be bought and sold as registered titles.

3.2.4   Profits *à prendre* in gross

Profits are also incorporeal hereditaments and, like easements, are often created for the benefit of other land. However, unlike easements, profits can exist in gross, ie in their own right without benefiting a dominant tenement. Examples of profits *à prendre* in gross are profits of hunting and shooting game, pasture and piscary, ie fishing rights. Under the previous law profits in gross, as with franchises, could only be protected against a registered estate by entering a notice or caution against the registered title. Under the Act, a profit *à prendre* in gross may now be registered with its own title if it is held for an interest equivalent to a fee simple absolute in possession or a term of years absolute with more than seven years unexpired (s 3(1)(d), (3)). So, like franchises, these often valuable rights can also be bought and sold as registered titles.

3.2.4.1   *Manors no longer registrable*

The Act contains no power to register a manor, ie the lordship of the manor. Manors impose no burden on the land within the manor and they sometimes create practical difficulties for the Land Registry. The Consultative Document therefore recommended that they should cease to be registrable. In addition, the Act allows the registered proprietor of a manor to apply for the manor to be removed from the register (s 119). (Similarly, advowsons ceased to be registrable as a result of the Patronage (Benefices) Measure 1986, s 6(2).)

3.3   COMPULSORY REGISTRATION (WHEN TITLE MUST BE REGISTERED)

Whereas the Land Registration Act 1925 listed 'dispositions' that triggered compulsory first registration, the 2002 Act refers to 'events'. This is wider in its ambit and will permit greater flexibility in the future (see s 5, which permits new events to be added later). Section 4(1) lists the events that trigger compulsory registration. These largely replicate the old law as laid down in the Land Registration Act 1925 and the Land Registration Act 1997. In line with the old law, mines and minerals held apart from the surface are excluded from registration (s 4(9)).

The events which induce compulsory first registration are covered at 3.3.1 to 3.3.8 below.

3.3.1   Transfers of a qualifying estate

A 'qualifying estate' is either a legal freehold estate in land or a legal lease, which has more than seven years to run. As we explained in the context of voluntary registration (3.2 above) the reduction from 21 years to seven years is significant and will result in many more business leases becoming registered. Registration is compulsory if the transfer is made:

(a)   for valuable or other consideration;
(b)   by way of gift;
(c)   in pursuance of an order of any court; or
(d)   by means of an assent (including a vesting assent).

As far as gifts are concerned, s 4(7) make it clear that no gift element exists where a landowner creates a nomineeship. A transfer (or grant) by way of gift includes:

(a)   a transfer or grant by a settlor which constitutes a trust under which the settlor does not retain the whole of the beneficial interest (s 4(7)(a)); and

(b)   a case where a beneficiary becomes absolutely entitled to unregistered land that is held on trust for him or her, and the beneficiary requires the trustees to convey the legal estate to him or her (s 4(7)(b)).

Thus under (a), a conveyance of unregistered land by a settlor (S) to trustees to hold on trust for S as S's nominee will not induce compulsory registration because there is no gift element. But if the trustees were to hold on trust for S for life and thereafter to X absolutely, the conveyance to the trustees would involve a gift element and would therefore trigger compulsory registration.

Even if the estate transferred has a negative value it is still regarded as having been transferred for valuable consideration (s 4(6)). This might be the case on an assignment of a lease where the current rent exceeds the market rent due to the operation of a rent review clause.

For the avoidance of doubt, s 4 also makes it clear that the following events will *not* induce compulsory registration:

(a)   transfer by operation of law, eg where a deceased's property vests in his or her personal representatives (s 4(3));

(b)   assignment of a mortgage term, ie where the mortgage is by demise or sub-demise (these are very rare and the Act prohibits any more being created that affect registered property) (s 4(4)(a));

(c)   lease merger, ie assignment or surrender of a lease to the immediate reversion where the term is to merge in that reversion (s 4(4)(b)).

3.3.2   Transfers to which the Housing Act 1985, s 171A applies

Section 4(1)(b) replicates the position under the old law. A transfer falls within the Housing Act 1985, s 171A, where a person ceases to be a secure tenant of a dwelling house because his or her landlord disposes of an interest in that house to a private-sector landlord. In such circumstances, the tenant's right to buy under the Housing Act 1985, Pt 5 is preserved. Such a transfer is subject to compulsory registration even if it would not otherwise be.

3.3.3   Leases granted for a term of more than seven years from the date of grant

The reduction in the length of leases subject to compulsory registration is an important change in the law. We commented on this in the context of voluntary registration (see 3.2.1 above). Importantly it will bring many business leases onto the register and thus enable third parties to inspect the lease and its title.

Section 4(1)(c) provides that registration is compulsory if a lease is granted out of a qualifying estate of an estate in land:

(a)   for a term of more than seven years from the date of grant; and

(b)   for valuable or other consideration, by way of gift, or in pursuance of an order of any court.

Leases for the grant of a mortgage term, ie a mortgage by demise or sub-demise, are not compulsorily registrable (s 4(5)). Neither are public-private partnership (PPP) leases for the proposed future running of the London underground railway (see s 90(2) and 7.4.3).

The grant of a lease will be regarded as a gift in the same circumstances as a transfer of a lease (see s 4(7) and our comments at 3.3.1 above). Similarly, if the lease granted has a negative value, it will still be regarded as having been granted for valuable consideration (see s 4(6) and 3.3.1 above).

3.3.4   Reversionary leases taking effect in possession more than three months after the date of grant

A new category of lease that is subject to compulsory registration is the reversionary lease. This is a right to possession under a lease that takes effect at a future date. A reversionary lease of any term granted to take effect in possession more than three months after the date of grant is required to be registered (s 4(1)(d)). Under the old law a buyer of land affected by such a reversionary lease may not have discovered it because the tenant was not in possession. However, the buyer might still have been bound by it as an overriding interest under the Land Registration Act 1925, s 70(1)(k). The change in the law overcomes this convey-ancing problem. It should be noted that reversionary leases taking effect within three months are not required to be registered. On this point the Law Commission explains, 'it is . . . normal for leases to be granted to take effect a short time after they are created, and these cause no significant conveyancing difficulties'.

3.3.5   Grant of a 'right to buy' lease under the Housing Act 1985, Pt V

Section 4(1)(e) replicates the old law found in the Housing Act 1985, s 154, the relevant parts of which are repealed in Sch 13 of the Act. The grant of a 'right to buy' lease under the Housing Act 1985 is subject to compulsory registration, regardless of whether the lease would otherwise be registrable because of it length.

3.3.6   Grant of a lease to which the Housing Act 1985, s 171A applies

Section 4(1)(f) replicates the old law for grants of leases to which s 171A applies in the same way as for transfers. See our comments at 3.3.2 above in relation to such transfers.

3.3.7   Protected first legal mortgages of a qualifying estate

The Land Registration Act 1997 introduced first mortgages of unregistered land as an additional trigger for compulsory registration. This is confirmed in s 4(1)(g) of the Act which refers to 'the creation of a protected first legal mortgage of a qualifying estate'. As we have seen, the change here is that a qualifying leasehold estate is now one with more than seven years to run, rather than 21. For the avoidance of doubt, s 4(8)(a) provides that a legal mortgage is 'protected' if it takes effect on its creation as a mortgage to be protected by the deposit of documents relating to the mortgaged estate. Further, s 4(8)(b) provides that a first legal mortgage is one which, on its creation, ranks in priority ahead of any other mortgages then affecting the mortgaged estate.

3.3.8   Crown land

Special provision is made for compulsory registration after the Crown has made a grant of a freehold estate out of demesne land (s 80). Demesne land is land which the Crown holds as feudal lord paramount and in which it has no estate.

3.3.9   Power to add new trigger events

Section 5 permits the Lord Chancellor by order to add new events that will trigger compulsory registration. The Lord Chancellor may also make such consequential amendments of any legislation, 'as he thinks appropriate'. Before exercising this power the Lord Chancellor must 'consult such persons as he considers appropriate' (s 5(4)). Any future event that may be added must be an event relating to an unregistered interest that is an interest of any of the following kinds: estate in land, rentcharge, franchise, or profit á prendre in gross (s 5(2)). A mortgagee cannot be required to register its interest, as there would be little point if the title to the affected estate remained unregistered (s 5(3)).

3.3.10   The duty to register

The time limit for applying for first registration is the same as under the old law, namely within two months of the relevant event (s 6(4)). Also in line with the old law, the registrar may extend this period if satisfied that there is good reason for doing so (s 6(5)). Unless the registrar extends the period, failure to register within the time limit will result in the transfer becoming void. In this event, the transferor will hold the legal estate on a bare trust for the transferee (s 7(2)(a)). Similarly, any grant of a lease or creation of a protected mortgage will become void and take effect instead as a contract for valuable consideration to grant or create the lease or mortgage concerned (s 7(2)(b)).

If it becomes necessary to repeat the transfer, lease or mortgage (because the previous one was void), the transferee, grantee or mortgagor is liable to the transferor, grantor or mortgagee for the proper costs involved (s 8(a)). They must also indemnify them for any other liability reasonably incurred as a result of the failure to register (s 8(b)).

3.4 DIFFERENT CLASSES OF TITLE AND THE EFFECT OF FIRST REGISTRATION

The classes of title that may be registered are the same as those under the Land Registration Act 1925. For freehold estates they are absolute, qualified or possessory titles. For leasehold estates they are absolute, qualified, possessory or good leasehold titles. The Act does not change the substance of what amounts to these different classes of title.

3.4.1 Absolute freehold

Almost all freehold titles are registered with absolute title. Section 9(2) provides that a person may be registered with absolute freehold title if the registrar considers that the title is such as a willing buyer could properly be advised by a competent professional adviser to accept. Even if the title is defective the registrar may still grant absolute title if he or she considers that the defect will not cause the holding under the title to be disturbed (s 9(3)). This means that an absolute title will be given if the title is a good title (one that can be forced on an unwilling buyer under an open contract) or a good holding title (technically a bad title, but the holding under which is unlikely to be challenged). It may even be given if the title is doubtful (one that the applicant cannot prove to be good). In practice, it is very unusual for a freehold title to be registered with anything other than absolute title.

The effect of registration with an absolute title is somewhat different from the previous law. As far as benefits are concerned, the legal estate is vested in the proprietor together with all the interests subsisting for the benefit of the estate, eg easements (s 11(3)). As far as burdens are concerned, the proprietor takes subject only to the interests set out in s 11(4) affecting the estate at the time of first registration. These are:

(a)   Interests which are the subject of an entry in the register in relation to the estate. (These can only be registered charges, notices, and restrictions because cautions and inhibitions are prospectively abolished under the Act.)

(b)   Unregistered interests which fall within any of the paragraphs of Sch 1 (see 12.2 for an examination of interests which override first registration).

(c)   Interests acquired under the Limitation Act 1980 of which the proprietor has notice. This provision is new and is worthy of explanation.

3.4.1.1 *Interests acquired under the Limitation Act 1980 of which the proprietor has notice*

The Law Commission introduced this provision to meet the following problem that can arise on first registration. Assume a landowner (A) owns unregistered land, which is adversely possessed by a squatter (S). After 12 years' adverse possession A's title is extinguished and S becomes the true owner. S then abandons the land and A resumes possession and sells to a purchaser (P) who applies for first registration.

Under the old law the rights of S in this situation would be an overriding interest under the Land Registration Act 1925, s 70(1)(j) and would bind P. Under the new law this is not the case (unless S is protected by the Act's transitional provisions to protect vested rights, see 9.6). Section 11(4)(c) allows P to take free of S's interest unless, at the time of first registration, P had notice of it. If P is bound by S's interest, S can seek alteration of the register to show S as registered proprietor. (Note that such alteration is not a 'rectification' of the register permitting a claim for indemnity.)

In determining whether P has notice under s 11(4)(c) the word will have its usual meaning of either actual, constructive or imputed notice. In particular, it will include constructive notice of matters that the first registered proprietor ought to have discovered from reasonable inspections and inquiries.

3.4.2 Qualified freehold

A qualified title is very rare. It will be given where the registrar considers that the applicant's title can only be established for a limited period, or subject to certain reservations that are such that the title is not a good holding title (s 9(4)). An example of this might be where the transfer to the applicant was made in breach of trust. Registration with a qualified freehold title has the same effect as registration with an absolute title, except that it does not affect the enforcement of any estate, right or interest which appears from the register to be excepted from the effect of registration (s 11(6)).

3.4.3 Possessory freehold

In practice, a possessory title will be given either where the applicant's title is based on adverse possession or title cannot be proven because the title deeds have been lost or destroyed. The Act provides that possessory title will be appropriate where the applicant is either in actual possession or in receipt of rents and profits and there is no other class of title with which the applicant may be registered (s 9(5)). Registration with a possessory freehold title has the same effect as registration with an absolute title, except that it does not affect the enforcement of any estate, right or interest adverse to, or in derogation of, the proprietor's title subsisting at the time of registration or then capable of arising (s 11(7)).

3.4.4 Absolute leasehold

In practice, an absolute leasehold title will only be given if the superior title is either registered with absolute title or, if unregistered, has been deduced to the registrar's satisfaction. The Act provides that an absolute leasehold title will be given if the registrar considers that the title is one that a willing buyer could properly be advised by a competent professional adviser to accept and the registrar also approves the lessor's title to grant the lease (s 10(2)). As with absolute freehold, even if the leasehold title is defective the registrar may still grant absolute title if he or she considers that the defect will not cause the holding under the title to be disturbed (s 10(4) and see 3.4.1 above).

Registration with an absolute leasehold title has the same effect as registration with an absolute freehold title (see 3.4.1 above) except that the estate is vested in the leaseholder subject to implied and express covenants, obligations, and liabilities incident to the estate (s 12(3), (4)). These will be apparent from an inspection of the lease (eg lessee's covenants).

3.4.5   Qualified leasehold

Like a qualified freehold title, a qualified leasehold title is very rare. It will be given where the registrar considers that the applicant's title (or the lessor's title) can only be established for a limited period, or subject to certain reservations that are such that the title is not a good holding title (s 10(5)). An example of this might be where the grant to the applicant was made in breach of trust. Registration with qualified leasehold title has the same effect as registration with absolute title but subject to the exceptions and qualifications explained at 3.4.2 above in relation to qualified freehold titles (s 12(7)).

3.4.6   Possessory leasehold

In practice, a possessory title will be given either where the applicant's title is based on adverse possession or title cannot be proven because the title deeds have been lost or destroyed. The Act provides that possessory title will be appropriate where the applicant is either in actual possession or in receipt of rents and profits and there is no other class of title with which he or she may be registered (s 10(6)). Registration with possessory leasehold title has the same effect as registration with absolute title but subject to the exceptions and qualifications explained at 3.4.3 above in relation to possessory freehold titles (s 12(8)).

3.4.7   Good leasehold

Although much rarer than an absolute title, a good leasehold title is more common than a qualified or possessory leasehold title. It is appropriate where the superior title is neither registered nor deduced to the registrar's satisfaction. The Act provides that a good leasehold title may be given if the registrar considers that the title is such as a willing buyer could properly be advised by a competent professional adviser to accept (s 10(3)). A good leasehold title may be given even if the title is open to objection, provided the registrar considers that the defect will not cause the holding under it to be challenged (s 10(4)). Registration with good leasehold title has the same effect as registration with absolute title, except that it does not affect the enforcement of any estate, right or interest affecting, or in derogation of, the title of the lessor to grant the lease (s 12(6)).

3.4.8   Other rule-making powers

Other rule-making powers relating to first registration are conferred on the Lord Chancellor and will take the form of land registration rules. Section 13 relates to dependant estates. It allows for rules to be made for an entry on the register to show that a registered proprietor has the benefit of a legal estate (eg easement or profit) over unregistered land. In addition, rules may make provision for the registration of someone as proprietor of an unregistered legal charge which is a charge on a registered estate. For example, certain local land charges do not need to be registered to have effect at law. Section 14 allows for rules to be made regarding the mechanics of first registration. These may cover such matters as applications for registration, the functions of the registrar, and the effect of entries made by the registrar.

3.5   CAUTIONS AGAINST FIRST REGISTRATION

Sections 15 to 22 of the 2002 Act deal with cautions against first registration. As the name implies, these cautions provide a means by which a person with an interest in unregistered land can be informed of an application for first registration of the title to that land. (Note: the Act prospectively abolishes cautions against dealings in registered land.) Cautions against first registration are a useful form of protection for someone claiming an interest in unregistered land who wishes to prevent the land becoming registered without first being given an opportunity to substantiate their claim. An example would be someone claiming an interest under an implied trust, which cannot be protected by the registration of a land charge. Section 15 deals with the right to lodge cautions.

Cautions against first registration have of course been with us for a long time, but some innovations are made under the new law. The principal changes are as follows.

(a) *Cautions register.* As well as cautions being recorded in the Index (formerly index map, see 6.7.2), the Act creates a new cautions register (s 19(1)). Previously, details of cautions were held on a 'caution title' at the land registry. Land registration rules will determine how the register is to be kept (s 19(2)), and the rules are likely to deal with the information that may be recorded on the register and the form and arrangement of that information. The register is also likely to be in dematerialized form, ie held electronically. To correct a mistake or for updating purposes, the court (or registrar) may order an alteration of the cautions register (see ss 20(1), 21(1); see 6.11.5). This is analogous with the alteration provisions for the register of title. The detail of such alteration powers will be set by land registration rules. Any person who suffers loss as a result of a mistake in the cautions register will be entitled to an indemnity from the state (Sch 8, para 1(1)(g)).

(b) *One cannot register a caution against one's own land.* Two years after s 15 comes into force, persons will be prevented from lodging a caution against first registration against their own estate, where that estate is registrable, eg where they hold an unregistered freehold or a lease with more than seven years to run. This should act as an inducement for voluntary registration and is part of the ultimate aim to achieve total registration. See generally s 15(3) and Sch 12, para 14(1).

3.5.1　Applications to lodge a caution

Any person having an interest in unregistered land can lodge a caution against first registration (s 15(1), (2)). This codifies the practice under the old law. Examples of persons who might lodge a caution are someone with a charging order or option over an unregistered freehold, a tenant over an unregistered freehold reversion or a beneficiary under an implied trust of unregistered land. However, as mentioned above, a new and significant exception to this principle is that a person cannot lodge a caution against his or her own estate, where that estate is registrable (s 15(3)). Thus a caution cannot be used as a substitute for first registration and what that person should do is register his or her estate. This should act as an inducement for voluntary registration. It is important to note that a transitional provision provides that the exception under s 15(3) will not take effect until two years after the provisions on first registration have come into force (see Sch 12, para 14(1)).

As was previously the case, the right to lodge a caution is exercised by an application to the registrar (s 15(4)). Land registration rules will be made to determine the form, content, and manner of the application. A person may not exercise his or her right to lodge a caution without reasonable cause (s 77(1)(a)) and a breach of this statutory duty will be actionable by anyone who suffers loss as a result (s 77(2)). The cautioner may of course apply to the registrar to withdraw the caution (s 17).

The Act makes special provision in relation to cautions against first registration of the Crown's demesne land (see s 81 and Sch 12, para 15).

3.5.2　Objections

Anyone may object to the application for a caution against first registration. If the objection is not groundless and cannot be disposed of by agreement, the registrar must refer the matter for determination to the adjudicator (s 73(1), (6), (7)). (See chapter 11 for further commentary on the powers of the adjudicator.) The owner of the legal estate to which the caution relates is the person most likely to object to the caution and this person can apply for cancellation of the caution in any event (s 18(1) and see 3.5.4 below).

3.5.3　The effect of a caution against first registration

The effect of a caution is contained in s 16:

(a) First, the registrar must give notice to the cautioner (by virtue of s 22 this is the person who lodged the caution or such other person as rules may provide eg the cautioner's personal representatives) of any subsequent application for first registration and of the cautioner's right to object to it (s 16(1)). Rules will be made specifying the period within which the cautioner may object.

(b) Secondly, the registrar must not deal with the first registration application until the end of that period, unless the cautioner has previously objected or advised the registrar that he or she will not object (s 16(2)). If the cautioner objects, the registrar must refer the matter to the adjudicator unless the objection is groundless or agreement can be reached (s 73(6), (7)).

(c) Thirdly, the caution has no effect on the validity or priority of any interest that the cautioner may have in the legal estate to which the caution relates (s 16(3)).

(d) Lastly, the section provides that an agent of the applicant for first registration may give notice to the cautioner as if the notice had been given by the registrar (s 16(4)). This effectively allows the applicant's solicitor to give notice without having to wait for the registrar to do it and will thus assist in speeding up the conveyancing process. Land registration rules will be made in this respect and are likely to stipulate that only solicitors and licensed conveyancers may act as agents in these circumstances.

3.5.4 Cancellation of cautions

Certain persons may apply to the registrar to cancel a caution against first registration. They are the legal estate owner to which the caution relates, and persons of such other description as land registration rules may provide (s 18(1)). Such other persons are likely to include those with interests in the land such as mortgagees and receivers. The registrar must serve notice of such application on the cautioner and warn the cautioner that the registrar will cancel the caution unless the cautioner objects to the application within a specified time (to be set by rules) (s 18(3), (4)). It is only the cautioner who may object to the application to cancel the caution. Unless agreement can be reached or the objection is groundless, the registrar must refer the matter to the adjudicator in the normal way (s 73(6), (7)). If the estate owner has consented to the lodging of the caution in the first place then he or she will not normally be allowed to object to it. This applies also to the estate owner's successor in title by operation of law, eg personal representatives (s 18(2)). However, rules are likely to provide that an estate owner's objection will be permitted in certain circumstances, eg where the interest protected by the caution has ended.

3.6   KEY POINTS FOR THE PRACTITIONER

- The length of leases that are subject to compulsory registration is reduced from more than 21 years to more than seven years.

- This period is likely to be reduced even further in future to more than three years.
- As a result, most business leases will now be brought onto the register and ultimately be subject to electronic conveyancing. Importantly, the lease itself will be open to public inspection.
- Profits *à prendre* in gross (eg fishing or shooting rights) and franchises (eg the right to hold a market) may now be registered with their own titles.
- A reversionary lease of any term granted to take effect in possession more than three months after the date of grant must be registered with its own title.
- After prior consultation the Lord Chancellor may add new trigger events for compulsory first registration.
- The Law Commission aims to achieve total registration for the whole of England and Wales 'in the comparatively near future'. To this end, the Law Commission has declared that the ways in which this can be achieved will be re-examined five years after the Act is brought into force.
- The classes of title that may be registered under the Act are the same as those under the Land Registration Act 1925. The Act does not change the substance of what amounts to these different classes of title, eg absolute, good leasehold.
- The effect of registration with an absolute title is somewhat different from the previous law. In particular, a new provision makes the registered proprietor bound by interests acquired under the Limitation Act 1980 of which the proprietor has notice (s 11(4)(c)).
- Cautions against first registration are to be recorded on a new cautions register which may be altered by analogy with the provisions applicable to the register of title.
- Two years after s 15 comes into force a person cannot register a caution against first registration against their own estate where that estate is registrable, eg if you hold an unregistered freehold or a lease with more than seven years left to run.

Chapter 4
Dispositions of Registered Land

4.1 INTRODUCTION

In this chapter we consider the matters covered in Pt 3 of the Act. These are:

(a) the powers of disposition of a registered proprietor (or someone entitled to be registered as proprietor);

(b) registrable dispositions, i.e. dispositions of a registered estate or charge that must be registered; and

(c) the effect that dispositions of registered land have on the priority of interests in such land.

4.2 POWERS OF DISPOSITION

One of the aims of the Act is to make it possible for title to land to be investigated on-line. To this end it is important that the register provides all the necessary information concerning the title. However one way in which a disposition of land may be challenged is that the party who made it was acting outside his or her powers in some way. One example of this would be where trustees are acting outside the terms of their trust. Another would be where a statutory body, eg local authority, makes a disposition that is ultra vires because the sale is not for the best price. Previously it had been assumed that a registered proprietor had all the powers of disposition that an absolute owner of a registered estate or charge had under the general law, unless there was some entry in the register, such as a restriction, which limited those powers. The Act now gives statutory effect to that assumption by laying down four guiding principles:

(a)   A registered proprietor should be taken to have unlimited powers of disposition. These powers apply equally to a person entitled to be registered as proprietor, such as the executor of a deceased registered proprietor or a disponee who has yet to be registered as proprietor.

(b)   If those powers are limited in some way, that limitation should be noted by an entry on the register, eg by a restriction (cautions and inhibitions are abolished under the Act).

(c)   If there is no entry on the register, any disponee may assume that there are no limitations on the powers of the disponor.

(d)   If such limitations exist but are not noted on the register, the disponee's title cannot be challenged. However, this does not make the disposition lawful. As a result, claims can still arise against the disponor in relation to an improper exercise of that power (or against the disponee if he or she was privy to the disponor's conduct).

4.2.1   Owner's powers

In relation to a registered estate, the Act adopts the term 'owner's powers'. A person may exercise owner's powers if he or she is either the registered proprietor of an estate or charge or is entitled to be so registered (s 24(1)). 'Owner's powers' are defined in s 23 as power to:

(a)   make a disposition of any kind permitted by the general law in relation to the interest the person has (excluding a mortgage by demise or sub-demise of a registered estate (which are now abolished) or a legal sub-mortgage of a registered charge); and

(b)   charge the estate at law with the payment of money (in the case of a registered estate) or to charge at law with the payment of money, indebtedness that is secured by the registered charge.

4.2.2   Protection for disponees

To prevent the title of the disponee being questioned the Act provides that a person's right to exercise owner's powers is unlimited unless there is some limitation reflected by an entry on the register or other limitation imposed by or under the Act (s 26). However, the disposition does not render the disposition lawful.

The notes to the Act suggest the following example of how this might operate in practice. Assume that W and X hold land on a bare trust as nominee for Y on terms that no disposition of the land should be made without Y's consent. Although in actual occupation, Y fails to protect her interest under the trust by entering a restriction on the register. In breach of trust, W and X fraudulently charge the land to Z (the mortgagee) without Y's consent. The result is that the charge to Z is valid and cannot be called into question by Y. This is because W and X's right to exercise owner's powers is taken to be free of limitation as there was no restriction on the register. Y's actual occupation is irrelevant and Y cannot claim an overriding interest under Sch 3, para 2 (interests of persons in actual occupation, see 12.3.2) because her consent to the charge was not obtained.

4.3   REGISTRABLE DISPOSITIONS

4.3.1   Introduction

Section 27(2) of the 2002 Act lists the dispositions of a registered estate that must be completed by registration. Section 27(3) does the same in respect of dispositions of a registered charge. Section 27(1) makes it clear that if the disposition of a registered estate (or charge) is required to be registered then it will not operate at law until it is so registered. Practitioners should bear in mind that once e-conveyancing is introduced this principle will, in effect, be superseded. This is because under e-conveyancing the making of the transaction and its registration will be simultaneous and the 'registration gap' will disappear (see chapter 8 for further details). Land registration rules may prescribe the form and content of any registrable disposition. These rules must be complied with if the disposition is to have effect (s 25). Rules may also make provision about applications to the registrar for the purposes of meeting registration requirements under s 27 (s 27(6)).

4.3.2   Dispositions required to be registered

The general policy of the Act is that all dispositions of registered land that create or transfer a legal estate should, in principle, be registrable unless there are good reasons why this should not be the case. Thus, subject to limited exceptions (see below), any transfer of or grant or reservation of any legal estate out of a registered estate or registered charge is a registrable disposition and must be so registered (s 27(2)(a), (3)(a)). See 3.3 for a list of registered estates that must have their own registered titles (eg freeholds, leases granted for more than seven years). Schedule 2 of the Act sets out the registration requirements for the specified dispositions, eg in respect of a transfer of whole or part the name of the transferee must be entered in the register as proprietor (Sch 2, para 2).

4.3.2.1   Transfers
Transfers of a registered estate must be registered. As mentioned above, however, there are exceptions to the general principle that a transfer of a registrable disposition must be registered. These exceptions, which also apply to the transfer of registered charges, involve dispositions by operation of law. They are as follows:

   (a)   A transfer on the death of a sole individual proprietor (eg to executors).

   (b)   A transfer on the bankruptcy of a sole individual proprietor (eg to the trustee in bankruptcy).

   (c)   A transfer on the dissolution of a sole corporate proprietor (which vests in the Crown *bona vacantia*).

4.3.2.2 Leases
In addition to transfers, the grant of most leases is a registrable disposition and must be completed by registration (eg leases granted for more than seven years). See 3.3 for commentary on the different types of registrable leases. Schedule 2, para 3 confirms that the grantee of a registrable lease (or the grantee's successor) must be entered in the register as the proprietor of the lease. A notice of the lease must also be entered in the register of the superior title. Two categories of lease are not registrable. They are the grant of a lease for seven years or less (unless it falls within a class of lease listed at 3.3) and a public-private partnership (PPP) lease for the London underground (see 7.4.3). Both take effect as overriding interests.

4.3.2.3 Leases of franchises or manors
A grant of a lease of a franchise or manor which is itself a registered estate is a registrable disposition (s 27(2)(c)). If the term of the lease is for more than seven years the grantee of the lease (or the grantee's successor) must be entered in the register as proprietor of the lease; a notice of the lease is also entered on the superior title (Sch 2, para 4). If the term of the lease is for seven years or less then it is only necessary to enter a notice of it in the register of the superior title (Sch 2, para 5).

4.3.2.4 Express grant or reservation of an easement, right or privilege
A further registrable disposition is described in s 27(2)(d) as 'the express grant or reservation of an interest of a kind falling within s 1(2)(a) of the Law of Property Act 1925, other than one which is capable of being registered under the Commons Registration Act 1965'. This effectively means that easements and profits à prendre, whether in gross or appurtenant to an estate, are registrable. Rights of common are excluded. This is because the Commons Registration Act 1965, s 1(1) prohibits such rights from being so registered. For the avoidance of doubt, the grant of easements, rights or privileges arising under s 62 of the Law of Property Act 1925 are not to be regarded as 'express' grants for these purposes, and are therefore not registrable (s 27(7)).

As explained in chapter 3, legal profits à prendre in gross are now registrable with their own titles. Thus the grantee of such a profit (or the grantee's successor in title) will be entered as proprietor of the interest created (and a notice of it is also entered in the register). For other interests under this heading, eg the grant or reservation of an easement, it is only necessary to enter a notice of it in the register. The register of the land benefiting from the interest will show the proprietor of the land as being also the proprietor of the interest (Sch 2, para 7).

4.3.2.5 Express grant or reservation of rentcharge or legal right of re-entry
A further registrable disposition is described in s 27(2)(e) as 'the express grant or reservation of an interest of a kind falling within s 1(2)(b) or (e) of the Law of Property Act 1925'. These are rentcharges and rights of re-entry in respect of a

lease or rentcharge. The grantee (or the grantee's successor) of the rentcharge is entered in the register as the proprietor of the interest created (except where a rentcharge term does not exceed seven years). A notice of the rentcharge is also entered on the register (Sch 2, para 6). For rights of re-entry (and rentcharges for seven years or less), it is only necessary to enter a notice of the interest on the register (Sch 2, para 7(2)(a)). As with easements, the register of the land benefiting from the interest will show the proprietor of the land as being also the proprietor of the interest. It should be noted, however, that it is not current land registry practice to record the benefit of a right of a re-entry on the title of the reversion to the lease, and this will be reflected in land registration rules.

4.3.2.6 Legal charge

A grant of a legal charge is, of course, also a registrable disposition and this is confirmed in s 27(2)(f). The chargee (or the chargee's successor in title) is registered as proprietor in the charges register. However the creation of a legal charge that is also a local land charge does not require registration (s 27(5)(c)). This is because local land charges are binding on disponees of registered land as overriding interests in any event (Sch 3, para 6). (As an aside, it should be noted that local land charges that are charges on land to secure the payment of money, eg a charge for executing street works under the Highways Act 1980, s 212, cannot be enforced as charges unless they are so registered (see s 55 and 5.6.3).)

A transfer of a legal charge is also a registrable disposition (s 27(3)(a)). This means that the transferee (or successor in title) is registered as proprietor of the charge (Sch 2, para 10). The creation of a sub-charge is also a registrable disposition (s 27(3)(b)). Here the sub-chargee is registered as proprietor.

4.4   EFFECT OF DISPOSITIONS ON PRIORITY

In the 1998 Report the Law Commission concluded that there was no need to implement a new scheme for determining the priority of interests in registered land. This was because under the future e-conveyancing system the date of creation of an interest and its registration will be one and the same and the register will thus become conclusive as to the priority of such interests. However the Commission considered that there should be a clear statutory statement of the relevant principles of law. These are contained in ss 28–31 of the 2002 Act, considered below.

4.4.1   Priority under the Act

Section 28(1) states the general principle of priority under the Act. This is that the priority of an interest affecting a registered estate or charge is not affected by a disposition of the estate or charge. An example of this would be an overriding interest which would bind a purchaser. Moreover, it makes no difference whether the interest or disposition is registered or not (s 28(2)). Thus, for cases falling within the general principle, the priority of *any* interest in registered land is determined by the date of its creation. This reflects the general law expressed by the maxim, 'where the equities are equal, the first in time prevails'.

Importantly, however, and in common with the position before the Act, this general principle will not apply where a registered disposition is for valuable consideration (this is analogous to the Land Registration Act 1925, s 20). The reason for this is the general proposition that interests which are not protected on the register will not bind a purchaser unless they are overriding interests. Moreover the question of whether a purchaser has notice of interests is generally irrelevant in the context of registered land.

Accordingly, s 29(1) provides that if 'a registrable disposition of a registered estate is made for valuable consideration, completion of the disposition by registration has the effect of postponing to the interest under the disposition any interest affecting the estate immediately before the disposition whose priority is not protected at the time of registration'. Following this, s 29(2) goes on to state when the priority of an interest *would* be protected against a registered disposition for valuable consideration. This will be the case where the interest:

(a)   is a registered charge;
(b)   is the subject of a notice in the register;
(c)   is an unregistered interest that overrides a registered disposition under Sch 3 (see chapter 12 concerning overriding interests);
(d)   appears from the register to be excepted from the effect of registration (ie where title is other than absolute, eg possessory); or
(e)   is incident to a leasehold estate, eg lease covenants — these are not entered on the register but simply discovered from reading the lease.

To reduce the number of overriding interests, once an interest is protected by a notice in the register it cannot later revert to an overriding interest, even if the notice were removed from the register by mistake (ss 29(3), 30(3); see 12.5).

If between completion and registration a purchaser created an interest in favour of a third party, the purchaser could not claim priority over it and the general principle in s 28 would apply. It would be patently unfair for a purchaser to create an interest in this way and then claim not to be bound by it simply because it had not been registered before the purchaser had become registered as proprietor of the land. This problem will disappear once electronic dispositions and their registration become simultaneous under the e-conveyancing system (see generally chapter 8).

Note that the Act changes the law as far as the definition of 'valuable consideration' is concerned. As before, valuable consideration excludes a nominal consideration in money, but the change is that it no longer includes the anachronism of marriage consideration (s 132(1)). The reason for this is because a transfer of land in consideration of marriage is usually a wedding *gift* and there can no longer be any justification for treating it any differently from other gifts of land.

The priority of registered charges on the same registered estate or charge, ie how they rank between themselves, is examined in chapter 5 (see 5.6).

The grant of a lease out of a registered estate that is not a registrable disposition (eg for a term of seven years or less) also falls within the exception to the general principle in s 28. In other words, these types of leases are treated as if they were registrable dispositions for the purposes of s 29 (s 29(4)).

4.4.2 Priority special cases

4.4.2.1 *Inland Revenue charges*
There are special rules for Inland Revenue charges on land in respect of unpaid inheritance tax (s 31). Where there is a disposition of property subject to an Inland Revenue charge, generally it takes effect subject to that charge (Inheritance Tax Act 1984, s 237(6)). In the absence of a notice on the register protecting it, however, the charge will attach to the proceeds of sale (unless the purchaser was not acting in good faith or paid only a nominal consideration; see the Inheritance Tax Act 1984, ss 238(1)(a), 272).

4.4.2.2 *Rights of pre-emption*
A right of pre-emption is a right of first refusal. The grantor of the right agrees that if he or she decides to sell the subject property, it will first be offered to the grantee. This is different from an option where the grantee can force the grantor to sell the land to him or her. The Act provides that a right of pre-emption in relation to registered land has effect from the time of its creation as an interest capable of binding successors in title (subject to the above rules about the effect of dispositions on priority) (s 115(1)). This means that it takes its priority from the date of its creation (when it becomes an interest in land). This is contrary to the view expressed by a majority of the Court of Appeal in *Pritchard v Briggs* [1980] Ch 338 where it was suggested that a right of pre-emption only became an interest in land once the grantor decided to sell. The Act therefore changes the law in this respect (in any event as far as registered land is concerned). The new rule is not retrospective and applies only to rights of pre-emption created on or after s 115 comes into force (s 115(2)).

4.4.2.3 *Equities arising by estoppel*
Similarly, s 116 provides that, in relation to registered land, an equity by estoppel has effect from the time when the equity arises as an interest capable of binding successors in title (subject to the above rules about the effect of dispositions on priority). Thus in relation to the doctrine of proprietary estoppel, the interest in land will arise at the point when the innocent party has acted to his or her detriment in reliance on the promise, ie before the court has made an order to that effect. This is known as an 'inchoate equity'. Section 116 reinforces the weight of judicial authority in this area. Generally the courts have favoured the view that even though the equity is merely inchoate, a proprietary interest in land does exist (rather than merely a personal right against the promisor). (See *Sen v Headley* [1991] Ch 425 at 440A per Nourse LJ and *Voyce v Voyce* (1991) 62 P & CR 290, 293.)

4.4.2.4 Mere equities

A mere equity is an equitable proprietary right that is capable of binding successive owners of land. The term is used to denote a claim to discretionary equitable relief in relation to property. Examples include a right to set aside a transfer for fraud or undue influence, a right to rectify an instrument for mistake and a right to seek relief against forfeiture of a lease after a landlord has peaceably re-entered. In unregistered land, a mere equity is not binding on a bona fide purchaser for value of a legal estate or an equitable interest without notice of it (*Mid-Glamorgan County Council v Ogwr BC* (1993) 68 P & CR 1, 9). In registered land, the notice rule has no application in relation to a purchaser of a legal estate. However, despite no clear authority on the point, it would seem that a mere equity will be defeated by the buyer of a later *equitable* interest without notice of that equity (mirroring the position in unregistered land). The Law Commission considered this situation to be anomalous, given that notice ought to be irrelevant as to the priority of interests in registered land. Accordingly, mere equities are dealt with in the same way under s 116 as equities arising by estoppel. Thus, in registered land, a mere equity has effect from the time the equity arises as an interest capable of binding successors in title (subject to the above rules about the effect of dispositions on priority). This change in the law means that, in registered land, a mere equity will not be defeated by a later equitable interest that is created for valuable consideration, where the grantee was a buyer in good faith and without notice of the mere equity.

4.5   KEY POINTS FOR THE PRACTITIONER

- If in future title is to be investigated on-line it is important that the register provides all the necessary information about the title.
- As a result of this, a registered proprietor may be assumed to have unlimited powers of disposition unless a limitation, eg restriction, is noted on the register.
- A person may exercise 'owner's powers' if he or she is either the registered proprietor of an estate or charge or is entitled to be so registered.
- Essentially, 'owner's powers' are the ability to dispose of the owner's interest and to charge it.
- All dispositions of registered land that create or transfer a legal estate should, in principle, be registrable unless there are good reasons why not.
- If the disposition of a registered estate (or charge) is required to be registered then it will not operate at law until it is so registered.
- In general terms, the dispositions required to be registered are: (a) transfers, (b) leases granted for more than seven years, (c) leases of franchises or manors, (d) express grants or reservations of easements, rights or privileges, (e) express grants or reservations of rentcharges or legal rights of re-entry, and (f) legal charges.
- The general principle with regard to priorities is that the priority of an interest affecting a registered estate or charge is not affected by a disposition of the estate or charge (s 28).

- For cases falling within the general principle, the priority of any interest in registered land is determined by the date of its creation.
- Importantly this general principle will not apply in the case of registered dispositions for valuable consideration (s 29). This is because, in general terms, interests which are not protected on the register will not bind a purchaser (unless they are overriding interests).
- Interests which bind a purchaser are:
  — a registered charge;
  — an interest protected by a notice in the register;
  — an overriding interest;
  — one that appears from the register to be excepted from the effect of registration (ie where title is other than absolute, eg possessory); or
  — one that is incident to a leasehold estate, eg lease covenants.
- Valuable consideration no longer includes marriage consideration.
- There are special priority rules for Inland Revenue charges in respect of unpaid inheritance tax.
- In registered land, a right of pre-emption has effect from the time of its creation as an interest capable of binding successors in title ('overruling' *Pritchard v Briggs* [1980] Ch 338).
- In respect of proprietary estoppel, the interest in registered land will arise at the 'inchoate equity' stage, ie at the point when the innocent party has acted to his or her detriment in reliance on the promise.
- Similarly, a mere equity has effect from the time the equity arises as an interest capable of binding successors in title.

Chapter 5
Notices, Restrictions and Charges

5.1   INTRODUCTION

This chapter will cover Pt 4 of the 2002 Act concerned with notices and restrictions (ss 32–47). It will also cover Pt 5 of the Act relating to charges (ss 48–57). The Act decreases from four to just two the protective entries that practitioners can make for the protection of third-party interests over registered land. They are notices and restrictions. These are dealt with below after a brief review of the existing law. Thereafter, Pt 5 of the Act is considered in detail as it relates to charges and the changes made to the law for registered charges.

5.2   THIRD-PARTY PROTECTION, THE EXISTING LAW

The 1925 legislation provided that third-party rights that are not protected as overriding interests or by being registered charges on the title are known as minor interests. If the list of overriding interests set out in the Land Registration Act 1925, s 70, does not cover the third-party interest in question then it can only be a minor interest. A clear example of such an interest is an estate contract. In such a case the minor interest *must* be protected by a registration, ie by an entry on the register of the relevant title. If there is no such registration then a buyer will take free of the third-party interest, and the question of notice for that buyer is quite immaterial. Minor interests can include equitable interests behind a trust of the legal estate, although such interests can be overreached. Just what form that protective registration might take in each case is covered by the four categories listed below.

5.2.1 Notices

A notice is a specific entry on the charges register protecting a particular interest. Notices are used to protect restrictive covenants, leases not capable of being registered in their own right, and, where the seller concurs, an estate contract. The support of the registered proprietor is required because a fundamental requirement for the registration of a notice is that the owner's land or charge certificate must be lodged with the notice at the time of application to the Land Registry for registration. Alternatively the certificate could be placed on deposit to meet the application for the registration of the notice. (However, there is one principal exception to this, which is a notice protecting a spouse's right of occupation pursuant to the provisions of the Family Law Act 1996.) The effect of the registration of a notice is that it is good notice to all and remains on the title with no further action required for the maintenance of the registration. If the registered proprietor refuses to support the application to register a notice then a caution can be used instead. The Act retains notices but in a different format.

5.2.2 Cautions (including cautions against first registration)

A caution is a protective entry that may be seen in the proprietorship register. It can be used to protect the same type of third-party interest as can be protected by a notice. The main difference between a caution and a notice is that with a caution you do not need to lodge the land or charge certificate with the caution application. Accordingly, a caution is used in hostile situations where the cooperation of the title owner is not going to be forthcoming. The effect of having a caution registered is to afford the cautioner a terminable period of protection. When a caution is registered the Land Registry will give notice to the cautioner of any imminent dealing with the land comprised in the subject title. This is termed 'warning the caution'. In effect the Registry warns the cautioner of the intended registration or dealing, and gives notice to the cautioner that if no steps are taken to show why the caution should remain, then within 14 days of giving the warning the caution will be removed and the pending registration or dealing will proceed. The cautioner must take steps to commence action within the 14-day notice period and to seek a hearing before the registrar. It is imperative that any cautioner acts swiftly once a 'warning-off' notice has been received otherwise the protection of the caution will be lost. By the Land Registration Act 1925, s 56(3) any person lodging a caution without reasonable cause will be liable to pay compensation to any other person who has as a consequence of the improper registration suffered loss or damage. Cautions against dealings are abolished by the Act.

A caution against first registration is different from mainstream cautions in that it exists only in relation to unregistered titles. A person who wishes to advance a claim against an unregistered title may wish to object to that title being submitted for first registration, as registration could adversely affect the person's interest in the land in question. If a caution against first registration is lodged and accepted, the registrar will advise the cautioner of an application for first registration that affects all or part of the land in dispute. The cautioner will then have a limited period during which to show cause why first registration should not be allowed. The usual period during which the cautioner must respond is 14 days but the notice can state a longer period. A typical example would be where there are two adjoining unregistered titles and there is a dispute about the line of their common boundary. If one party wanted to be sure that registration of the other title did not take place before the question of the boundary line was resolved, a caution against first registration would assist. A caution against first registration is registered with its own caution title number and details of the caution are set out in the caution title including relevant information from the supporting statutory declaration. The changes made by the Act to cautions against first registration are covered in chapter 3.

5.2.3 Restrictions

Registration of a restriction will prevent dealings with the registered title until there has been conformity with a particular requirement. For example, a consent may be required to the transfer of a registered lease from the management company that looks after the estate in which the property is located. The most commonly seen restriction is that for a tenancy in common, where the restriction will highlight the fact that no disposition by one proprietor of the land under which capital moneys arise is to be registered except under an order of the court or the registrar. Another common restriction is that in favour of a registered lender, which will effectively stop any disposition of the land without the approval of that lender. Some restrictions will be automatic, eg where a charity is the proprietor, and some will be voluntary, as is the case mentioned above involving the lender. A restriction registration application requires the proprietor's land or charge certificate to be lodged at the Registry. A restriction will appear in the proprietorship register. The Act retains restrictions but in a different format.

5.2.4 Inhibitions

An inhibition is a comparatively rare form of registration as it is draconian in its effect. It stops all dealings with the property. As a result it is really only seen where the registered proprietor is an individual who is adjudged bankrupt. In these circumstances a bankruptcy inhibition will be registered pursuant to a receiving order in bankruptcy. Otherwise an inhibition can only be entered on the title pursuant to an order of the court or the registrar and then only for wholly exceptional circumstances such as suspected forgery (see *Ahmed v Kendrick* (1987) 56 P & CR 120, CA). The Act gets rid of inhibitions.

5.3   NOTICES AND RESTRICTIONS, THE NEW REGIME — AN INTRODUCTION

The Law Commission in the 1998 Report were critical of the existing law because they felt it was unduly complicated. They said, 'there are four different methods of protecting minor interests. These overlap with each other and it is often possible to protect a right by more than one means' (see para 6.44 of the 1998 Report). Furthermore the case of *Clark v Chief Land Registrar* [1993] Ch 294 (Ferris J); [1994] Ch 370 (CA) makes it clear that a caution fails to protect in one particularly significant way. This is because it does not protect the proprietary interest because it does not preserve the priority of the right. Cautions merely give the cautioner a right to be notified of an impending dealing with the registered land. This is a major failing of such a protective entry. For this and other reasons in the Reports of 1998 and 2001 the changes set out below were recommended.

The 2002 Act abolishes inhibitions and cautions. (Although there are transitional arrangements contained in Sch 12 relating to inhibitions and cautions against dealings. For example existing cautions will remain in the register as a result of the transitional provisions contained in Sch 12, paras 1, 2(3)). Notices and restrictions remain but in a different format. Notices will be used to protect encumbrances on land that are intended to bind third parties. Typical encumbrances that will be protected by notices are easements or restrictive covenants. Restrictions regulate the circumstances in which a disposition of a registered estate or charge may be the subject of an entry in the register. The major change in the law introduced by the Act is that either can be applied for without the permission of the registered proprietor. However, the registered proprietor must be informed of the application and will be at liberty to seek the cancellation of the notice, or object to an application for a restriction. There is no reference in the Act to minor interests. Interests that are to be protected by an entry in the register have the mouthful of a title of being interests protected by an entry on the register!

Both notices and restrictions will now be considered in more detail.

5.4   NOTICES

Sections 32–39 of the 2002 Act cover notices that can be one of two types, either consensual or unilateral. The distinction between the two is discussed further below. The Law Commission, in the 2001 Report, considered that a notice may be entered on the register in at least five circumstances, namely:

(1)   On the first registration of an estate, in respect of an interest that burdens it;
(2)   Where it appears to the registrar that a registered estate is subject to an overriding interest;
(3)   Where it is necessary to complete the registration of a registrable disposition;
(4)   Where such an entry is necessary to update the register; and
(5)   On application to the registrar.

5.4.1   Introduction

Section 32(1) states that, 'A notice is an entry in the register in respect of the burden of an interest affecting a registered estate or charge.' Section 32(2) then stipulates that the registration of the notice will be on the title to which it relates or indeed against any registered charge affected by the burden of the interest. This is the same as was required by the 1925 legislation. Section 32(3) then makes it clear that the registration of a notice does not by itself ensure the validity of the interest. All that the registration does is to say that if the interest is valid, then the priority of the interest is protected for the purposes of the Act and in particular for the purposes of ss 29 and 30. (See chapter 4 concerning these two sections with regard to the effect of registered dispositions.) Section 77 of the Act imposes a duty of reasonableness. A person must not exercise the right to apply for the entry of a notice without reasonable cause. The duty is owed to any person who suffers damage should there be a breach of this duty to act reasonably.

The Act will make it possible to enter either a notice or apply for a restriction without the consent of the registered proprietor. However, in such a situation, the proprietor will be notified of its entry and will be able to apply for its cancellation. Section 39 makes it clear that there will be rules made about the form and content of notices in the register.

5.4.2   Excluded interests

Section 33 of the Act lists interests that cannot be protected by a notice. They are called excluded interests. They are:

(a)   a trust of land;

(b)   a settlement under the Settled Land Act 1925;

(c)   a lease for a term of three years or less from the date of the grant and which is not required to be registered;

(d)   a restrictive covenant made between a lessor and lessee so far as it relates to the property leased;

(e)   an interest which may be registered under the Commons Registration Act 1965;

(f)   an interest in coal or a coal mine and rights attaching under the Coal Industry Act 1994;

(g)   although not within s 33, there is another excluded interest. This is excluded by s 90(4) which states that no notice may be entered in the register in respect of an interest under a public-private partnership (PPP) lease relating to transport in London.

The first two excluded interests are included to prevent notices being used to protect beneficial interests behind a trust. They are better suited to the protection of a restriction. This is because their interest may be overreached with the payment of purchase moneys of a trust property to two or more trustees. (See the case of *State Bank of India v Sood* [1997] Ch 276 for further details about overreaching. In this case there was no actual capital money paid to the trustees. However, the Court of Appeal held that the overreaching took effect on the execution of the mortgage in question and at that point in time the interests of the beneficiaries became attached to the equity of redemption.) The third excluded interest relates to short-term leases. Although registration triggers cover leases for more than seven years, s 33(b) relates to leases of three years or less. In theory it is still possible to register a notice in respect of a lease with a term of more than three years but less than eight years. However, if the promise of e-conveyancing is fulfilled then the Lord Chancellor may reduce the cut-off point for registering leases down to more than three years. By doing so the timings will then coincide. The fourth excluded interest covers leasehold covenants and this is because the lease terms will make the covenants apparent.

5.4.3   Applications for the entry of a notice

If a party claims to be entitled to an interest affecting a registered title then, provided the interest is not an excluded interest, that party can apply to the registrar to enter a notice (see s 34(1)). The application will be one of two types, agreed or unilateral (s 34(2)). If the application is to proceed on the basis of an agreed notice then it must fall within one or more of the three types listed in s 34(3)(a)–(c). They are where:

(a)   the applicant is either the registered proprietor or the person entitled to be registered as proprietor of the estate or charge that is burdened by the interest to be noted;
(b)   either the registered proprietor or the person entitled to be registered as proprietor of the estate or charge consents to the entry of the notice; and
(c)   the registrar is satisfied as to the validity of the applicant's claim.

Practitioners should note at this point the complete absence of any requirement for the land certificate to be produced to enable the registration to proceed. Even though the first two types listed above are clearly consensual even there the certificate is not required for registration of the notice. As to the third type, the entry will be with the approval of the registrar. It would seem likely that a spouse's charge in respect of his or her matrimonial home rights under the Family Law Act 1996, s 31(10) would fall within this category. Currently the effect of the registration of a matrimonial homes rights notice is that it is good notice to all and remains on the title with no further action required for the maintenance of the registration. This would seem to necessitate their future home being within s 34(3)(c).

If the notice is by way of a unilateral notice then ss 35 and 36 specifically apply. This form of notice will take over where the abolished cautions left off. Because all notices, whether agreed or unilateral, will protect the priority of an interest, if valid, as against a subsequent registered disposition, this gives more protection to an applicant than was the case with cautions. If the registrar enters a unilateral notice in the register, notice of the entry must be given to the proprietor of the registered title or charge to which the entry relates. (Section 35(1)(b) also provides that notice of the entry must also be given to 'such other persons as rules may provide'. Those rules have yet to be made.) A unilateral notice must identify itself as a unilateral form of notice and indicate who is the beneficiary of the notice. This is all that is required within the notice. This would seem to be so as to ensure an element of confidentiality in the register.

Section 36 deals with the cancellation of unilateral notices. This section includes a right to challenge notices made by an applicant for a unilateral notice. This section therefore provides that a proprietor affected by the notice or person entitled to be registered as proprietor of the subject estate (or charge) may apply for cancellation of a unilateral notice. The cancellation application is by way of an application to the registrar. The party entitled to the benefit of the notice will be entitled to oppose such an application under the general right conferred by the Act to object to an application to the registrar. If the dispute cannot be resolved by agreement, then it must be referred to the adjudicator for settlement. If the beneficiary of the notice does not make any objection to the application made by the proprietor seeking cancellation of the unilateral notice then the registrar must cancel the notice (s 36(3)).

Section 37 deals with 'unregistered interests'. This section states that if the registrar encounters a registered title that is subject to an unregistered interest being an unregistered interest that overrides first registration (and is not an excluded interest under s 33), then the registrar may enter a notice in the register concerning that interest. The effect of this is to promote the registration of overriding interests (see 12.5). This statutory approval of the noting of overriding interests is part of the attempt by the Law Commission and the Land Registry to eliminate such interests so far as possible. Section 37(2) provides that the registrar must give notice of such an entry to parties that may be covered by rules that have yet to be made. (Section 39 covers rule making by providing that rules may make provision about the form and content of notices in the register.)

Section 38 is concerned with registrable dispositions. The Act provides that, where a person is registered as proprietor of an interest under a disposition of any of the following kinds, the registrar must enter a notice in the register regarding that interest. To identify the interests in question, s 38 refers back to s 27(2)(b)–(e) and relates to:

(a)   the grant of any registrable lease;

(b)   where the registered estate is a franchise or manor, the grant of any lease of that franchise or manor;

(c)   the express grant or reservation of an easement, right or privilege for an interest equivalent to an estate in fee simple absolute in possession or a term of years absolute. However, there is a specific exclusion of a right of common which is capable of being registered under the Commons Registration Act 1965;

(d)   the express grant or reservation of a rentcharge in possession which is either perpetual or for a term of years absolute;

(e)   the express grant or reservation of a right of entry exercisable over or in respect of a legal lease, or annexed, for any purpose, to a legal rentcharge.

The effect of this provision is to require the registrar to enter notices of the listed interests, and the notices will be entered against the title or titles of the estates out of which the interests were granted or reserved.

5.5   RESTRICTIONS

5.5.1   Introduction to restrictions

Section 40(1) states that, 'A restriction is an entry in the register regulating the circumstances in which a disposition of a registered estate or charge may be the subject of an entry in the register'. It can be used for many purposes, for example to ensure that where consent is required for a particular transaction, it is obtained. The most frequently encountered example of this kind of restriction will occur when there is a management company and there is a restriction in the register indicating that no registration of a transfer may be made without the consent of an officer of the management company. This is entered in the register to make sure that other arrangements are completed with the transferee, such as a deed of covenant to pay management charges and to comply with repairing obligations, before the transfer of ownership can be concluded, ie by registration. Accordingly, s 40(2) states that a restriction may prohibit the making of an entry and that prohibition may be indefinite, for a period specified in the restriction or until a specified event occurs (s 40(2)(a)–(b)). The events which may be specified include the giving of notice, the obtaining of consent, and the making of an order by the registrar or the court (s 40(3)(a)–(c)). The restriction is to be made against the registered estate or charge to which it relates (s 40(4)). Practitioners will no doubt recall restrictions they have encountered which fit the descriptions above, but such restrictions will certainly include entries relating to mortgages restricting further entries without the permission of the proprietor of the first charge. It is clear from the wording of the Act that the nature of restrictions is not limited to those listed above. Restrictions may take many forms and contain various different restrictive elements beyond those listed in the Act.

The Act will make it possible to either enter a notice or apply for a restriction without the consent of the registered proprietor. However, in such a situation, the proprietor will be notified of the application, to which the proprietor may then object. Section 77 of the Act imposes a duty of reasonableness. A person must not exercise the right to apply for the entry of a restriction without reasonable cause. The duty is owed to any person who suffers damage should there be a breach of this duty to act reasonably.

5.5.2 The effect of restrictions

Section 41 of the Act sets out the effect of the appearance of a restriction in the register. This is that no entry in respect of a disposition to which the restriction applies may be made unless the disposition/entry complies with the terms of the restriction. There is one express exemption to this rule. Section 41(2) states that the registrar may make an order disapplying a restriction relating to a disposition specified in the order. An example given in the notes to the Act of where it might be appropriate for the registrar to exercise this power is if the restriction requires consent by a named individual and he or she has disappeared. Alternatively the registrar may make an order that the restriction applies but with modifications (s 41(2)(b)), in effect repeating what presently appears in existing restrictions. This is because they are currently shown on the register with the following wording included at the start of the restriction, 'Except under an order of the registrar . . .'. However, s 41(3) makes it clear that the power to make such an order is only exercisable on the application of a party who appears to the registrar to have a 'sufficient interest in the restriction'. This will be a question of fact and will depend upon evidence produced to the registrar. It will be the subject of rules yet to be made.

5.5.3 The powers of the registrar to register notices

The registrar may enter a restriction if it appears that it is necessary or desirable to do so for three specific reasons set out in s 42(1)(a)–(c) of the Act. They are to:

(a) prevent invalidity or unlawfulness relating to transactions affecting a registered estate or charge. (The example quoted in the notes to the Act is of breach of trust, where the trustees of the land are required to obtain the consent of some person to a disposition.)

(b) ensure that interests which are capable of being overreached are actually overreached. (The example given is of interests under a trust of land (or settlement under the Settled Land Act 1925). To ensure they are overreached there could be a restriction to the effect that the proceeds of any registered disposition must be paid to at least two trustees or a trust corporation.)

(c) protect a right or claim regarding a registered title or charge. (Such a claim or right need not be proprietary. The kind of entry might be a restriction entered in respect of an order appointing a receiver. The notes to the Act state that it could also be a restriction entered in respect of a charging order relating to an interest under a trust.)

Section 42(1) gives the registrar the power to enter a restriction. (In comparison s 44 (see 5.5.5 below) imposes a duty on the registrar to register a restriction in particular circumstances.) Although as has been seen above in 5.4 above a notice can have priority, a restriction is not intended to confer priority. Consequently, s 42(2) states that no restriction may be made to protect a right or claim that is intended to protect the priority of an interest and which otherwise could be the subject of a notice instead. That is not to say that the same interest could not have two forms of protection. For example a notice could protect the priority of a right of pre-emption and at the same time a restriction could be made to ensure that the registered proprietor first offers to sell the land to the grantee of the right before selling elsewhere. The registrar is required by s 42(3) to give notice of restrictions made under the whole section to the proprietor of the estate or charge. This does not apply to entries made pursuant to the provisions of s 43 (see 5.5.4 below).

5.5.4 Applications for restrictions

These can be made by the registered proprietor or with the consent of the registered proprietor where a restriction may be entered by the registrar, rather than one that is an obligatory restriction. Alternatively a person may apply to the registrar for a discretionary restriction where the applicant 'has a sufficient interest in the making of the entry' (s 43(1)(c)). There is to be a power to make rules that will require that an application be made in such circumstances and by such persons as the rules may provide. The rules will also cover the nature of the consent required of the registered proprietor. They will also define and specify standard forms of restriction (s 43(2)). Section 43(3) provides that if a person entitled to apply for a restriction applies for a form of restriction not prescribed by rules, then the registrar may only approve the application:

(a)   if it appears to the registrar that the terms of the restriction are reasonable; and

(b)   that the application of the proposed restriction would be straightforward and not place an unreasonable burden on the registrar.

5.5.5 Obligatory restrictions

The power to enter a restriction is in fact strengthened by s 44 in the Act that imposes a duty to enter a restriction in the particular case of legal co-ownership. When the registrar enters two or more persons in the register as the proprietor of a registered estate, the effect of s 44 is to require the registrar to enter a restriction in the register. The nature of the restriction will be covered by rules that will ensure that interests which are capable of being overreached on a disposition are overreached. An example given in the notes to the Act effectively covers co-ownership and the trust element of owning a property jointly. So, if two registered proprietors were to hold an estate on trust for several beneficiaries, a restriction could be entered to ensure that the proceeds of any registered disposition are paid to at least two trustees. If one of the trustees were to die, this would ensure that no disposition could be made until another trustee was appointed.

Section 44(2) allows for restrictions required by statute. They shall be the subject of rules as to their form. Section 86(4) also contains a statutory obligatory restriction. After registration of a bankruptcy order the registrar must enter in any affected title (ie owned by the bankrupt) a restriction reflecting the effect of the Insolvency Act 1986. (This restriction is preceded by a notice that is registered upon the registration of a petition in bankruptcy.)

5.5.6 Notifiable applications

Section 45 of the Act is meant to protect registered proprietors against unwarranted restrictions being entered upon the register. If an application for a restriction is 'notifiable', and the nature of such a restriction is defined by s 45(3), then the registrar must serve notice on the registered proprietor and such other persons as rules may prescribe (s 45(1)(a), (b)). The application is notifiable unless it is made with the consent of the registered proprietor, made under an order of court, or required under the rules. Anyone receiving such a notice can by reason of s 73 object to the application to the registrar. If it is not possible to dispose by agreement of an objection then the registrar must refer the matter to the adjudicator.

5.5.7 Restrictions made by order of court

Section 46 gives courts the power to protect a right or claim by making an order requiring the registrar to enter a restriction on the register. No such order can be made to protect the priority of an interest that must be protected by a notice. However the court can direct that the entry made as a result of the order have overriding priority. Where, under the present law, the court would order the entry of an inhibition, it is under the Act most likely to order the entry of a restriction. The notes to the Act refer to the operation of this section on the basis of an example whereby a restriction overrides the priority protection given to an official search or the entry of a notice in respect of an estate contract.

5.6   CHARGES

The 2002 Act seeks to simplify and in some respects change the law relating to registered charges. One type of mortgage is abolished for registered land. A mortgage by demise or sub-demise is no longer possible for a registered property. Section 23(1)(a) of the Act specifically excludes the possibility from the list of owner's powers set out in that section. Furthermore s 25 makes it clear that rules can be made to control the form and content of a mortgage deed. This will need to be the case once e-conveyancing is the norm.

By s 132 of the Act a 'charge' is defined as 'any mortgage, charge or lien for securing money or money's worth'. (The same section defines a 'legal mortgage' as having the same meaning as in the Law of Property Act 1925, see s 205(1)(xvi) of that Act.) The definition has been drafted in this wide manner to ensure that it should include both charges to secure the discharge of some obligation as well as charges imposed by statute. (Indeed there are two specific sections dealing with statutory charges, being ss 50 and 55, and these are discussed at 5.6.1 and 5.6.3 below).

Sections 48–50 deal with the relative priority of charges, while ss 51–53 cover the powers of a chargee. Sections 54 and 55 deal with the realization of the security while two miscellaneous sections, 56 and 57, relating to charges follow these. They will all now be considered in turn.

5.6.1 Relative priority

Section 48 sets out how the order of priority of registered charges can be ascertained from a registered title. The basis of priority of charges is that they are 'to be taken to rank as between themselves in the order shown in the register' (s 48(1)). Therefore the first registered in time has, in the absence of any evidence to the contrary, the position of being first in priority against all others that appear subsequently in the register. As is the case with many other sections in this Act there is provision for rules affecting charges. These rules will make provision about how priority is to be shown in the register and about applications for registration regarding priority. In effect the rules will enable the creation of alternatives to the main proposition set out in s 48(1). The rules will therefore be concerned with how the register will show that order of priority and how applications can be made to register a different order that has been agreed between several chargees/applicants, see s 48(2)(a), (b).

Section 49 is concerned with tacking and further advances. A registered lender may make a further advance in priority to any subsequent registered charge if the first lender making the further advance has not received from the subsequent lender notice of that later loan. This section therefore allows a lender to make a further advance on the security of an existing charge if that first lender has not received notice from another lender that a subsequent charge has been created (s 49(1)). There will be rules governing how the receipt of the notice shall be effected (s 49(2)). However, the section does not stop there. It also allows further benefit to first lenders who make further advances in two further ways.

First the lender may also make a further advance that ranks in priority if the advance is made as a result of an obligation to do so in the original mortgage deed and that obligation was noted in the register. Thus, the lender can obtain the same priority for two loans if the original mortgage terms contained an obligation for the further sum to be advanced and that obligation was noted in the register (see s 49(3)). This is a repeat of the present law. However, there is a new provision that will benefit lenders. Section 49(4) allows a lender to make a further advance ranking in priority if the parties to the original charge agree a maximum amount for the security for the loan, and where that agreement as to a maximum was noted in the register (s 49(4)(a), (b)). As long as the sums due to the first lender do not exceed the maximum loan amount specified, in accordance with rules, the subsequent loan or loans up to the agreed maximum will take the same priority over any subsequent charge.

Section 50 deals with statutory charges and a duty of notification. Perhaps the most common form of statutory charge is a charging order made pursuant to the terms of the Charging Orders Act 1979, or by some other enactment that imposes a charging order such as the Criminal Justice Act 1988, s 78. If the registrar registers a charge made pursuant to statute which has priority over a previously registered charge, then the registrar must give notice of the statutory charge to parties listed in rules yet to be made. As to their identity, the notes to the Act helpfully indicate that they are likely to be mortgagees whose interests are protected in the register. The change made by the section is to ensure that lenders have notice of statutory charges. In doing so it will allow lenders to consider whether they should make further advances arising from the 'postponed' registered charge. They may not wish to, as the statutory charge may very well reduce the value in the security because of the priority attaching to the statutory charge.

5.6.2   The lender's powers — powers as chargee

Section 51 states the obvious. On completion of the registration process a registered charge has effect as a charge by deed by way of legal mortgage. In this way whatever the loan documentation may be called, all mortgages of registered land will take effect as 'a charge by deed by way of legal mortgage'. Conveyancers should remember that s 25 of the Act also enables the creation of rules that control requirements as to the form and content of a registered charge.

Section 52 covers how the Act legislates for the protection of someone in whose favour a disposition is made by a chargee. The section has much in common with s 26 that covers the same area in relation to dispositions of registered land. If nothing to the contrary is noted in the register, the chargee is taken to have all the powers of disposal of a legal mortgagee under the Law of Property Act 1925 so that the rights and interests given by the disposition cannot be contested. This does not mean that there cannot be disputes and claims between lender and buyer on the terms of a loan because s 52(2) makes it clear that the provision does not affect the lawfulness of a loan, it simply prevents the title of a disponee being questioned.

Section 53 repeats and extends the current law by providing that the proprietor of a sub-charge has in relation to the subject property the same powers as the sub-chargor. This can also apply to a registered sub-sub-charge.

5.6.3   Realization of security

Section 105 of the Law of Property Act 1925 regulates the mortgagee's duties in relation to the application of proceeds of sale paid on a sale by a lender — in particular what happens to a surplus that may exist once a lender has taken from the proceeds all moneys properly payable to the lender as a result of the mortgage terms. Any surplus is held on trust for 'the person entitled to the mortgaged property' (Law of Property Act 1925, s 105). Where a lender has a surplus, and if that lender does not know of any subsequent lenders, theoretically that lender should account to the defaulting borrower. So s 54 of the Act provides that for the purposes of s 105, in its application of the proceeds of sale, the party with the proceeds must proceed on the basis of anything in the register immediately before the sale. The effect of this is that the lender who holds a surplus after effecting a mortgagee's sale will have to consult the register to determine who is entitled to the surplus. This should ensure that, whether they have notice or not of subsequent loans, if they are protected by an entry or entries on the register they will be entitled to receive the surplus.

Section 55 makes it clear that a charge over registered land that is a local land charge may only be realized if the title to the charge is registered. These local land charges take effect as overriding interests as is confirmed by their inclusion in Sch 1 and Sch 3 of the Act. Those that are charges on land are typically to secure money due to the local authority. Common examples are charges to cover moneys paid by a local authority arising from non-compliance with a repairs notice under the Housing Act 1985, s 193 or street works under the Highways Act 1980, s 212. Thus, they will only be enforceable as charges if they are registered charges on the register.

5.6.4   Miscellaneous matters

Section 56 covers the power to give a valid receipt for moneys secured by a registered charge where there are joint proprietors of the registered charge. A valid receipt in these circumstances may be given by:

(a)   the registered proprietors; or
(b)   the survivor or survivor of the registered proprietors; or
(c)   by the personal representative of the last survivor of the registered proprietors.

This provision has a lot in common with the existing law set out in s 32 of the 1925 Act.

Finally s 57 states that rules may be made to cover the right of consolidation in relation to a registered charge. (The current rule is the Land Registration Rules 1925, r 154.) Consolidation of mortgages arises from the doctrine that a mortgagee who holds several mortgages by the same borrower, but perhaps on different properties, can insist on the redemption of them all if the borrower seeks to redeem any of them.

5.7   KEY POINTS FOR THE PRACTITIONER

- The 2002 Act abolishes inhibitions and cautions against dealings (although there are transitional arrangements contained in Sch 12 relating to inhibitions and cautions against dealings).

- Notices will be used to protect encumbrances on land that are intended to bind third parties.
- Restrictions regulate the circumstances in which a disposition of a registered estate or charge may be the subject of an entry in the register.
- Either notices or restrictions can be applied for without the permission of the registered proprietor. However, the registered proprietor must be informed of the application and will be at liberty to seek the cancellation of the notice, or object to an application for a restriction.
- There is no reference in the Act to minor interests. These interests are to be known as interests protected by an entry in the register.
- Notices will be either agreed or unilateral in nature. Affected parties can apply to the registrar to cancel a unilateral notice.
- Section 33 of the Act lists excluded interests that cannot be protected by a notice. They include a trust of land, a lease for a term of three years or less from the date of the grant and which is not required to be registered, and a restrictive covenant made between a lessor and lessee relating to the property leased.
- A person must not exercise the right to apply for the entry of a restriction or a notice without reasonable cause. The duty is owed to any person who suffers damage should there be a breach of this duty to act reasonably.
- Where, under the present law, the court would order the entry of an inhibition, it is under the Act most likely to order the entry of a restriction.
- A mortgage by demise or sub-demise is no longer possible for a registered property.
- The priority of mortgages is by the first in time at registration as shown on the register. There will be rules to enable variations to this by agreement between lenders.
- The registrar must give notice of a registered statutory charge that has priority, to parties listed in rules yet to be made. They are likely to be mortgagees whose interests are protected on the register.

Chapter 6

Registration Generally

6.1   INTRODUCTION

In this chapter we consider various miscellaneous matters relating to the register and registration generally. These include the conclusiveness of registration, boundaries, quality of title, accessing information, priority protection, applications, and land and charge certificates. We also examine the provisions in the 2002 Act relating to the alteration of the register, rectification, and indemnity (indemnities also appear in chapter 10; see 10.5.2 for further details). For the record, s 1(1) of the Act confirms that a register of title shall continue to be kept. Section 1(2) goes on to provide that rules can be made regarding the information to be included in the register, the form in which the information is to be kept, and the arrangement of that information (most titles are already held in electronic form). The other main parts of the Act that are considered in this chapter are Pt 6 (ss 58–78), s 120 and Sch 4.

6.2   CONCLUSIVENESS OF REGISTRATION

It is well established that the act of registration vests the legal estate in the
registered proprietor. Accordingly s 58(1) of the 2002 Act provides that if, on the
entry of a person in the register as proprietor of a legal estate, the legal estate
would not otherwise be vested in that person, it shall be deemed to be vested in
him or her as a result of the registration. From this it follows that even if a transfer
is a nullity, eg because of fraud, the estate will still vest in the transferee if his or
her name is on the register (although of course an application can be made to alter
the register, see 6.11 below). Section 58(2) creates an exception to this guiding
principle. It provides that the legal estate will not vest in the registered proprietor
if there is a registrable disposition and some further entry is still required to meet
the registration requirements set out in Sch 2. So, for example, on the grant of a
long lease the registry is required to enter a note of the lease on the superior
registered freehold title. If it fails to do so, then by virtue of s 58(1), the leasehold
legal estate will not vest in the lessee (although it will do so in equity and the
lessee can apply to the registrar to correct the mistake). Section 59 goes on to
confirm that certain entries must be made in relation to certain dispositions, eg the
owner of a legal estate must be registered as the proprietor of the estate and
the owner of a legal charge must be entered as the proprietor of the charge. The
effective date of registration is the time of the making of the application (s 74).
This accords with the land registry's 'real time priority' system under which an
application's priority is determined by the time at which it is entered on the day
list.

6.3   BOUNDARIES

The 2002 Act preserves the general boundaries rule. This is that the boundary lines
shown on the filed plan are not conclusive, ie they do not show the exact line of
the boundary (s 60(1), (2)). However rules may make provision for the exact line
of a boundary to be fixed (see s 60(3)). In the past, applications to fix boundaries
have been rare, due perhaps to the risk of creating a boundary dispute where none
existed and also due to the costs involved (the Registry needs to investigate
adjoining landowners' titles as well). The Law Commission believes that fixed
boundaries will become more common in future for two reasons. First, because the
development of modern mapping techniques will make the means of fixing
boundaries less demanding. Secondly, because the adverse possession reforms will
prevent a 'boundary creeper' type squatter succeeding if the boundary is fixed
(Sch 6, para 5(4)(b)). This may act as an incentive for property owners to stop
encroachers by fixing their boundaries (see 9.3). Rules may also be made requiring
a successful boundary creeper who becomes registered to have his or her boundary
fixed so that he or she (or a successor in title) cannot encroach again.

6.4   ACCRETION AND DILUVION

Accretion and diluvion ensue from the forces of nature and occur where land is bounded by water, eg a river. Accretion is where land previously covered by water is added over time to an adjoining owner's land, eg through the retreat of the water. Diluvion is the opposite and occurs where land over time is gradually lost into adjoining water through erosion or the advance of the water (see generally *Southern Centre of Theosophy Inc v State of South Australia* [1982] AC 706, 716). Section 61(1) gives effect to the common law doctrine of accretion and diluvion. It provides that the fact that a registered estate is shown as having a particular boundary does not affect the operation of accretion and diluvion, ie the boundary may fluctuate over time. This doctrine applies whether the general boundaries rule applies or whether the exact boundary has been fixed (see 6.3 above). Parties may of course contract-out of the statutory provision if they wish. Section 61(2) provides that they may enter into an agreement concerning the operation of accretion or diluvion in relation to a registered estate provided it is registered in accordance with land registration rules. Thus, if two registered estates have, say, a brook dividing them, the respective owners can agree that the boundary is in a particular place notwithstanding any changes that may be made by the brook.

6.5   UPGRADING CLASS OF TITLE

The different grades of registered title found under the old law are preserved in the 2002 Act and we have considered them at 3.4, eg absolute, possessory, etc. Readers may recall that the Land Registration Act 1925, as amended by the Land Registration Act 1986, contained provisions for the upgrading of titles, eg from possessory to absolute, or from good leasehold to absolute leasehold. Section 62 of the Act replicates the previous law with some amendments. It effectively empowers the registrar to upgrade a class of title if certain conditions are met and these are now considered.

First, a possessory title may be upgraded to an absolute title in two situations:

(a)   If the registrar is satisfied as to the title to the estate (s 62(1)). This might occur where a person was initially registered with possessory title because his or her title deeds were missing. If subsequently those deeds come to light the registrar can upgrade the title to absolute if he or she is otherwise satisfied with them.

(b)   If the title has been registered with possessory title for 12 years and the proprietor is still in possession, the registrar can upgrade the title to absolute (s 62(4)). (For the meaning of 'proprietor in possession' see s 131 and 6.11.2 below). Section 62(9) permits the Lord Chancellor by order to alter the 12-year period. This might happen in future if, say, the limitation period for the recovery of unregistered land is reduced from 12 years to ten (see chapter 9 generally regarding adverse possession).

The Act provides for upgrades in respect of other classes of title. A qualified title can be upgraded to absolute if the registrar is satisfied as to the title to the estate (s 62(1)), eg where the cause of the registrar's original objections is subsequently shown to no longer threaten the holding under that title. There is provision for upgrading qualified leasehold titles as well (s 62(3)). A good leasehold title can be upgraded to an absolute title if the registrar is satisfied as to the superior title (s 62(2)), eg where the superior title is itself registered for the first time. A possessory leasehold title can be upgraded to good leasehold if the registrar is satisfied as to the title to the estate (s 62(3)(a)) or the title has been registered as possessory for 12 years and the proprietor is in possession (s 62(5)). A possessory leasehold title can be upgraded to absolute if the registrar is satisfied both as to the title to the estate and as to the superior title (s 62(3)(b)).

Section 62(6) provides that none of the powers conferred by the Act to upgrade a title may be exercised by the registrar if there is any outstanding adverse claim to the registered proprietor's title. This is a claim which is made by virtue of an estate, right or interest whose enforceability is preserved by virtue of the existing entry about the class of title. Such adverse claims must therefore be resolved before an upgrade can proceed.

The categories of persons who may apply to upgrade a title are widened under the Act. Whereas the Land Registration Act 1925, s 77 referred to the registrar acting on his own initiative or 'on application by the proprietor', s 62(7) lists the following persons who may apply:

(a)   the proprietor of the estate to which the application relates;

(b)   a person entitled to be registered as the proprietor of that estate (eg an executor in respect of the testator's land prior to sale);

(c)   the proprietor of a registered charge affecting that estate (ie prior to exercising its power of sale); and

(d)   a person interested in a registered estate which derives from that estate (eg a subtenant).

As before, there would be nothing to stop other persons interested in the registered estate from requesting the registrar to exercise his or her power to upgrade a title.

Unlike the Land Registration Act 1925, the effect of upgrading a title is set out expressly in s 63 of the Act. First, where a freehold or leasehold title is upgraded to absolute, 'the proprietor ceases to hold the estate subject to any estate, right or interest whose enforceability was preserved by virtue of the previous entry about the class of title' (s 63(1)). This principle also applies where leasehold is upgraded from possessory or qualified title to good leasehold. However, the upgrade does not affect or prejudice the enforcement of any estate, right or interest affecting, or in derogation of, the lessor's title to grant the lease (s 63(2)).

Any person who had previously had the benefit of an estate, right or interest and who suffers loss as a result of the upgrade is entitled to be indemnified by the state for that loss. This is because that person is deemed to have suffered loss by reason of the rectification of the register (see Sch 8, para 1(2)(a) and 6.12 below).

6.6   USE OF REGISTER TO RECORD DEFECTS IN TITLE

Section 64 contains important new provisions to record on the register certain defects in title where such defects would not previously have been recorded. It provides that the registrar, becoming aware that the right to determine (ie end) a registered estate has become exercisable, may enter this fact on the register. The most obvious example of this would be in a leasehold context where the lessee has breached a lease covenant and the lessor has become entitled to forfeit the lease. Another example would be where a rentcharge is unpaid in respect of a freehold estate and the rentcharge owner is able to exercise a right of re-entry. Both situations could potentially result in the loss of the estate. If the registrar notes the defect on the register, a prospective buyer will be alerted to the problem at a much earlier stage of his or her investigations (ie instead of finding out from replies to enquiries). This accords with the guiding principle of the 2002 Act, which is to have a conveyancing system in which title, as far as possible, can be investigated on-line. Section 64(2) allows for rules to make provision about the circumstances in which the registrar must exercise his or her power, how entries will be made and the removal of such entries. Once e-conveyancing is with us, network access agreements are likely to require solicitors and licensed conveyancers to disclose such defects affecting clients' estates to the Registry (which they would otherwise be reluctant to do). This will enable the appropriate entry to be made on the register.

6.7   ACCESSING INFORMATION

Section 112 of the Land Registration Act 1925 (as substituted by the Land Registration Act 1988) opened up the register to the public for the first time. This meant that it was no longer necessary for a registered landowner to give consent before his or her title could be inspected. Building on this, and in order to facilitate an e-conveyancing system in which enquiries will be made on-line, s 66 of the 2002 Act extends the scope of the open register. Section 66(1) provides that a person may inspect and make copies of, or any part of, the following:

(a)   the register of title;
(b)   any document kept by the registrar which is referred to in the register of title;
(c)   any other document kept by the registrar which relates to an application to him or her; or
(d)   the register of cautions against first registration.

Section 66(2) provides that the right to inspect and copy is subject to rules. These rules are likely to provide for exceptions and impose conditions, eg the payment of fees. The explanatory notes to the Act indicate that the rules may restrict access to documents of a private nature or which contain commercially sensitive information to those who have a good reason to see them. Protection of private information is likely to follow the scheme laid down in the Freedom of Information Act 2000.

The term 'office copies', familiar to conveyancers for decades, is replaced by the more user-friendly term 'official copy'. Section 67(1) provides that an official copy of the items listed above ((a)–(d)) is admissible in evidence to the same extent as the original. There is power for rules to make provision about the form of official copies, who may issue them, applications for them and the conditions to be met by applicants, eg payment of fees (s 67(3)). A person who relies on an official copy in which there is a mistake is not liable for the loss suffered by another by reason of that mistake (s 67(2)). The person suffering loss is entitled to be indemnified by the state (see 6.12 below).

6.7.1   Conclusiveness of filed copies

Under the previous law, the Land Registration Act 1925, s 110(4) provided that the register was conclusive in relation to the abstracts and extracts from documents that were referred to in it. Thus, filed copies could be relied upon and it was unnecessary to see the originals. Section 120 of the Act does the same as the old s 110(4) but goes further to take account of the open register. Section 110(4) applied as between vendor and purchaser only, whereas the new provision benefits others as well. Section 120 applies in two situations:

(a)   First, where there is a disposition that relates to land to which a registered estate relates. This will include dispositions that require registration, eg a transfer of freehold, but also some that do not. The open register is open to everyone including those who are granted interests out of a registered estate that are not registrable and those who are parties to any subsequent dealings with those unregistered interests. Thus, for example, a lessee under a short lease (which is not registrable) may search and rely upon extracts from documents referred to in the register of the freehold title, eg freehold covenants that affect the lessee. The assignee of a short lease may do the same.

(b)   Secondly, where there is an entry in the register relating to a registered estate that refers to a document kept by the registrar which is *not* an original. An example might be leases — sometimes the Registry does not always retain originals of leases but just keeps copies. Thus, filed copies of the copies may also be relied upon as conclusive.

Section 120 goes on to provide that:

(a)   as between the parties to a disposition, the document kept by the registrar is to be taken to be correct and to contain all the material parts of the original document (s 120(2));

(b)   no party to the disposition may require the production of the original document (s 120(3)); and

(c)   no party to the disposition is to be affected by any provision of the original document which is not contained in the document held by the registrar (s 120(4)), ie it can be taken 'as read'. However, any person suffering loss as a result of a mistake in an unoriginal document referred to in the register will be entitled to an indemnity (see 6.12 below).

6.7.2   Index (formerly Index Map)

Readers will be familiar with the Land Registry Index Map from which it is possible to ascertain whether any parcel of land in England and Wales is registered and, if not, whether it is affected by any caution against first registration. As so much information is held by the Registry electronically (ie 'in dematerialised form') the Act drops the use of the word 'map' and simply provides for the registrar to keep an Index to enable the following matters to be ascertained in relation to any parcel of land (s 68(1)):

(a)   whether any registered estate relates to the land;

(b)   how any registered estate which relates to the land is identified for the purposes of the register;

(c)   whether the land is affected by any, and if so what, caution against first registration; and

(d)   such other matters as rules may provide.

Rules will be made regarding official searches of the Index and how the information in the Index is to be kept and arranged. It is likely to be kept in electronic form and possibly include more information than the Index Map does at present, eg concerning land use.

6.7.3   Accessing historical information

A new provision allows the registrar to provide information about the history of a registered title (s 69). The registrar has sometimes done this in the past (if the applicant can show good reason) but it has never been on a statutory footing. Historical information can of course be useful to conveyancers. They might want to know the extent of land that was intended to benefit from a restrictive covenant created many years ago. They might want to establish whether freeholds had previously been in common ownership, thus extinguishing restrictive covenants or easements. A point may also arise as to whether a former owner is liable on the covenants for title implied in an earlier transfer (see the Law of Property

(Miscellaneous) Provisions) Act 1994, s 7). Rules may make provision about applications to the registrar for the exercise of this power (s 69(2)). The Law Commission has stressed that a request for historical information should only be made if there is a sound conveyancing reason for doing so. It should never been seen as a routine enquiry! The concern is that such requests will simply slow down the conveyancing process. The Act imposes no obligation on the Registry to keep a complete historical record of a title, nor to keep any record of a title for an unlimited period; so applicants may not find what they want anyway.

6.7.4   Official searches

Section 70 allows for rules to make provision for official searches of the register, including searches of pending applications for first registration. The rules may in particular make provision about the form of application; the manner in which such applications may be made; the form of official search certificates; and the manner in which such certificates may be issued.

6.8   PRIORITY PROTECTION

Conveyancers will of course be aware of how official searches of the register confer priority protection in favour of an applicant. In a typical case, several days before completion a purchaser will carry out an official search of the register in order to update the office copy entries of the title. When the search certificate is issued the applicant will then have 30 working days in which to complete the transaction and apply to register the transfer at the Land Registry. Provided this is done in time, any entry made on the register during the priority period will be postponed behind the applicant's application to register the transfer. At present, official searches can be made by post, telephone, fax, direct access or in person.

Section 72 of the 2002 Act makes express provision for priority protection and, importantly, extends the circumstances in which it can be obtained. There is power for rules to make provision for priority periods in connection with:

(a)   (as is presently the case) official searches of the register, including searches of pending applications for first registration; or

(b)   (this is new) the noting in the register of a contract for the making of a registrable disposition of a registered estate or charge. This is linked to the introduction of e-conveyancing. Under the e-conveyancing system, in order for such an estate contract to be valid, it will be necessary to enter a notice of the contract on the register (see 8.5). At the same time, that entry will confer priority protection on the applicant.

Section 72(7) provides that the rules may, in particular, make provision as to:

(a)   the commencement and length of the priority period;

(b)   the applications for registration to which such a period relates (eg typically a transfer and a charge);

(c)   the order in which competing priority periods rank; and

(d)   the application of priority protection where more than one priority period relates to the same application (eg when a search is repeated).

Rules may also make provision for the keeping of records in relation to priority periods and the inspection of such records (s 72(6)(b)). This will (as now) allow someone to discover if there is any priority period in place in respect of another application on the subject title.

Section 72(2) confirms the general rule above that where an application for an entry in the register is protected, any entry made in the register during the priority period relating to the application is postponed to any entry made in pursuance of it. There are, however, two exceptions to this:

(a)   The first exception relates to the situation where someone (X) makes an official search shortly after another person (Y) has already done so. In this case, clearly X's subsequent application will not take priority over Y's subsequent application (see s 72(3)).

(b)   The second exception is where the court orders that a restriction be entered and directs under s 46(3) that it is to have overriding priority (s 72(4)), eg in order to freeze the register, see 5.5.7.

6.9   FORM AND CONTENT OF APPLICATIONS TO THE REGISTRY

As we have seen, the 2002 Act contains specific rules concerning particular kinds of application. Examples include the procedure on applications by a squatter in Sch 6, para 15 and rules concerning first registration applications in s 14. The Act also contains, in Sch 10, para 6, a general power to make rules concerning other matters including the form and content of applications under the Act. It will be possible to require all applications to be in a prescribed form and in future this is likely of course to be in electronic form. In respect of company charges, applications for registration at the Land Registry and the Companies Register may ultimately be combined. The Land Registry and Companies House are currently discussing possible ways in which the two systems can be linked electronically and s 121 allows for rules to be made regarding the transmission of information from the Land Registry to the Companies Registry.

6.10   LAND CERTIFICATES AND ABOLITION OF CHARGE CERTIFICATES

Under the 2002 Act there will no longer be a requirement for the registered proprietor to produce the land certificate to the Registry on a disposition of a registered estate or when applying to register a notice or restriction. This is because it is incompatible with the system of electronic conveyancing. Instead there are special procedures to enable the registered proprietor to secure the cancellation of a notice (s 36, 5.4.3) and object to the entry of a restriction (s 45, 5.5.6). Indeed, the Act says very little about land certificates at all. The only provision is in Sch 10, para 4 in which there is a power by rules to make provision about:

(a)   when a certificate of registration of title may be issued;
(b)   the form and content of such a certificate; and
(c)   when such a certificate must be produced or surrendered to the registrar.

As the register alone is conclusive as to the state of the title, the entries in the land certificate may be out of date. Because of this the Law Commission envisage that a land certificate will probably in future no longer contain a copy of the register. It will merely certify the registration of a parcel of land and identify the name of the registered proprietor.

Perhaps more significantly for practitioners is the abolition of the charge certificate once the Act comes into force. Registered charges can already be discharged electronically under the END (Electronic Notification of Discharge) system and it is likely that the creation of registered charges will be one of the first dispositions that can be effected electronically. As a result, charge certificates will become redundant.

6.11   ALTERATION AND RECTIFICATION OF THE REGISTER

Whereas the Land Registration 1925 talks about 'rectification' of the register the 2002 Act provides for 'alteration', both of the register of title (s 65, Sch 4) and (this is new) the register of cautions (ss 20, 21). Under the Act, rectification is just one kind of alteration and is defined as one which involves the correction of a mistake *and* which prejudicially affects the title of a registered proprietor (Sch 4, para 1). As a result of the latter, a right to indemnity will naturally flow from rectification (see 6.12 below).

The court and the registrar are both given powers under the Act to alter the register (Sch 4, paras 2–7). These are considered below. Of course alteration of the register will also be permitted under network access agreements in e-conveyancing, eg by practitioners (see generally chapter 8).

6.11.1   Alteration by the court

The court may order alteration of the register in three cases:

(a)   to correct a mistake, eg where a transfer has been forged;
(b)   to bring the register up to date, eg removing a leasehold title from the register following forfeiture; and

(c) to give effect to any estate, right or interest excepted from the effect of registration, eg where land is registered with possessory freehold title as a result of adverse possession but it later transpires that the land is leasehold.

Where a court makes an order for the register to be altered, the registrar will be under a duty to alter the register once the order is served on him or her. The equivalent provision in the 1925 Act applied only in relation to an order to *rectify* the register. Rules yet to be made will determine when a court can order alteration in cases which do not amount to rectification (Sch 4, para 4(a)). These are likely to restrict the court's duty to order an alteration to cases where it has made a determination in proceedings. So, for example, it would not extend to an incorrect entry which is discovered during proceedings but which is not relevant to the outcome of the particular case.

6.11.2 Protecting a proprietor in possession

The Land Registration Act 1925, s 82(3) protects registered proprietors who are in possession of their land by restricting the circumstances in which their titles can be rectified. If, for example, two adjoining landowners are both registered as proprietors of a strip of land on their common boundary the register will be rectified against the one who is *not* in possession of it. This reflects the reality on the ground. Schedule 4, para 3(2) continues this protection by preventing an order for the alteration of the register that amounts to rectification without the proprietor's consent where the proprietor is in possession. However, this protection will not apply in two cases (also mentioned in the 1925 Act):

(a) where the proprietor has by fraud or lack of proper care caused or substantially contributed to the mistake; or

(b) it would for any other reason be unjust for the alteration not to be made.

In the Act, the definition of a 'proprietor in possession' is clarified. A proprietor will be in possession where:

(a) the land is physically in his or her possession (s 131(1); *Chowood Ltd v Lyall (No 2)* [1930] 2 Ch 156);

(b) the land is physically in possession of a person who is entitled to be registered as proprietor (s 131(1)), eg trustee in bankruptcy or personal representative. However, a squatter who is entitled to be registered as proprietor under Sch 6 of the Act is not, for these purposes a person entitled to be registered (s 131(3)). The Law Commission thought it inappropriate to extend protection to trespassers;

(c) the registered proprietor is the landlord and the person in possession is a tenant (s 131(2)(a));

(d)   the registered proprietor is a mortgagor and the person in possession is the mortgagee (s 131(2)(b)). This reverses *Hayes v Nwajiaku* [1994] EGCS 106 which held that a mortgagee in possession was not in possession for the purposes of s 82(3) of the 1925 Act;

(e)   the registered proprietor is a licensor and the person in possession is a licensee (s 131(2)(c)); and

(f)   the registered proprietor is a trustee and the person in possession is a beneficiary under the trust (s 131(2)(d)).

Section 131(2) makes it clear that the second-named person in (c)-(f) above will also be in possession if he or she is *treated* as being in possession. So this would include a tenant who had sublet premises or a mortgagee who had exercised its power of leasing.

Where the court can order rectification of the register and the land is not in possession of the proprietor the court must make an order unless it considers there are exceptional circumstances which justify its not doing so (Sch 4, para 3(3)). This reflects the present law (see *Epps v Esso Petroleum Co Ltd* [1973] 1 WLR 1071).

6.11.3   Alteration by the registrar

In addition to the court, the registrar is given powers of alteration. The registrar may alter the register in four cases. The first three are the same as for the court (see 6.11.1 above). The fourth case is for the purpose of removing a superfluous entry. This would cover a case where a restriction on the powers of a registered proprietor had ceased to apply or perhaps where an interest protected by one entry on the register was adequately protected by another entry. With the arrival of e-conveyancing the registrar's power to remove superfluous entries is likely to become an important tool for the land registry. This is because, in future, authorized practitioners will be the ones actually registering dispositions, rights, and interests in registered land and the registry will want to remove unwanted entries that are cluttering up the register. Thus, the registrar will be able to carry out regular checks of registered titles and keep them up to date. This will help to achieve one of the main objectives of the Act, namely that the register should at all times be an accurate reflection of the true state of the title.

As with the court's powers, rules yet to be made will regulate when the registrar is under a duty to alter the register other than in cases of rectification. Contrary to the corresponding rule for the court (see above) this is likely to cover cases where the registrar discovers grounds for doing so irrespective of how those grounds came to light. Other rules will deal with the manner in which the registrar should exercise the power, applications for alteration of the register and the procedure for exercising the power of alteration, whether on application or not (Sch 4, para 7(b)–(d)).

If the registered proprietor objects to an application to alter his or her registered title, the registrar must, in the absence of agreement, refer the matter to the land registry adjudicator (s 73, see chapter 11). The provisions protecting a proprietor in possession referred to above (6.11.2) apply as much where the power to rectify is exercised by the registrar as they do in proceedings before the court (Sch 4, para 6). Similarly, where grounds for rectification exist and the land is not in the possession of the proprietor, the registrar must rectify the register unless he or she considers there are exceptional circumstances which justify not doing so (Sch 4, para 6(3)).

6.11.4   Costs in non-rectification cases

If the register is altered in a case not involving rectification, the registrar may pay such amount as he or she thinks fit in respect of any costs or expenses reasonably incurred by a person in connection with the alteration (Sch 4, para 9(1)). Ideally the consent of the registrar should first be obtained before any costs are incurred. Where the costs or expenses are incurred with the registrar's consent the registrar may always exercise this power. Even if the registrar does not give prior consent he or she may nevertheless pay costs and expenses where it appears to the registrar that they had to be incurred urgently and it was not reasonably practicable to apply for consent in advance. The registrar may also subsequently approve the incurring of them (Sch 4, para 9(2)). This power remedies a deficiency in the present law because there is currently no power to pay a party's costs in relation to an alteration that does not amount to rectification of the register. An example of when such costs may be incurred would be where a registered proprietor takes legal advice in connection with a request by the registrar concerning whether certain entries on the register are spent and can be removed.

6.11.5   Altering the cautions register

At 3.5 we explained the new register of cautions. Essentially this register is a record of cautions made against first registration in respect of unregistered legal estates (cautions against registered estates have of course been abolished under the Act). The person with the benefit of the caution against first registration who is claiming an interest in the unregistered land is given an opportunity to object before any application for first registration proceeds. Sections 20 and 21 of the Act allow for the court or registrar to alter the cautions register for the purpose of correcting a mistake or bringing the register up to date. An example might be where a court decides that the cautioner lacks the requisite interest in the land and thus orders the cancellation of the caution. Where the registrar alters the cautions register, the registrar may pay such amount as he or she thinks fit in respect of any costs reasonably incurred by a person in connection with the alteration (s 21(3)). Where a court orders an alteration, it can naturally award costs under the general rules found in the Civil Procedure Rules 1998, r 44. Rules yet to be made may stipulate when there is a duty to alter the register, the form and service of any order, applications to the registrar, and general procedure. When e-conveyancing is introduced, network access agreements may authorize practitioners to initiate the alteration of the cautions register (see generally chapter 8).

6.11.6   Alteration of documents

The Act contains a specific rule-making power to enable the registrar to correct a mistake in an application or accompanying document. In the circumstances prescribed in such rules, the correction will have the same effect as if made by the applicant or interested parties (Sch 10, para 6(e)). This effectively replicates the Land Registration Rules 1925, r 13, which presently allows the registrar to correct clerical errors. Given that the power is widely used, the Law Commission considered it appropriate to embody the power in primary legislation and hence the reference to it in the Act. In practice, the registrar serves notice on the interested parties of his or her intention to correct a mistake and then, provided there is no objection, simply goes ahead and makes the alteration.

6.12   INDEMNITY

The 2002 Act sets out eight circumstances in which a person who suffers loss is entitled to be indemnified (Sch 8, para 1(1)). Importantly, the substance of the indemnity provisions in the Act does not differ in any significant way from the existing indemnity provisions in the 1925 Act (as amended by the Land Registration Act 1997, s 2). A claimant can recover any loss that flows from the particular ground, whether that loss is direct or consequential.

The eight circumstances for indemnity are loss by reason of:

(a)   rectification of the register;

(b)   a mistake whose correction would involve rectification of the register;

(c)   a mistake in an official search;

(d)   a mistake in an official copy (formerly 'office copy');

(e)   a mistake in a document kept by the registrar which is not an original and is referred to in the register;

(f)   the loss or destruction of a document lodged at the registry for inspection or safe custody;

(g)   a mistake in the cautions register; or

(h)   failure by the registrar to perform his or her duty under s 50. This is a new duty — when the registrar registers a statutory charge that has priority over a prior charge on the register he or she has a duty to notify the prior chargee of that statutory charge (see 5.6.1).

As in the 1925 Act, no indemnity is payable on account of any mines or minerals or the existence of any right to work or get mines or minerals, unless (rarely) it is noted on the register of title that the title includes the mines or minerals (Sch 8, para 2).

Indemnity is considered further in chapter 10 at 10.5.2.

6.13 KEY POINTS FOR THE PRACTITIONER

- If, on the entry of a person in the register as proprietor of a legal estate, the legal estate would not otherwise be vested in that person, it shall be deemed to be vested in him or her as a result of the registration.
- The legal estate will not vest in the registered proprietor if there is a registrable disposition and some further entry is still required to meet the registration requirements, eg a note of a lease on the superior freehold title.
- The effective date of registration is the time at which the application is made, ie when it is entered on the Land Registry's day-list.
- The boundary lines shown on the filed plan are not conclusive unless they have been fixed (which is not common but may become so).
- The fact that a registered estate is shown as having a particular boundary does not affect the operation of accretion and diluvion, ie the boundary may fluctuate over time (although parties are free to contract-out).
- The power to upgrade a class of title is broadly in line with the old law, although the categories of persons who may apply to upgrade are widened.
- If the registrar becomes aware that the right to determine (ie end) a registered estate has become exercisable, he or she may enter this fact on the register, eg right to forfeiture on breach of lease covenant.
- E-conveyancing network access agreements are likely to require solicitors and licensed conveyancers to disclose title 'defects', such as the above.
- The scope of the open register is extended.
- The more user-friendly term 'official copy' replaces 'office copy'.
- A lessee under a short lease (which is not registrable) may search and rely upon extracts from documents referred to in the register of the freehold title, eg freehold covenants that affect the lessee.
- The 'Index' replaces the Index Map. The Index is likely to be kept in electronic form and include more information than the Index Map does at present, eg concerning land use.
- The Act formally permits the registrar to provide information about the history of a registered title which may be useful to practitioners, eg regarding land benefiting from covenants.
- Section 72 makes express provision for priority protection and extends the circumstances in which it can be obtained, eg priority for an estate contract following exchange.
- In future, applications to the Registry are likely to be in a prescribed electronic form.
- Rules will be made regarding the transmission of information from the Land Registry to the Companies Registry, eg in respect of company charges.
- In future a land certificate is unlikely to contain a copy of the register. It will merely certify the registration of a parcel of land and identify the name of the registered proprietor.
- Charge certificates are to be abolished.

- The Act essentially talks about 'alteration' of the register rather than rectification.
- The court and the registrar are both given powers under the Act to alter the register.
- Where a proprietor is in possession the register cannot be altered without the proprietor's consent unless the proprietor has by fraud or lack of proper care caused or substantially contributed to the mistake or it would for any other reason be unjust for the alteration not to be made.
- If the registered proprietor objects to an application to alter his or her registered title, the registrar must, in the absence of agreement, refer the matter to the land registry adjudicator for determination.
- If the register is altered in a case not involving rectification, the registrar may pay such amount as he or she thinks fit in respect of any costs or expenses reasonably incurred by a person in connection with the alteration.
- The court may order an alteration of, or the registrar may alter, the new cautions register for the purpose of correcting a mistake or bringing the register up to date.
- The Act contains a specific rule-making power to enable the registrar to correct a mistake in an application or accompanying document.
- Schedule 8 sets out eight circumstances in which a person who suffers loss is entitled to be indemnified. The substance of the indemnity provisions does not differ significantly from the existing indemnity provisions in the 1925 Act.

Chapter 7
Special Cases

7.1 INTRODUCTION

Part 7 of the 2002 Act is intended to deal with several areas deemed to be special cases where special provision is required. These special cases include various matters relating to the Crown and the treatment of pending actions, writs, orders and deeds of arrangement including bankruptcy petitions and orders.

Several definitions are in order at an early stage in this chapter. This is because arcane words and phrases will be encountered, especially in relation to Crown land. Demesne is defined as 'a sovereign's or state's territory; a domain'. The *Concise Oxford Dictionary* (9th edn, 1996) helpfully goes on to explain that in 'Law history — possession (of real property) as one's own'. The phrase then arises 'held in demesne' meaning (of an estate) occupied by the owner and not by tenants. The derivation explains all. It is Middle English via Anglo-French, the Old French being 'demeine' (later Anglo-French demesne) 'belonging to a lord' from Latin dominicus (as dominical). There is actually a statutory definition in the Act for demesne land. Section 132(1) defines 'demesne land' as 'land belonging to Her Majesty in right of the Crown which is not held for an estate in fee simple absolute in possession'. The meaning of all of this is considered further at 7.2.1 below.

Escheat appears in this part of the Act. 'Escheat' is defined as 'the reversion of property to the state, or (in feudal law) to a lord, on the owner's dying without legal heirs' (*Concise Oxford Dictionary*, 9th edn, 1996). Thus, the word is used to cover property affected by this and the word will also be used as a verb meaning 'hand over (property) as an escheat'. It is in effect the determination of freehold estate. Should escheat occur, the effect is that the lord out of or from whom that estate was held, becomes entitled to the land by his or her own right, free of the determined legal estate. This will be considered in detail in 7.2 below.

7.2 THE CROWN

The notes to the 2002 Act helpfully set out the main categories of Crown land, which are:

(a) Land belonging to government departments. This land is said to be 'in the name of' the Minister of the Crown for a particular government department. A typical example would be land used by the army and held by or for the Ministry of Defence. However, there may also be some land, which is said to be 'in the name of' the Queen. The Law Commission gave the example of ancient defence installations that existed at law in this format. The Law Commission also highlighted the existence of other 'semi-Government property', such as old lighthouses. Much of this kind of land or property is covered by specific legislation and the example given by the Law Commission was the Defence Act 1842. Where there is no specific legislation, the Law Commission thought that the Crown Lands Act 1702 applies.

(b) Land held by the monarch in right of the Crown (the Crown Estate). This is property or land forming the Crown estate and which is under the management of the Crown Estate Commissioners. This holding is said to be held by the Queen 'in right of the Crown in her political capacity'.

(c) The Crown's Private Estate. This Private Estate covers land or property that is owned by the Queen in her private capacity. The example given by the Law Commission of this type of holding is the Sandringham Estate. The provisions of the Crown Private Estates Acts 1800, 1862 and 1873 will therefore govern these properties.

(d) The two Royal Duchies of Cornwall and Lancaster.

(e) A residual category of land which includes the royal palaces and parks. These properties or the land in this category will be governed by the Crown Lands Act 1702. As well as the royal palaces and parks this category will also include any other Crown land not covered by any other arrangement. It is interesting to note that by the Crown Lands Act 1702, s 5 these lands are inalienable, ie they cannot be bought or sold, and the maximum length of lease that may granted of them is 31 years.

The notes to the Act make it clear that the statute addresses the following issues in relation to Crown land:

(a) registration of title to Crown land that is held by the monarch in demesne;
(b) escheat of registered land;
(c) representation in relation to Crown and Duchy land; and
(d) the disapplication of certain requirements relating to Duchy land.

Thus, s 79 covers provisions relating to the voluntary registration of demesne land, s 80 the compulsory registration of grants out of demesne land, while s 81 covers cautions against first registration and demesne land. Escheat is dealt with in s 82. In relation to both Crown and Duchy land s 83 describes who is to be considered the appropriate representative for notices, etc while s 84 covers the disapplication of particular requirements relating to the two Duchies of Lancaster and Cornwall. Finally s 83 covers the application of property when 'bona vacantia' applies. Each of these sections will now be considered in more detail.

7.2.1 Voluntary registration of demesne land

Section 132(1) defines 'demesne land' as 'land belonging to Her Majesty in right of the Crown which is not held for an estate in fee simple absolute in possession'. The meaning of this is considered below. (However it should be noted that s 132(2) goes on to state that in this statutory definition the reference to land belonging to Her Majesty does not include land in relation to which a freehold estate has determined but in relation to which there has been no act of entry or management by the Crown. This would exclude land subject to escheat but not yet controlled by the Crown.) Section 79 of the Act sets out detailed provisions relating to the voluntary registration of demesne land. There are five sub-sections. The basic stipulation in the whole section is set out in s 79(1) which provides that 'Her Majesty may grant an estate in fee simple absolute in possession out of demesne land to Herself'. To understand the purpose of this provision there is required a brief overview of the basic principles and history of English land law itself.

Gray states that 'at the heart of medieval theory lay the proposition that there could be no ownership of land, as such, outside the *allodium* — or prerogatival title of the Crown. The object of each tenant's ownership was instead an artificial proprietary construct called an "estate"' (S Gray and FS Gray, *Elements of Land Law* (Butterworths, 2001)). In other words, all land belonged to the Crown and lesser mortals could merely own an estate, now refined down to a freehold or leasehold estate, in land. Thus, estates are 'slices of time'. This was made clear in *Walsinghams Case* (1753). In this case it was said that 'the land itself is one thing, and the estate in the land is another thing, for an estate in the land is a time in the land, or land for a time, and there are diversities of estates, which are no more than diversities of time . . .'. In this way a freehold is unlimited in time while a leasehold is by its very nature granted for a defined and limited period of time. However, neither of the two modern forms of estate applies to the way the Crown holds land. This is an historic form of land holding where the notes to the Act make clear that 'the Crown has dominion over all land as lord paramount. Demesne land is land in which no fee simple subsists and so belongs to the Crown absolutely.' Demesne lands of the Crown will include many important parts of England and Wales including the foreshore around the country unless it has been vested in a private owner. Demesne land will also include land that has escheated to the Crown, see s 82 of the Act. The result of this anachronistic arrangement

regarding land ownership and the Crown is that much of Crown land is unregistered. This is as a direct result of the Land Registration Act 1925 failing to afford
a registration mechanism for the first registration of Crown land. The 2002 Act
changes the law so that s 79 allows voluntary first registration of demesne land.

   To enable the monarch to participate in the move to the registration of all land
in England and Wales, the monarch can register Crown land by granting to Herself
a freehold estate out of the demesne land. Any such application must be made for
registration of that new estate within two months or the grant will be invalidated.
Should an application be made on behalf of the Crown then the registrar may
extend the registration period of two months provided the registrar is satisfied that
there is good reason to do so. Section 79 goes on to provide that the power to grant
a freehold must only be used to ensure the first registration of the title to the subject
property. This should ensure that the Crown does not by mistake create a fee
simple in its own favour if, for any reason, the freehold grant is completed but
registration is not.

7.2.2   Compulsory registration of grants out of demesne land

Section 80 of the Act creates a framework within which it will be necessary to
apply for first registration for the following events:

   (a)   a grant by the Crown of a freehold out of demesne land not being a grant
to the Crown itself pursuant to s 79 (s 80(1)(a));
   (b)   a grant by the Crown out of demesne land of a leasehold estate of more
than seven years from the date of the grant for valuable or other consideration or
by way of a gift or by order of court (s 80(1)(b)(i), (ii)).

This provision is required because of the way that s 4 of the Act has been drafted
to cover when title must be registered. In effect this is because s 4 only applies to
certain dispositions or transfers of, and grants out of, existing estates. The problem
is that demesne land is not an estate in land. To get around this technical bar to
the registration of grants out of demesne land s 80 applies a compulsory trigger to
the events set out above. There is by s 80(4) a facility for the Lord Chancellor, by
order, to add to the events relating to demesne land that trigger compulsory
registration.

7.2.3   Demesne land: cautions against first registration

Section 15 of the Act permits persons to lodge a caution against the registration of
title to an unregistered legal estate if the applicant is allowed to do so under the
conditions set out in the section. Section 81(1) extends the effect of s 15 by stating
that it shall apply as if demesne land were held by the monarch by way of an
unregistered freehold estate. The need for this is once again dictated by the archaic
laws relating to Crown land and the fact that the Crown does not hold land by way

of an estate. Because there is no estate the Act deems its existence to allow there to be cautions against first registration that cover demesne land. Section 81(2) provides for the making of rules that may modify the provisions of the Act relating to cautions as they may apply to demesne land first registration cautions.

7.2.4   Escheat, etc

Escheat is defined as 'the reversion of property to the state, or (in feudal law) to a lord, on the owner's dying without legal heirs' (7.1 above). Thus, the word is used to cover property affected by this and the word will also be used as a verb meaning 'hand over (property) as an escheat'. It is in effect the determination (the termination) of freehold land. Should escheat occur, the effect is that the lord out of or from whom that estate was held, becomes entitled to the land by his or her own right, free of the determined legal estate.

The Law Commission noted that there are in the region of 500 cases of escheat every year and that they normally arise out of the insolvency of a company. The Law Commission went on to note that, 'In such cases, the liabilities that affect the land normally exceed its value!' In fact there are currently three modern situations where disclaimer can give rise to escheat:

(a)   As a result of the Companies Act 1985, s 654, when a company is dissolved, all its property passes either to the Crown (or one of the Royal Duchies), as *bona vacantia*. Section 656 of the 1985 Act permits the Crown, within 12 months, to disclaim any such property. If the Treasury Solicitor, on behalf of the Crown, disclaims, the effect is that, in the case of freehold land, the estate determines and therefore escheats to the Crown. Interestingly, the amusing effect of this is that if the Crown does disclaim land received as *bona vacantia* it receives it back as land that is subject to escheat!

(b)   Under the Insolvency Act 1986, s 315 a trustee in bankruptcy may disclaim onerous property. Onerous property is defined as 'any . . . property comprised in the bankrupt's estate which is unsaleable or not readily saleable, or is such that it may give rise to a liability to pay money or perform any other onerous act'. Consequently it is quite conceivable that a freehold that originally belonged to the bankrupt might be onerous. This could arise if it were subject to mortgages or other charges that greatly exceeded its market value.

(c)   The Insolvency Act 1986, s 178, is very much like s 315 (see (b) above), but relates to company failures. Section 178 states that a liquidator of a company that is being wound up may disclaim onerous property, and 'onerous property' has the same meaning as it does for individuals.

Accordingly it is still possible to see freeholds affected by disclaimer and thereby subject to escheat. When that happens, the defunct title has to be removed from the register because of course the estate, as a result of disclaimer and escheat, no longer subsists. It will be appreciated that the consequence of this is that every year a motley selection of properties will continue to fall outside the land registration process and will militate against the aims of the Act of complete registration of land in England and Wales. As a consequence s 82 of the Act seeks to resolve this problem.

The purpose of s 82 is to avoid a registered estate having to be removed from the register. It makes provision for rules to be possible about the determination of a registered freehold property. The notes to the Act make it clear that it is envisaged that when land escheats, an application will be made for the entry of a restriction in the register. This is likely to provide that no disposition is to be made of the estate except by order of the court, or possibly by or on the direction of the Crown Estate. When a new freehold is granted, then upon application it will be registered with a new title number. The old title will then be closed. Any encumbrances to which the former title was subject and which still subsisted in relation to the new estate will be entered in the register of the new title.

Section 82(2) makes it clear that the rules to be made under this section may in particular make specific provision underpinning the desire to avoid the loss of registered titles. Accordingly s 82(2)(b) states that rules may make provision for entries relating to a freehold to continue in the register, notwithstanding determination, and for such time as the rules may provide.

7.2.5   Crown and Duchy land: representation

This part covers cases where special landowners need to stipulate who will deal with registered land matters on their behalf. It follows the content of the original legislation. The Land Registration Act 1925, s 96 covered much the same area as s 83 of the Act. Section 96 allowed the monarch to appoint a representative to act in relation to the monarch's property. The same was the case for Duchy land. Section 83 of the Act sets out:

(a)   who may represent the monarch or Duchy for a particular property for all purposes of the Act;

(b)   who is entitled to receive a notice as the owner under the Act; and

(c)   who may make such applications and perform such other acts that an owner might under the Act.

Thus the Crown Estate will deal with Crown Land, the Chancellor of the Duchy will deal with the Duchy of Lancaster and for the Duchy of Cornwall it will be such person as the Duke of Cornwall appoints.

7.2.6   Disapplication of requirements relating to Duchy land

The Law Commission stated that 'the legal position in relation to both Duchies is in fact arcane and complex'. The Duchy of Cornwall's powers in relation to the sale and acquisition of land are governed by the Duchy of Cornwall Management Acts 1863 to 1982. Similar antediluvian provisions regarding land ownership and transfer apply to the Duchy of Lancaster. The notes to the Act explain that this section disapplies the requirement that a transfer of registered land by the Duchy of Cornwall needs to be enrolled in the Duchy office within six months after it is made. This is because if this time limit is not adhered to then the transfer will not be valid and effectual against the Duke of Cornwall. The effect of this section is that a disposition of a registered estate or charge by or to either Duchy can be made in the usual way, without regard to the requirements that would otherwise apply under any legislation affecting the Duchies.

7.2.7 *Bona vacantia*

It is the case currently that registered estates and charges will pass to the Crown as *bona vacantia* when there is no other person or company entitled to become the beneficial owner of that estate or charge. Practitioners will immediately recognize that the most familiar example is where a limited company has been liquidated and a registered estate or charge belonging to it has not been dealt with and as such the estate or charge remains in the name of the liquidated company. (For example where a property is subject to several leases it is common to vest the freehold of the property in a management company owned by the leaseholders. Sadly they neglect filing requirements at Companies House whereupon the management company is struck off. At that point the registered estate in theory passes to the Crown as *bona vacantia*.) Where this kind of difficulty arises the registered estate or charge is not determined but vests in the Treasury Solicitor on behalf of Her Majesty or in the Duchies of Cornwall or Lancaster. (Contrast the position when land escheats to the Crown on disclaimer, 7.2.4 above.) Consequently s 85 enables the making of rules about how the passing of a registered estate or charge as *bona vacantia* is to be dealt with for the purpose of the Act.

7.3   PENDING ACTIONS, ETC

Section 86 of the 2002 Act covers matters relating to bankruptcy and s 87 deals with pending land actions, writs, orders and deeds of arrangement. Each will now be considered in turn.

7.3.1 Bankruptcy

Section 86 deals with matters relating to bankruptcy and makes special provision for the effect of bankruptcy, to reflect the provisions of the Insolvency Act 1986. Currently if a petition in bankruptcy is filed the court must apply to register the petition as a land charge in the register of pending actions, see the Land Charges Act 1972, s 5(1)(b). The registrar will on receipt of such a registration then seek to make an appropriate entry in all registers of registered land that appear to relate to the registration, ie the proprietor is the party named in the petition. This is made all the easier by the fact that the Land Registry handles the work of the Land Charges Registry as well as the registers for registered land. The registrar will therefore register a creditor's notice in the affected title of any land so affected by the petition. Section 86(2) repeats this by providing that after the registration of a petition in bankruptcy as a pending action under the Land Charges Act 1972, the registrar must enter in the register of any registered estate or charge which appears to the registrar to be affected a notice in respect of the pending action. A notice made under s 86(2) continues in force until a restriction is entered pursuant to a bankruptcy order (see below) or a trustee in bankruptcy is registered as proprietor (s 86(3)).

Section 86(4) mimics the provisions of s 86(2) but in relation to the final bankruptcy order. So, after the registration of a bankruptcy order under the Land Charges Act 1972, the registrar must enter in the register of any registered estate or charge which appears to the registrar to be affected a restriction reflecting the effect of the Insolvency Act 1986. (Currently, the registrar is required to enter a bankruptcy inhibition. Under the Act, because inhibitions are abolished, the registrar must protect a bankruptcy order by the entry of a restriction.)

Section 86(5) gives protection to buyers in relation to bankruptcy petitions and orders, by following the approach adopted in the Insolvency Act 1986 which protects a bona fide purchaser for value without notice. Thus, in the case of a bankrupt debtor, a transferee to whom a registrable disposition is made is not subject to a 'better' claim by the debtor's trustee in bankruptcy, provided that:

(a)   the disposition is made for valuable consideration;

(b)   he or she acts in good faith;

(c)   at the time of the disposition, no notice or restriction was entered in relation to the registered estate or charge; *and* the person to whom the disposition was made had no notice of the bankruptcy petition or the adjudication, see s 86(5)(a)–(c).

There is a caveat to the protection and that is in s 86(7) which says that nothing in the section requires a person to whom a registrable disposition is made to make any search under the Land Charges Act 1972. Accordingly a buyer of registered land is not required to check on the financial condition of the seller by completing a bankruptcy search against the seller. This reinforces the core aspect of the Act that the register must reflect the true and current position regarding the status and condition of the title and the proprietor. In this way s 86(5) makes it clear that, where the proprietor of a registered estate is adjudged bankrupt, provided the above conditions (a), (b) and (c) are satisfied, and where the registration requirements have been complied with, the title of his or her trustee in bankruptcy is void against a transferee. This will hopefully resolve some uncertainty in this area of conveyancing.

7.3.2   Pending land actions, writs, orders and deeds of arrangement

Section 87 deals with pending land actions, writs, orders and deeds of arrangement and so covers the topics that, in the case of unregistered land, may be registered under the Land Charges Act 1972, ss 5–7. (Section 5 of the 1972 Act covers the register of pending actions, s 6 deals with the register of writs and orders affecting land and s 7 deals with the register of deeds of arrangement affecting land.) The obvious exception is of course bankruptcy matters that are covered by s 86 (see 7.3.1 above in relation to bankruptcy petitions and orders in bankruptcy). The Land Registration Act 1925, s 59 covered much the same area as s 87 but provided for such matters to be protected by a caution against dealings. This form of protection is abolished by the Act. Under the new regime their priority has to be protected by means of an entry in the register, either as a notice or a restriction. A couple of these miscellaneous matters cannot be protected by a notice, eg a deed of arrangement and an order appointing a receiver. The consequence of this is that the only way of protecting such a deed or order is by means of a restriction.

7.4 MISCELLANEOUS SPECIAL CASES

Section 88 of the 2002 Act deals with incorporeal hereditaments, s 89 covers settlements and s 90 PPP leases relating to transport in London.

7.4.1 Incorporeal hereditaments

'Incorporeal' means 'of or relating to property or an asset that does not have value in material form, as a right or patent' (*Concise Oxford Dictionary*, 9th edn, 1996) and hereditaments covers property that can be inherited. Together incorporeal hereditaments are intangible objects such as tithes or easements. Accordingly s 88 states that the Act shall cover four specifically listed matters:

(a)   rentcharges;
(b)   franchises (a liberty or privilege sometimes granted by the Crown, such as a right to hold a market or maintain a ferry);
(c)   profits *à prendre* in gross (rights of taking the produce or part of the soil from the land of another person, eg a right of pasture or a right of common); or
(d)   manors.

The application of the Act with regard to the four listed matters may be modified as rules yet to be made will provide.

7.4.2 Settlements

Section 89 is concerned with settlements under the Settled Land Act 1925. Since 1 January 1997 life interests take effect not under the Settled Land Act 1925 but under the Trusts of Land and Appointment of Trustees Act 1996. However, life interests in land that were created prior to the 1 January 1997 are still governed by the Settled Land Act 1925. Accordingly there will still be examples of settled land but inevitably they will be diminishing in number as time passes.

As a consequence of this, s 89 provides for rules to make provision for the purposes of the Act in relation to the application to registered land of the enactments relating to settlements under the Settled Land Act 1925. This means that rules, yet to be made, will be formulated to deal with settled land transactions as they relate to registered land, rather than setting out the detailed provisions in the Act. (Section 89(3) makes it clear that for the purposes of this section of the Act, 'registered land' means an interest the title to which is, or is required to be, registered.) Rules relating to settled land transactions may include provisions modifying any of those enactments mentioned above so far as they may relate to registered land.

7.4.3   PPP leases relating to transport in London

The present government has set out extensive plans to change the way that the London Underground system is administered, funded and managed. Part of this new system involves London Transport Public-Private Partnership leases, i.e. PPP leases. (Section 90(6) makes it clear that 'PPP lease' has the meaning given by the Greater London Authority Act 1999, s 218 that made provision about leases created for public private partnerships relating to transport in London.) They will, once the system gets up and running, arise out of the arrangements for the future administration, funding, and management of the London underground or tube structure. These PPP leases will include underground railway lines, stations and other relevant installations such as the signaling equipment. They are in effect leases of the infrastructure of the actual tube lines themselves. Under the terms of the Act and in particular s 4(c) leases such as these PPP leases could be subject to compulsory first registration being for a term greater than seven years in duration. However, s 90 states that no application for voluntary registration may be made under s 3 of the Act and that the requirement of compulsory registration does not apply on the grant or transfer of a leasehold estate in land under a PPP lease. Furthermore the section states that s 27 of the Act (dispositions requiring to be registered) will not apply to PPP leases. Indeed no notice may be entered in the register in respect of an interest under a PPP lease. However, s 90(5) states that Sch 1 and Sch 3 of the Act have effect as if they included a paragraph referring to a PPP lease. Accordingly a PPP lease will be recognized under the terms of the Act as an overriding interest. The Law Commission felt that the reason for taking PPP leases outside the registered system in this way is as follows.

Such leases are likely to be granted for a comparatively short period, namely 30 years. They will be virtually inalienable. Although it would no doubt be possible to produce accurate plans for such leases, it is thought that the costs would be enormous and disproportionate to the benefits that would accrue from so doing.

No doubt the present government believe that when any such PPP leases determine, presumably by effluxion of time, the assets that are required to run the tube line will be available to the relevant public authority empowered to be responsible for the running of the tube line services. It is assumed that this is part of the reasoning behind the decision to exempt these PPP leases from the otherwise mandatory system of first registration. In any event the number of leases involved is likely to be somewhat limited in number.

7.5 KEY POINTS FOR THE PRACTITIONER

- Section 79 covers provisions relating to the voluntary registration of demesne land, s 80 covers the compulsory registration of grants out of demesne land, while s 81 covers cautions against first registration and demesne land.
- Escheat is dealt with in s 82. The purpose of s 82 is to avoid a registered estate having to be removed from the register.
- In relation to both Crown and Duchy land, s 83 describes who is to be considered the appropriate representative for notices, etc while s 84 covers the disapplication of particular requirements relating to the two Duchies of Lancaster and Cornwall.
- Section 85 covers the application of property when *bona vacantia* applies. Section 85 enables the making of rules about how the passing of a registered estate or charge as *bona vacantia* is to be dealt with for the purpose of the Act.
- Section 86(5) gives protection to buyers and in relation to bankruptcy petitions and orders, the Act follows the approach adopted in the Insolvency Act 1986 which protects a bona fide purchaser for value without notice.
- Section 87 deals with pending land actions, writs, orders and deeds of arrangement, covering topics that, in the case of unregistered land, may be registered under the Land Charges Act 1972, ss 5–7.
- Section 88 states that the Act shall cover rentcharges, franchises, profits *à prendre* in gross, or manors. The application of the Act with regard to these four may be modified as rules yet to be made will provide.
- Section 89 provides for rules to be made in relation to settled land that is registered land.
- In relation to PPP leases, s 90 states that no application for voluntary registration may be made under s 3 of the Act and that the requirement of compulsory registration does not apply on the grant or transfer of a leasehold estate in land under a PPP lease. Furthermore, the section states that s 27 of the Act (dispositions requiring to be registered) will not apply to PPP leases.

Chapter 8

Electronic Conveyancing and Other Conveyancing Reforms

8.1   INTRODUCTION

One of the main purposes of the 2002 Act is to usher in electronic conveyancing within the next three to five years. The new legislation aims to create the necessary legal framework that will allow registered land conveyancing to be conducted electronically. It is therefore worth repeating that the main aim of the Act is that, under a system of electronic dealing with land that it seeks to create, the register should be a complete and accurate reflection of the state of the title of the land at any given time, so that it is possible to investigate title to land on-line, with the absolute minimum of additional enquiries and inspections. This is all predicated upon a system of electronic dealings making possible on-line title investigation. This is in effect e-conveyancing. However, practitioners need to note:

(a)   That e-conveyancing is to be introduced in stages, with the simplest transactions first. As a result the Act authorizes the Lord Chancellor to regulate, by rules, transactions that can be effected electronically. The first transactions to be effected electronically will be covered by the descriptions e-lodgement, e-discharges and e-charges. Since 18 February 2002 practitioners who use the Land Registry Direct system have been able to lodge applications to change the register electronically. This is e-lodgement (the next two are really self-explanatory, e-discharges cover the electronic release of registered charges and e-charges will cover electronically created mortgages) which covers the following applications:

(i)   severance of a joint tenancy by notice,
(ii)   change of a property description,
(iii)   change of the proprietor's address.
(iv)   change of the proprietor's name by deed poll or marriage, and
(v)   death of a joint proprietor.

There will then follow a move towards the acceptance of discharges and charges being lodged electronically. This development should be possible by the summer of 2003.

(b)   The Act also gives the Lord Chancellor the power to make e-conveyancing compulsory. While the Act contemplates a transitional period, where paper-based conveyancing will co-exist alongside e-conveyancing, there is a clear intention to terminate paper-based conveyancing sooner rather than later. At present the timescale seems to anticipate the full system being released around 2006 at the earliest, when the two approaches to registered conveyancing will run concurrently. The Registry already has a working model for e-conveyancing. It is currently in the process of consulting with interested parties and should produce a report in the early part of 2003. Systems will then have to be built and prepared for a pilot scheme in, hopefully, 2005 with the full release a year later.

(c)   The Land Registry will control permitted access to the e-conveyancing network. This means that conveyancers will in practice need the continued approval of the Registry to be able to effect e-conveyances. Let us hope the Chief Land Registrar exercises this control on a practical and reasonable basis having regard to the demands of the modern cost-effective conveyancing practice. There is a right of appeal to the newly created adjudicator, see chapter 11.

(d)   The Land Registry will be required to make the necessary arrangements to allow individuals to carry out their own conveyancing, ie there will still be a place for the 'do-it-yourself' conveyancer. In principle this seems sensible but quite how it will be carried out in practice is unclear. Will there be computer terminals that will be made available to the public? If not how will the system operate? No doubt the draft rules anticipated later this year (2002), will throw further light on this particular area of concern.

(e)   The suggested system for e-conveyancing does not appear, at present, to accommodate auction contracts. How they are to be dealt with is unclear and this will need to be resolved before the final system is completed. It will be one area to be covered in the consultation process about the model for e-conveyancing that is to be conducted by the Registry during 2002 and the early part of 2003. This is also the case for sales by tender.

(f)   E-conveyancing will abolish the 'registration gap'. With paper-based conveyancing, normally on the contractual day of completion, the deed of transfer and any mortgages are completed. Thereafter they must be submitted to the Land Registry to ensure the completion of the process of recording those deeds and charges in the registers. The time between the completion of the transaction together with the deeds and their registration at the Land Registry is called the 'registration gap'. Electronic conveyancing will abolish this gap in time as completion will include a simultaneous registration by the electronic update of the register, see 8.5 below.

(g)   If practitioners have any questions about e-conveyancing they can contact the Land Registry's electronic conveyancing task force on 020 7416 4721 or questions can be posed via an e-mail to <mailto:questions@e-conveyancing. gov.uk>. There is also an informative and helpful website at <http://www. e-conveyancing.gov.uk/Default.asp> that has been set up by the Land Registry to underpin the consultation process as well as the gradual changeover to e-conveyancing.

8.2   SECTION 8 OF THE ELECTRONIC COMMUNICATIONS ACT 2000

At present, in England and Wales contracts for the sale or creation of interests in land have to be made in writing and signed by the parties. Similarly, deeds must be in writing and the signature of the party or parties making the deed must be witnessed. All conveyances, transfers, leases, mortgages and legal charges must be deeds. Thus, notwithstanding the growing use of electronic communication at all the other stages of a conveyancing transaction, the two key stages of making the contract and completion must be achieved by using paper documents. Most subsequent applications for registration at the Land Registry must therefore also be made on paper.

In March 2001 the Lord Chancellor's Department issued a consultation paper entitled *Electronic Conveyancing — A draft order under section 8 of the Electronic Communications Act 2000*. The first part of these guidance notes (8.2) is taken from that consultation paper. The Electronic Communications Act 2000 gives Ministers the power to change the law to authorize or facilitate the use of electronic communication and electronic storage. The proposal is to use this power to improve the conveyancing process by permitting the creation of electronic conveyancing documents such as contracts, transfers, conveyances, leases and mortgages. The use of the electronic conveyancing documents will be voluntary, but they will in general only be permitted for registered land. The purpose of the draft order is to remove the legal obstacles that may prevent the use of electronic forms of communication in relation to dealings with land. Those obstacles are the formal requirements that apply to most dispositions of land and to contracts for the sale or other disposition of land, eg they must be in writing.

If made, the order will create a new system of formalities for the creation and disposal of interests in land and establish a new legal framework in which electronic conveyancing documents will have the same effect as their paper equivalents. If made effective the order will make these changes by amending the Law of Property (Miscellaneous Provisions) Act 1989. The amendment will enable contracts to be created electronically despite the requirement of the 1989 Act that contracts for the sale and purchase of land must be in writing. New land registration rules and stamp duty legislation will also be needed before this proposal can be brought fully into force. The draft order proposes the insertion of a new s 144A into the Land Registration Act 1925. Practitioners need to bear in mind that this provision was issued prior to the Land Registration Bill 2001 and may prove to be superfluous now that the 2002 Act has been passed.

An electronic document which satisfies the requirements of the proposed new section will satisfy any statutory requirement of writing, signature and, in the case of a corporation, sealing. The document will also be regarded as a deed. The draft order also inserts a new s 2A into the Law of Property (Miscellaneous Provisions) Act 1989 so that an electronic contract will be as effective as an equivalent paper contract if it meets the conditions set out in the new section. These are that all the terms of the contract are set out, or referred to, in the document; the contract states when it will take effect; and the contract is signed with the certificated signature of each signatory. It will be possible to make electronic contracts in relation to both registered and unregistered land.

Electronic conveyancing documents will have to be electronically signed with a certificated electronic signature and will have to specify when they are intended to take effect. Electronic documents, other than contracts, will also have to be made in a form prescribed by HM Land Registry. The format of the e-conveyancing documentation will be issued as the processes are prescribed.

The consultation process was due to end on 25 June 2001. Since then the Land Registration Act 2002 has been passed which could make an order under s 8 of the Electronic Communications Act 2000 irrelevant for registered land. This is because the Act covers the areas originally intended for the proposed order. In any event, it should be remembered that these details are only proposals and will only come into force if an order is made. The order, by a statutory instrument, must be laid before Parliament for approval by resolution of each House of Parliament. However, it may be put to one side allowing the 2002 Act and subsequent registration rules to take centre stage for the framework for electronic conveyancing.

There is a continuum between the 2000 statute and the Act in that s 91(10) of the Act dealing with the formalities of electronic dispositions makes it clear that definitions will be the same for both enactments. In detail the section provides that references to an electronic signature and to the certification of such a signature are to be read in accordance with the Electronic Communications Act 2000, s 7(2), (3). Section 7(2) provides that for the purposes of that section, an electronic signature:

. . . is so much of anything in electronic form as—

(a)   is incorporated into or logically associated with any electronic communication or electronic data; and

(b)   purports to be incorporated or associated for the purpose of being used in establishing the authenticity of the communication or data, the integrity of the communication or data, or both.

8.3   E-CONVEYANCING ARISING FROM THE LAND REGISTRATION ACT 2002

The main aim of the 2002 Act is to put in place the necessary framework to ensure that e-conveyancing can prove to be more than just a mere proposal. To do this the Land Registry must put in place an effective system to handle electronic dealings with land. This will come about from the land register being a complete and accurate reflection of the state of the title of the land at any given time. The underlying reason for this arrangement is to ensure that practitioners and the general public can investigate title to land electronically, with the absolute minimum of other additional inquiries and inspections. Moreover when consulted the register should show accurately the true and up to date state of the title at the time of consultation. This is the very essence of e-conveyancing. Much of the following is based upon the detail and proposals set out in Law Commission reports and in particular, '*Land Registration for the Twenty-First Century — a Conveyancing Revolution*', Law Com No 271 (2001).

The Act puts in place an outline of the structure in which it will be possible to generate and transfer estates and/or interests in registered land by electronic conveyancing. This outline will be fleshed out by subsequent rules that have yet to be issued by the Registry. The statute creates the outline by authorizing the execution of formal deeds and documents electronically. The Act also contemplates the formation of a secure electronic computer network within which to carry out e-conveyancing. It is envisaged that the execution of all such deeds and documents together with their registration will be simultaneous. To do this the process of registration will be initiated by conveyancing practitioners. However, there is a novel element of state control that will affect all conveyancers. The Land Registry control who may access the computer network and how. The Registry will also exercise control over the changes that can be made to the land register. The Act also provides for the Lord Chancellor to regulate by rules transactions that can be carried out electronically. Furthermore, the Act gives the Lord Chancellor power to make the use of e-conveyancing compulsory. Compulsory e-conveyancing will only arise after a period of consultation and after a transitional period when conveyancers will move from the existing paper-based system to an electronic system. As such there will necessarily be a period of time while the two systems co-exist.

The Act is intended to make it impossible to create or transfer many rights in or over registered land except by registering them. Investigation of title should be effected entirely on-line. It is intended that the Registry will also provide a means of managing a chain of transactions by monitoring them electronically. This is an important innovation. It will enable the cause of delays in any chain to be identified. Once identified, steps will no doubt be taken to put pressure on the delaying party to make sure the bottleneck to progress is removed. Quite how this will be done remains to be seen. The Law Commission anticipated that as a result of this supervision by the Registry far fewer chains will break in consequence and that conveyancing will be considerably expedited. The involvement of the Registry is anticipated at a very early stage in most if not all registered land transactions, as will be highlighted below in 8.5.

Part 8 of the Act deals with electronic conveyancing. There are just five sections to this part of the Act, ss 91–95, that cover merely two sides of A4. For a major reform of conveyancing the source is remarkably slight. Section 91 covers the formalities of electronic dispositions, s 92 the land registry network, s 93 the powers to require simultaneous registration, s 94 electronic settlement, and s 95 covers rule making provisions in a supplementary section. Section 92 refers to Sch 5 of the Act and covers detailed provisions relating to the land registry network. (In particular the schedule covers, *inter alia*, access to the network, terms of access, termination of access and appeals arising from termination. This schedule is considered at 8.10 below.) Each of these five sections will now be considered in turn.

8.3.1   Electronic dispositions: formalities

Section 91 contains ten sub-sections the first of which (s 91(1)) makes clear in what circumstances the whole section applies to a document in electronic form. This will be the case where the document purports to effect a disposition that falls within the provisions of s 91(2) and where the conditions of s 91(3) are met. Thus, there are two requirements: first that s 91(2) is complied with and then secondly those conditions in s 91(3) are complied with. The approach is uniform, ie it will apply equally to deeds under seal or agreements made under hand. To comply with s 91(2) a disposition falls within the section if it is:

(a)   a disposition of a registered estate or charge;
(b)   a disposition of an interest which is the subject of a notice in the register; or
(c)   a disposition of unregistered land triggering first registration.

All of which will be of a kind that will be specified by rules, as elsewhere in the Act, yet to be made. The conditions in s 91(3) are that:

(a)   the document includes a provision for the date and time of when it is completed;
(b)   the document includes the electronic signature of each person by whom it purports to be authenticated;
(c)   each electronic signature is certified; and
(d)   such other conditions as rules may provide are met.

The preconditions of an electronic document are, therefore, that it includes the date and time when it is to take effect, and the certified electronic signatures of all the parties, along with other conditions that may be imposed by rules. These rules are, as elsewhere in the Act, yet to be made. The first pre-condition is unexceptional in that it is vital that if only for priority purposes the date and time of the electronic document must be clear especially as the completion of the e-document will coincide with the registration of that document. This first precondition sets aside the paper-based requirement for 'delivery'. A contract is made when it is delivered at exchange. As to a document under seal, signing and delivering it makes a deed. This will be set aside in the age of e-conveyancing and thus each document will need to include a time and date for the purposes of registration.

As to the electronic equivalent of a pen-based signature, this is going to be a wholly different matter in the digital age. An e-document will be a document that includes the electronic signature of each person by whom it purports to be authenticated. It is authentication that is required. As the notes to the Act points out, 'It is the means by which an electronic document can be authenticated as that of the party making it.' Thus, the Act is not being very prescriptive. All it refers to is an electronic signature. In the words of the Law Commission, 'An electronic signature is not a "signature" in the ordinarily accepted sense. It is a means by which an electronic document can be authenticated as that of the party making it.' So, as the technology develops it should enable rules to be made to prescribe what mechanisms the registry accepts, as appropriate digital forms of signature authentication. As a safeguard any digital signature needs to be certified. This is the authentication of the form of electronic signature itself. It is the security apparatus for the digital signature.

Section 91(4) makes it clear that a document to which this section applies will be considered as having been made in writing and signed by each person or sealed by a company whose electronic signature is included. The effect of this is to ensure that the existing law relating to conveyancing documentation is deemed to apply to e-documentation. Accordingly s 91(5) indicates that a document to which the section applies, an e-document, is to be regarded for the purposes of any statute as a deed. In this way, for example, if a statute requires a document to be in writing then it is deemed to be by the operation of this section. This would therefore include e-contracts within the provisions of the Law of Property (Miscellaneous Provisions) Act 1989 and in particular s 2 (which states that, 'A contract for the sale or other disposition of an interest in land can only be made in writing . . .'). Similarly, where statute requires a deed this too will be deemed to be included for e-conveyancing purposes, eg the Law of Property Act 1925, s 52(1) states that, 'All conveyances of land or any interest therein are void for the purpose of conveying or creating a legal estate unless made by deed.' This is further extended by the effect of s 91(6) of the Act. This covers the effect of agency authentication. Thus, where an e-document is covered by s 91(6) and is authenticated by an agent, it is to be regarded as having been authenticated by that agent under the written authority of the agent's principal. However, the consequences of this will have considerable relevance to conveyancing practitioners. The effect of the section means that once in force it will not be possible to question the existence of authority from a client to give their conveyancing practitioner the entitlement to effect an electronic signature on their behalf. If the practitioner makes the electronic signature on their behalf then they will be deemed to have had authority as a result of the effects of s 91(6). As a matter of professional practice it is therefore apparent that conveyancing practitioners will need to reconsider their procedures for taking instructions from their clients to make quite sure that they are properly authorized to effect electronic signatures on behalf of clients. The clients need to be made fully aware that their practitioner will by statute be given authority to act in this way and the clients need to give their informed consent to this. This is of considerable significance for practitioners.

Section 136 of the Law of Property Act 1925 allows anyone to expressly transfer the benefit of any contract to which they are a party and this covers contracts affecting land. Section 136(1) of the 1925 statute requires notice in writing to be given to the other party to the agreement of the form of assignment. This is turn could come within the context of e-documentation. Consequently, s 91(7) states that if notice is given electronically it will be deemed to have been given in writing (and as such it will come with the Law of Property Act 1925, s 136). Thus, if there is an option to purchase land registered as a notice on the register then, pursuant to s 136(7), an e-notice will be required and will be deemed to be in writing.

Section 75 of the Law of Property Act 1925 allows a purchaser to have, at his or her own cost, the execution of the conveyance attested by someone appointed by the purchaser. Bearing in mind the nature of the execution and completion of e-documents this provision is redundant and as a result s 91(8) indicates that s 75 attestation will not apply to e-documents.

This part of the Act also covers the execution of deeds and documents by a company. At present a company can complete legal documentation in various ways. A company is no longer required to have a common seal and thus a deed can be properly executed by the signatures of a director and secretary, or two of the company's directors (see the Companies Act 1985, s 36A added by the Companies Act 1989, s 130 which came into force on 31 July 1990). Alternatively, the company's common seal can still be used (and typically is). If either of the above methods of execution is adopted, the buyer from a company incorporated in England and Wales is entitled to assume that proper execution has occurred (s 36A(6) of the 1985 Act). Section 91(9) deals with e-documents made by a company and executed without a seal. It makes it clear that the protection afforded by s 36A(6) will apply to an e-document that has been electronically authenticated on behalf of the company.

8.3.2   Land Registry network

In this context a network is a system of inter-linked computers that access the same pool of electronic data; it is in effect 'a chain of interconnected computers, machines, or operations'. Section 92 makes provision for the Land Registry network that will be required for e-conveyancing to be a reality. Section 92 also refers to Sch 5 of the Act and covers detailed provisions relating to the land registry network. (The schedule covers, among other things, access to the network, terms of access, termination of access and appeals arising from termination. This schedule is considered at 8.10 below.) Section 92 simply states that the registrar may provide or arrange for the provision of an electronic communication network. The network is for use for such purposes as the registrar thinks fit relating to registration or the carrying on of transactions which:

(a)   involve registration; and
(b)   are capable of being made electronically (s. 92(1)).

The Law Commission considered that the purposes of the network will, therefore, include:

(1)   the provision of information to the registrar or to any party to a transaction or proposed transaction that will involve:
   (a)   some disposition of registered land or of an interest in registered land; or
   (b)   a disposition of unregistered land that will trigger compulsory first registration;
(2)   the preparation of conveyancing documents in electronic form in relation to (1)(a) or (b) above; and
(3)   the registration of any disposition.

The network will exist to conduct the public face of land registration. It will allow the public to view the register, to update the register and to create new title and interests electronically. It will extend to the public the information, plans and data that make up the millions of registered titles to property across England and Wales.

8.4   STAMP DUTY AND E-CONVEYANCING

Stamp duty is a healthy source of revenue for the government. However, it is a Victorian form of tax and as such is collected in a somewhat Dickensian fashion. Stamps are literally impressed upon deeds to confirm payment. Accordingly, currently stamp duty on land transactions depends upon the existence of deeds and documents in paper-based format. On 8 November 2000, the Inland Revenue indicated that there would be legislation to extend the stamp duty regime to cover transfers of land that are made electronically, by e-conveyancing. A detailed set of proposals, containing drafts of any necessary clauses and regulations, is to be published in due course. The Revenue recently issued a consultation paper entitled, *Modernising Stamp Duty on Land and Buildings in the UK*, and this paper can be

seen on the Inland Revenue web site at < www.inlandrevenue.gov.uk/consult_
new/mod_stamp_duty.pdf >. The paper includes proposals to cover stamp duty in
the era of e-conveyancing.

8.5   THE ANTICIPATED MODEL OF E-CONVEYANCING

The computer e-conveyancing network will only be accessible by contractually
authorized professionals, whether they are solicitors, licensed conveyancers, estate
agents or mortgagees. The e-conveyancing network will not just be used for the
several conveyancing stages of each transaction, but also for the provision of
property information and to co-ordinate and manage chains of registered land
dealings.

We anticipate that the Land Registry will be made responsible for managing
chains of transactions in order to smooth the progress of them. When a buyer or a
seller instructs a conveyancing practitioner to act on his or her behalf where there
is likely to be a chain of transactions, that practitioner will be required to notify
the Land Registry 'Chain Manager' of their instructions. Thereafter the practitioner
will also be obliged to advise the Registry of the completion of the several stages
in the conveyancing procedure so that the chain manager can log them. In this way
each step can be shown in a matrix thereby building up a complete picture in the
chain of what point each transaction has reached. This process should enable all
those involved in a transaction to identify bottlenecks within the chain that can be
addressed so as to try to expedite the process.

The proposed system of chain management will require practitioners to provide
information to the Registry. Clients may instruct their conveyancing practitioner
not to divulge such information. In theory this could give rise to a conflict of
interests for practitioners, especially when practitioners note that Sch 5, para 6 of
the 2002 Act makes it clear that network access obligations prevail where there
may be a conflict of obligations. It is believed that the information that a
practitioner will be required to supply will relate to progress only and not to
personal or financial information. For example, the system will want to know if a
mortgage offer is required and, if so, if the lender has issued it to the borrower/
purchaser; it will not need to know the details of the mortgage offer itself.

This information will be made available via the secure registry intranet to all
parties in the chain. (An intranet, unlike the internet, is a network of computers
that is not open to the public but is only available to a limited and defined number
of parties entitled to access the data contained within the intranet network, eg
within a closed section of the registry network.) This will be by way of the chain
matrix, an example of which is set out below. It is a concept graphic prepared by
the Land Registry and reproduced with their kind permission:

Target Completion
17 May 2002

Chain Progress Chart

Firm		Contract Issued	Searches Requested	Enquiries Raised	Searches In	Enquiries Completed	Contract Approved	Mortgage Offer	Contract Exchanged	Contract Released/ Contract Exchanged
John Chalkley & Co. Ref: JC 12657/1	S	●				●	●		●	●
Griffiths Williams Ref: JRW 87643/4	P	●	●	●	●	●	●	●	●	●
Griffiths Williams Ref: JRW 87643/5	S	●				✖	●			✖
Messrs Adams Thompson Ref: ATD 785432/P	P	●	●	●	●	✖	✖	●		✖
Messrs Adams Thompson Ref: ATD 785432/S	S	●				●	●		●	●
Messrs Thomas & Perry Ref WJP109247/1	P	●	●	●	●	●	●	✖		✖
Messrs Thomas & Perry Ref WJP109247/2	S	●				●	●		●	●
Messrs Serpell Ref RM4563/Jon/P	P	●	●	●	●	●	●	●	●	●
Messrs Jones & Davies Ref RM4563/Jon/S	S	●				●	●		●	●
Messrs Roper & Kenward Ref: AHT 32673/5	P	●	●	●	✖	●	✖	●		✖

When the seller and buyer have agreed the terms of the contract, they will send a copy in electronic form to the Land Registry, where it will be checked electronically. This will enable any inconsistencies in the agreement on factual matters such as the property address, title number and seller's name to be identified and corrected before the contract is made binding. The contract will be made in electronic form and signed using a digital signature, ie electronically by the seller and buyer. As is the case now, estate contracts should be protected in the register by the entry of a notice (currently a caution). This noting in the register should be made electronically at the same time as the establishment of the binding contract. An example of an e-conveyancing contract is set out below and is a concept graphic prepared by the Land Registry and reproduced with their kind permission on p 104.

With regard to the notice and in relation to official searches, s 72 of the Act makes express provision for priority protection and, importantly, extends the circumstances in which it can be obtained. There is power for rules to make provision for priority periods in connection with the noting in the register of a contract for the making of a registrable disposition of a registered estate or charge. This is of course linked to the introduction of e-conveyancing. Under the e-conveyancing system, in order for such an estate contract to be valid, it will be necessary to enter a notice of the contract on the register (see 6.8 for further details about priority protection). At the same time, that entry will confer priority protection on the applicant.

The draft transfer and any mortgage will be prepared in electronic format and in relation to the transfer will first be agreed between the seller and buyer. As was the case for the contract, the draft will be submitted to the Registry for scrutiny. The particulars in the transfer will be checked electronically against the contract to ensure that there are no inconsistencies. The Registry in consultation with the seller and buyer will indicate the form that the land register will take when the transaction is completed by it then assembling a pre-completion draft register.

Agreement

Incorporating the Standard Conditions of Sale **(Third Edition)**

Agreement Date [   ] (dd/mm/yy)   Completion Date [   ] (dd/mm/yy)

Seller's Name(s) [John Andrews   ]   Buyer's Name(s) [   ]

The seller sells in his/her capacity of [Registered Proprietor(s) ▼]

Seller's Address
```
55 Devonia Gardens
Enfield
London N18 1AE
```

Buyer's Address
```


```

Title Number [MX20890]

Property Address
```
55 Devonia Gardens
Enfield
London N18 1AE
```

Tenure [Freehold ▼]   Title Guarantee [Full ▼]

Purchase Price [34000 ▼]   Deposit [34000 ▼]

Chattels [15000 ▼]   Balance [307500 ▼]

The following clause(s) will be included in the transfer to the buyer:

```
The transferee hereby covenants with the transferor to observe and
perform the covenants referred to in the charges register of the
above title and to indemnify the transferor for any breach thereof
```

The following special conditions are incorporated in this contract

[None ▼]

The Seller will sell and the Buyer will buy the propert for the Purchase Price

[Send]   [View Register]   [Delete]

Completion, when it takes place, will entail the following actions happening concurrently:

(a)   the execution of the transfer and any charges in electronic form and their transmission to the Registry, where they will be stored;

(b)   the registration of the dispositions so that the register conforms with the notional register previously agreed with the Registry; and

(c)   the appropriate (and automatic) movement of funds and the payment of stamp duty and Land Registry fees.

The transfer of fees will entail the involvement of several different agencies but will need to be effected electronically. Electronic Funds Transfer (EFT) is being seriously considered by the Land Registry to ensure that the movement of funds electronically can match the intended efficiency of the e-conveyancing system. The number of different parties involved complicates EFT. However, the Register believe that a model can be produced that will provide the framework for the successful transmission of moneys electronically. The Land Registry believes that the conveyancing market could adopt a system based on the CRESTCo system of electronic share transfer used in the financial markets. (CRESTCo is a company that operates instant or real-time settlements in the international finance markets, settling large volumes of transactions in several different currencies.) An example of an e-statement of funds (an e-completion statement), involved at completion is set out below and is a concept graphic prepared by the Land Registry and reproduced with their kind permission:

		£	
	Price	331,500	
	Deposit	33,000	Seller's Solicitor
	Balance	298,500	
	Stamp Duty	9,900	Inland Revenue
	LR Fees	300	Land Registry
	Sols. Fees	850	Buyer's Solicitor
		309,550	
New Lender	Mortgage	125,000	
		184,550	
Sale Proceeds	From Sale	182,950	
Buyer's Bank	Shortfall	1,600	

The beneficial effect of this system of e-conveyancing is that the time lag between completion and registration that arises in the paper-based system will be eradicated. Changes to the register will be made automatically as a consequence of electronic deeds and documents and applications created by conveyancing practitioners on behalf of their client sellers and buyers.

In respect of company charges, applications for registration at the Land Registry and the Companies Register may ultimately, with the advent of e-conveyancing, be combined. The Land Registry and Companies House are currently discussing possible ways in which the two systems can be linked electronically and s 121 allows for rules to be made regarding the transmission of information from the Land Registry to the Companies Registry.

8.6   E-CONVEYANCING AND FIRST REGISTRATION

The effect of e-conveyancing on the practice of first registration is unlikely to be of any great consequence. We assume that the transfer inducing first registration will be possible in electronic format. In essence while the transaction will be conducted on a paper-based system the transfer deed will be prepared electronically so that it can then be adopted for the purposes of the first registration application to the Registry. Secondly, where first registration is voluntary, it will be possible to make the application for electronic voluntary first registration. In both cases the supporting title deeds will have to be physically delivered to the Registry to enable it to approve and first register the newly registered title.

8.7   STATE CONTROL OF CONVEYANCERS AND CONVEYANCING

Substantial state control of the conveyancing process and those who conduct that process is put in place by the proposed model of e-conveyancing. Only those solicitors or licensed conveyancers who have been authorized to do so will be permitted to conduct electronic conveyancing. The relationship with the Registry will be contractual, under a 'network access agreement', and the Registry will be obliged to contract with any solicitor or licensed conveyancer who meets specified criteria.

Those specified criteria will be the subject of wide consultation and discussion with the relevant professional and other interested bodies. It may be that the intention of the Act is to raise the standards of conveyancing. It may achieve that. But what it certainly achieves is the state control of conveyancers and conveyancing. Presumably if an authorized e-conveyancer is identified as someone who regularly causes bottlenecks in chains of transactions, he or she could be at risk of losing their authorization. Perhaps they will then have to limit their work to unregistered transactions!

8.8   PITFALLS OF E-CONVEYANCING

E-conveyancing is not without potential difficulties. Several have been anticipated in legal and computing journals. One recent article looked at the potential abuse and misuse of digital signatures by unauthorized third parties. See, 'The cost of e-conveyancing' (2002) 99/11 LS Gaz 43, and 'The perils of non-repudiation' (2001) 98/39 LS Gaz 45. Practitioners should also consider the warnings about security and computer virus attacks set out in 'The BadTrans virus and e-conveyancing' December 2001/January 2002 *Computers & Law* 8. In that article the author Raymond Perry says, 'The Government has already given an indication that in cases where a solicitor is negligent in protecting his digital signature as a result of which the register is altered then the Land Registry may look to the solicitor for an indemnity if compensation has to be paid.' This means that solicitors will need to be sure that they have taken all reasonable steps to protect their IT systems from third-party attack and misuse of their digital signatures. Failure to do so could be expensive. The future will clearly require conveyancing practitioners to be experts in 'software updates and virus warnings' as well as the law and practice of conveyancing.

The Land Registry has made it clear that it will be seeking to create the highest levels of security for the process of e-conveyancing and for this reason the Registry say that it is unlikely that the e-conveyancing system will be internet based. It is more likely to be a closed system open only to those authorized under network access agreements, see Sch 5 of the Act. However, it is the view of the Land Registry that 'it must be stressed that any electronic system of conveyancing is unlikely to be less secure and fraud resistant than the existing paper-based system, and hopefully will be much more so'.

It is possible that practitioners will be conducting conveyancing transactions in such a way that, as a result of e-conveyancing practice, practitioners will be responsible for automatic changes to the register. This additional responsibility will potentially have an effect on the cost of professional indemnity insurance. The Registry believes that, although there may be areas where the practitioner may be exposed to greater risk than at present, there are also areas where the risks will be greatly diminished. A good example of where liability could be lessened is with the elimination of the registration gap. Nevertheless, the Registry is aware of these concerns and intends to consult with the Law Society as a result.

8.9   A COMPARISON BETWEEN PAPER-BASED CONVEYANCING AND E-CONVEYANCING

It may assist practitioners to see how stages in a conveyance compare as between the present paper-based system and its likely successor, e-conveyancing. The comparison will follow the five stages in a normal conveyance for a purchaser:

(a)   estate agent/marketing stage;
(b)   pre-contact stage;
(c)   contract stage;
(d)   post-contract but pre-completion stage;
(e)   completion and post-completion stage.

Paper-based conveyancing	E-conveyancing
Estate agent/marketing stage	*Estate agent/marketing stage*
Traditional marketing methods used by private sellers or their agents, eg adverts, boards signs, lists, etc.	Traditional marketing methods used by private sellers or their agents, eg adverts, boards signs, lists, etc. There could be additional e-marketing on the internet through agents or possibly the National Land Information Service (NLIS). If the 'seller's pack' becomes law then the agents will need to be able to provide it.
Pre-contact stage	*Pre-contact stage*
1 Buyer makes an offer that the seller accepts. Their respective conveyancers are instructed.	1 Buyer makes an offer that the seller accepts. Their respective conveyancers are instructed. There may be a requirement to notify the Land Registry of a potential transaction so that the chain matrix can be formed, the notification made by the seller or the estate agent by e-mail.
2 Several searches required, all requested by post.	2 Several searches required, all requested electronically via the NLIS.
3 Paper-based enquiries issued and answers reviewed.	3 Enquiries made by e-mail and answers received by e-mail and reviewed.
4 Survey commissioned.	4 Survey commissioned.
5 Mortgage arrangements made.	5 Mortgage arrangements made on-line.
6 Paper contract approved and signed by the hand of the contracting party and held by practitioners.	6 E-contract approved by the practitioners and then by the Land Registry and electronic signatures arranged. At the same time any requisitions of the Registry must be raised and answered before exchange.

7 Where a chain of transactions exists practitioners acting for buyers and sellers in the chain arrange a proposed completion date and seek to make a series of coordinated exchanges.	7 Guided by the Land Registry chain manager and by reference to the on-line chain matrix a completion date is agreed and contracts are ready to be electronically concluded. The registry may before exchange enter the proposed new title entries in draft form on the register in readiness for exchange — the notional register.
Contract stage	*Contract stage*
Contracts exchanges usually following one of the Law Society formulas (either A, B or C) and usually by telephone between practitioners involved in the chain of transactions.	Electronic exchange based upon electronic signatures and the approved e-documentation based on the on-line matrix information. Deposits paid by EFT (Electronic Funds Transfer) system. Completion financial e-settlement arrangements to be prepared. A note of the contract is entered on the relevant title at the time of exchange and the title freezes. The registry will after exchange enter the proposed new title entries in draft form on the register in readiness for completion — the notional register.
Post-contract but pre-completion stage	*Post-contract but pre-completion stage*
Requisitions on title. Drafting and approval of transfer deed. Final searches.	No need for requisitions on title. The e-transfer will be approved by the practitioners and the Land Registry, and draft changes to be made to the register are approved by the Registry. No need for final land registry search, the title is frozen and there is an entry protecting the contract but a bankruptcy search will be required against the borrowers to protect any lenders. (A company search will still be required if the seller is a company — it can be completed on-line at Companies House.)

The seller signs the transfer in readiness for completion.	No further signatures required.
Completion and post-completion stage	*Completion and post-completion stage*
1 Completion The transfer deed is signed, dated and delivered to effect completion and the deeds passed over to the buyer's practitioner with undertakings to pay off mortgages and to pass over forms DS1 or END1.	*1 Completion* There is no need for a transfer and there are no deeds. Once all parties are advised, the land registry will complete the change of ownership by making the draft entries, the formal details of title and ownership on the e-register.
Payments are made either by bank transfer, bankers draft or cheque.	Payments are made by e-settlement including redemption moneys, fees, stamp duty and costs (EFT) Electronic Funds Transfer system.
2 Post completion Stamp duty paid. Land registration application made hopefully within the priority period. The Registry update the title and issue either a land or charge certificate.	*2 Post completion* Unless the title is for first registration there is nothing further to be done. The title has been instantly updated at completion. The title can be accessed electronically on the open-to-the-public land register.

8.10   SCHEDULE 5 OF THE ACT — THE LAND REGISTRY NETWORK

This schedule contains ten parts covering the mechanics of the proposed land registry network. (A network in computer terms is a system of computers that are interconnected by various means including telephone cables in order to share information between users). These various parts cover:

(a)   access to the network;
(b)   term of access;
(c)   termination of access;
(d)   appeals against decisions by the registrar;
(e)   network transaction rules;
(f)   the overriding nature of network access obligations;
(g)   do-it-yourself conveyancing;
(h)   presumption of authority;
(i)   management of network transactions; and
(j)   various miscellaneous supplementary matters.

Each will now be considered below.

8.10.1   Access to the network

It is the view of the Land Registry and indeed it is the thrust of the Act that conveyancers intending to participate in e-conveyancing will need to be given appropriately regulated access to the Land Registry network. Paragraph 1 of the schedule indicates the basis upon which parties can apply for access to the network. Such access can only be allowed by means of an agreement with the registrar. The agreement is called in the Act a 'network access agreement' and it will authorize access for:

   (a)   the communication, posting or retrieval of information;
   (b)   the making of changes to the register of title or cautions register;
   (c)   the issue of official search certificates;
   (d)   the issue of official copies; or
   (e)   such other conveyancing purposes as the registrar thinks fit.

The notes to the Act make it clear that it is envisaged that different levels of access might be given to different types of users of the system, depending on the part they play in the conveyancing transaction. Typically, therefore, there could be different levels of access for estate agents, mortgage lenders and conveyancers.

   Paragraph 1 also states that the registrar must, on application, enter into a network access agreement with an applicant if that applicant meets such criteria as rules yet to be made may provide. This is clearly of consequence to conveyancing practitioners as it would be possible for those rules to exclude parties that fail to meet these unwritten criteria who presently are able to carry out conveyancing as part of their practice. It will be imperative to review these rules and to ensure that, through lobbying by professional bodies, the criteria are as wide as possible so as to allow easy access to all solicitors and licensed conveyancers. Paragraph 4 of the schedule provides for appeals against refusal of access, see 8.10.4 below for further details. Somewhat reassuringly, rules made under this paragraph are subject to greater Parliamentary scrutiny than normal land registration rules as s 128(5) provides that rules under s 93 or para 1, 2 or 3 of this schedule shall not be made unless a draft of the rules has been laid before and approved by resolution of each House of Parliament. Furthermore the Lord Chancellor must also consult before making the rules. Under para 11, the Lord Chancellor must have regard to the need to secure confidentiality of private information held on the network, competence of the use of the network (in particular for the purposes of making changes), and the adequacy of insurance arrangements for potential liabilities.

8.10.2   Terms of access

Paragraph 2 of Sch 5 covers terms of access and states that the terms shall be such as the registrar thinks fit. Importantly this includes charging for access to the network. These powers and entitlements accruing to the registrar are to be used to:

(a)   regulate the use of the network;

(b)   ensure that users use the network to carry on qualifying transactions specified in the agreement (see below for the meaning of 'qualifying transaction');

(c)   effect other matters relating to qualifying transactions as rules may provide; and

(d)   monitor network transactions.

It will be a condition of a network access agreement that the user must comply with any rules for the time being in force and made pursuant to para 5 of this schedule. (See 8.10.5 below for further details.)

8.10.3   Termination of access

Paragraph 3 covers termination either by the user of the system or by the registrar. If the user wishes to terminate the network access agreement he or she may do so at any time by notice to the registrar. This is the easier part of the paragraph. Termination by the registrar whereby a practitioner could lose his or her livelihood is the harder and more complex arrangement covered by the paragraph. Rules may make provision about the termination of a network access agreement by the registrar and may make provision about:

(a)   the grounds of termination;

(b)   the procedure to be followed in relation to termination; and

(c)   the suspension of termination pending appeal.

Furthermore rules may authorize the registrar to terminate a network access agreement if the user granted access:

(a)   fails to comply with the terms of the agreement;

(b)   ceases to be a user with whom the registrar would be required to enter into a network access agreement; or

(c)   does not meet such conditions as the rules may provide.

Bearing in mind the gravity of a termination order by the registrar, rules made under this paragraph are subject to greater Parliamentary scrutiny than normal land registration rules as s 125(5) provides that rules under s 93 or para 1, 2 or 3 of this schedule shall not be made unless a draft of the rules has been laid before and approved by resolution of each House of Parliament. Furthermore the Lord Chancellor must also consult before making the rules. Under para 11, the Lord Chancellor must have regard to the need to secure confidentiality of private information held on the network, competence of the use of the network (in particular for the purposes of making changes), and the adequacy of insurance arrangements for potential liabilities.

It may well be possible that rather than terminate the agreement the registrar may, where there is a breach of the agreement by a user, utilize contractual remedies against a party to a network access agreement which the registrar can pursue without actually terminating the agreement itself.

8.10.4   Appeals against decisions by the registrar

Paragraph 4 of Sch 5 covers appeals from decisions made by the registrar. A person who is aggrieved by a decision of the registrar about entry into or termination of a network access agreement can appeal against the decision to the adjudicator. (The adjudicator's powers and functions are detailed in ss 107–114 of and Sch 9 to the Act.) When exercising this appellate power the adjudicator can give such directions as he or she considers appropriate to give effect to his or her decision. Therefore the adjudicator would be expected to handle disputes about whether the registrar had acted properly when deciding that an applicant did not meet the criteria for the level of access sought or, in relation to a user of the network, the termination of their network access agreement. There will be rules, as yet unseen, that make provision about appeals under this paragraph. There is one further right of appeal but only on a point of law from the adjudicator's decision. Section 111(2) makes it clear that in the case of a decision on an appeal under para 4 of Sch 5 an appeal on a point of law alone is possible.

8.10.5   Network transaction rules

Network transaction rules, as yet unmade, will be of considerable practical importance, as they will in effect detail how e-conveyancing is to be conducted or performed. Paragraph 5 of the schedule simply states that rules may make provision about how to go about network transactions. This is probably the shortest and simplest way of saying that e-conveyancing will be regulated totally by rules and that these rules of conduct will give explicit direction as to how an e-conveyancer must conduct his or her business over the Land Registry network. The rules will therefore require users to submit information as well as conduct themselves in such a way so as to comply with these transaction rules. These rules will inevitably cover not just registered titles but also unregistered titles that are to be submitted for first registration.

8.10.6   The overriding nature of network access obligations

Paragraph 6 of Sch 5 is quite brief. It states that to the extent that an obligation not owed under a network access agreement conflicts with an obligation owed under such an agreement by the person granted access, the obligation not owed under the agreement is discharged. We have previously noted that the proposed system of chain management will require practitioners to provide information to the registry. Clients may instruct their conveyancing practitioner not to divulge such information. In theory this could give rise to a conflict of interests for practitioners especially when practitioners note that Sch 5, para 6 of the Act makes it clear that network access obligations prevail where there may be a conflict of obligations.

The notes to the Act give further examples of where this kind of conflict might arise. For example, the rules are likely to require the disclosure of other information that a registered proprietor might not wish to have disclosed, such as the fact that a right to determine a registered estate in land has become exercisable, ie forfeiture of a registered lease. Similarly a conveyancer who has entered into a network access agreement may be required to provide specified information about a dealing, and, in particular, information about interests the priority of which is protected without the need for registration. In these circumstances, the situation may arise where a conveyancer could be required to act contrary to the wishes of his or her client. Paragraph 6 of the schedule makes it quite clear that where conflicting obligations do arise the obligation under the network access agreement prevails and discharges the other obligation to the extent that they conflict. This will be an important professional conduct issue.

8.10.7   Do-it-yourself conveyancing

If there is a Land Registry network Sch 5, para 7 states that the registrar has a duty to provide such assistance as he or she thinks appropriate for the purpose of enabling persons who wish to do their own conveyancing to do so by means of the network. This will obviously involve such persons in the conduct of a 'qualifying transaction' (see 8.10.10 below for the meaning of a 'qualifying transaction'), over the Land Registry network and not via a conveyancing practitioner. There is a qualification to this duty and that is that it does not extend to the provision of legal advice! Accordingly the duty covers procedural and practical elements of the conveyancing process and therefore extends to affording 'do-it-yourselfers' access to the network to enable them to conduct a qualifying transaction without professional assistance. We presume that to enable this duty to be performed the registrar will carry out the electronic transactions at the direction of the do-it-yourself conveyancers and that this service will be made available from district registries or other approved locations with access to the Land Registry network.

8.10.8   Presumption of authority

The existing law means that a conveyancer does not have an implied authority to sign an agreement on behalf of his or her client. The conveyancer must have explicit written authority to sign any agreement for and on behalf of the client. Paragraph 8 of Sch 5 has been included to avoid the need for the exchange of paper-based authorities before contracts can be concluded electronically. Where a user of the Land Registry network purports to sign an agreement on behalf of their client then the conveyancer shall be deemed to be so acting in favour of any other party provided the following two conditions are fulfilled:

(a)   that the contract purports to be authenticated by the conveyancer as agent; and

(b)   that the contract contains a statement to the effect that the conveyancer is acting under the authority of his or her principal.

No doubt the rules to be made under para 5 (8.10.5 above) will require a network user, the conveyancing practitioner, to obtain all necessary authorities to allow him or her to comply with these two conditions. The failure of the practitioner to obtain such authorities would then put him or her in breach of the network access agreement and thus in jeopardy of losing the right of access to the network.

8.10.9   Management of network transactions

Network access agreements will require users to supply information about transactions they are dealing with. This will be required for various reasons but the main one being to enable the registry to deal with a chain matrix and to allow the chain manager to do his or her job. As a result of Sch 5, para 9 the registrar may use monitoring information (ie information arising from the provisions of a network access agreement), for the purpose of managing network transactions. The registrar may disclose such information to persons authorized to use the network. The registrar can also authorize the further disclosure of that information if the registrar considers it necessary or desirable to do so. The notes to the Act rather disarmingly comment that 'The "chain manager" will not have any direct coercive powers but will be able to identify the link in the chain that is causing delay and will then be able to encourage that party to proceed with due dispatch.' We wonder how long it will be before patience is exhausted and the rules are changed to allow chain managers to accrue coercive powers?

Network access agreements will impose other duties upon conveyancing practitioners. One involves the recording of defects in title. Section 64 of the Act contains important new provisions to record on the register particular defects in title where such defects would not previously have been recorded. It provides that if the registrar becomes aware that the right to determine (ie end) a registered estate has become exercisable, he or she may enter this fact on the register. Section 64(2) allows for rules, as yet unmade, to make provision about the circumstances in which the registrar must exercise his or her power, how entries will be made and the removal of such entries. Once e-conveyancing is with us, network access agreements are likely to require conveyancing practitioners to disclose such defects affecting clients' estates to the Registry. This will enable the appropriate entry to be made on the register.

8.10.10   Various miscellaneous supplementary matters

The final section of the schedule covers three various supplementary matters. First para 10 states that the registrar may provide, or arrange for the provision of, education and training in relation to the use of the Land Registry network. This is an excellent inclusion within the Act, as it will almost certainly be required to ensure that the system is used properly and in accordance with the spirit of the Act.

Paragraph 11 makes it clear that any rules made relating to paras 1, 2 or 3 of the schedule are to be made by the Lord Chancellor who must consult with other parties before making rules. In particular for para 1 or 3 the Lord Chancellor must have regard to the need to secure:

(a)   the confidentiality of private information kept on the network;
(b)   competence in relation to the use of the network; and
(c)   adequate insurance covering liabilities arising from the use of the network.

Finally, para 12 lists several definitions relating to the Land Registry network. This includes a 'qualifying transaction' which is a transaction that involves registration and is capable of being effected electronically.

8.11   OTHER CONVEYANCING REFORMS

Apart from the potentially massive changes that e-conveyancing will bring to the law and practice of conveyancing, the 2002 Act makes one or two other changes that deserve specific scrutiny. The changes relate to:

(a)   the proof of title to registered land;
(b)   when a registrable lease is to be granted out of unregistered land; and
(c)   covenants for title relating to registered property.

Each will now be considered.

8.11.1   Proof of title to registered land

At present deducing title to registered land is governed by s 110 of the Land Registration Act 1925. This section requires the seller to supply the buyer with a copy of the entries on the register of title and a copy of the filed plan. It also requires the seller to supply an abstract or other evidence of matters about which the register is not conclusive (eg overriding interests), and copies or abstracts of any documents noted on the register. An example of the last item would be a conveyance containing restrictive covenants, which would be noted on the charges register. Charges or encumbrances which will be discharged or overridden at completion, such as the seller's mortgage, do not need to be supplied (although details will be seen in the charges register).

Section 110 does not require the seller to supply office copies; mere photocopies of the entries inside the land or charge certificate would be sufficient. However, both Standard Condition 4.2.1 and the Law Society Conveyancing Protocol require the seller at his or her own expense to provide the buyer with office copies. This is best practice in any event because office copies show the current position of the register whereas the land or charge certificate may not have been updated for many years. Since 29 May 2001 office copies show a time of issue as well as a date, eg 1 June 2002 12:34:56. The need for a time of issue arises as a result of Land Registry searches and applications now acquiring priority on a 'real time' basis. Thus it is now possible for different versions of the register to exist on the same day.

The Law Commission recommended that the provisions of s 110 should not be replicated in the new Act and that parties should be left to make their own contractual arrangements as to how title should be deduced. To ensure that there are no abuses of this change they also recommended that there should be a rule-making power as to the proof of title that a buyer might require. Accordingly Sch 10, para 2 covers the regulation of title matters between sellers and buyers. It does so by indicating that rules as yet unmade may make provision about the obligations with respect to proof of title or perfection of title. This is restricted to the seller's title under a contract for the transfer or other disposition for valuable consideration of a registered estate or charge. Such rules can be overriding. Accordingly there is no section that is the exact equivalent of the old s 110 and practitioners must await rules to see what is expected of them in their contracts, failing which they must consider title in the context of each contract drafted by them. This will need to be done in the light of the nature of the registered title for the subject property.

8.11.2   Where a registrable lease is to be granted out of unregistered land

In the case of unregistered land the Law of Property Act 1925, s 44 provides that the buyer can insist upon seeing the lease of the property that is being purchased, supported by all deeds of assignment and other legal documents dealing with the legal estate representing a period of ownership for at least the last 15 years. In this respect the title is deduced in much the same way as is the case for freehold properties. However, the crucial difference is that where an existing unregistered lease title is to be deduced, the buyer cannot insist upon seeing details of any superior titles. If the buyer needs to submit the lease for first registration and has no details of the superior title, the lease will be registered with a mere good leasehold title. This could be unacceptable to a mortgagee.

The Act stops s 44 applying to either registered land or to a lease derived out of registered land, see Sch 11, para 2 of the Act. The Act goes on to make further provisions regarding a contract to grant a registrable lease out of an unregistered estate. The Law Commission wanted to ensure that all such leases were registered with an absolute title and thereby avoid the problem outlined in the paragraph above. The Act therefore stops s 44 applying to contracts to grant leases that are compulsorily registrable, see Sch 11, para 2 of the Act. The effect of this amendment is that where an owner of an unregistered title grants a registrable lease via a contract the grantor will have to deduce the details of the superior title for the statutory period of 15 years. This should enable the new lease to be granted with an absolute class of title.

In the context of commercial leases it should be remembered that the Law of Property Act 1925, s 44 applies to contract. Commercial leases are normally granted without the necessity for a contract. As the Act contemplates that leases of more than seven years be registrable it might still be possible that there will be leases granted that will not have an absolute title. Nevertheless the Law Commission expressed the hope that even these leases would be offered with details of the title to allow the lessee to apply for an absolute title. We suspect that their hope will not come to fruition as there are many commercial lessors who will not be predisposed to showing more than they have to about the ownership of their property.

8.11.3 Covenants for title relating to registered property

Since the Law of Property (Miscellaneous Provisions) Act 1994 came into force on 1 July 1995, it is no longer necessary to state the seller's capacity in the contract (eg beneficial owner, trustee, personal representative, etc). Presently the seller must decide whether to give a full title guarantee, a limited title guarantee or no title guarantee at all. The importance of the title guarantee is that covenants for title on the part of the seller are implied into the purchase deed. By definition, a limited guarantee will imply less extensive covenants for title than a full guarantee, and no guarantee will imply none. Full title guarantee is normally given where the seller owns the whole legal and equitable interest in the property and would, before July 1995, have sold as 'beneficial owner'. In the absence of any express provision in the contract, Standard Condition 4.5.2 provides that the seller will sell with full title guarantee. Limited title guarantee is normally given where the legal owner/seller is a personal representative, or a trustee holding on trust for others. Before July 1995 such a seller would have sold as 'personal representative' or 'trustee' respectively. The seller also has the option of giving no title guarantee at all and this is often done in circumstances where the seller has little or no knowledge of the property or the title history, or if the disposition is by way of gift. A mortgagee exercising its power of sale may offer no title guarantee but as a buyer's practitioner you should be wary of accepting this, especially where you are also acting for the buyer's mortgagee who might insist on a title guarantee. A seller would generally not wish to give any title guarantee where selling only a possessory title.

The Act inserts a new subs (4) into s 6 of the Law of Property (Miscellaneous Provisions) Act 1994, see Sch 11, para 31. Under s 6, a person making a disposition is not liable under the statutory implied covenants for anything that was within the prior knowledge of the person to whom the disposition was made. The new subsection is added to exclude liability for any information that was entered in the register of title relating to that interest at the time of the disposition. The reasoning for this is of course that the register of title is an open register and therefore open to public inspection.

8.11.4   Covenants implied on the assignment of a pre-1996 lease

For many years it was the position that the original lessor and original lessee were liable to each other under the covenants in their lease for the full term granted by the lease. As a consequence of the effects of privity of contract this liability remained enforceable in the courts even if the lessee had subsequently assigned the residue of the term of the lease. The practical effect of this used to be that a lessee could be sued for arrears of rent, even though that lessee had not been the tenant in occupation for many years and, indeed, even where there had been many other subsequent lessees liable to pay rent under the terms of the original lease. (In *Selous Street Properties Ltd v Oronel Fabrics Ltd* [1984] 1 EGLR 50 it was held that where a later tenant carries out improvements that increase the rental value, the original tenant must pay rent at that higher level even though the works were carried out after the original tenant ceased to be involved as a result of having assigned the residue of the term of the lease.) However, the provisions of the Landlord and Tenant (Covenants) Act 1995 have made a measure of reform but these provisions only apply to new leases created on or after 1 January 1996. (This Act applies to all leases granted on or after 1 January 1996. All other leases will not normally be affected by the Act. It reverses the general rule that prevailed before the Act was passed that a lessee remained liable under the lease covenants throughout the full term of the lease.) There will, however, still be many leases in existence that were granted prior to the change in the law.

In the context of such leases, ie those still in existence and which were granted prior to 1996, the Land Registration Act 1925, s 24(1)(b), (2) made provision for implied indemnity covenants on the part of the transferee in favour of the transferor. For example, where there is a transfer of a lease this 1925 legislation will create implied indemnity covenants on the part of the transferee in favour of the transferor.

As a result of the doctrine of privity of contract, an owner of land may continue to be liable under a covenant affecting the land even after the control of the land has passed to someone else, namely, the buyer or buyer's successor in title. In this situation the seller's practitioner must ensure that the buyer gives the seller an indemnity covenant against any future breaches of the covenant because the seller could in future be sued for breach of contract. However, a covenant limited to seisin (ie possession) will generally not bind the covenantor after disposal of the land. So in this situation an indemnity covenant from the buyer would be inappropriate. Therefore, in the sale of leasehold land the buyer's indemnity is normally implied (under the Land Registration Act 1925, s 24(1)(b), for registered land whether or not the assignment is for value).

Practitioners will recall that the Land Registration Act 1925, s 24(1)(b), (2) was repealed prospectively by the Landlord and Tenant (Covenants) Act 1995. However of key importance is that this repeal will only be in respect of 'new tenancies', ie those granted after 31 December 1995, when the 1995 Covenants Act was brought into force. The Act in effect replicates the effect of s 24(1)(b) and (2) in relation to the assignment of leases which are not 'new tenancies' for the purposes of the 1995 Act and the new provisions are set out in Sch 12, para 20 of the Act.

8.11.5   E-conveyancing and land and charge certificates

8.11.5.1   Charge certificates
Practitioners should note that the Act effects the abolition of the charge certificate once the Act comes into force. Registered charges can already be discharged electronically under the END system and it is likely that the creation of registered charges will be one of the first dispositions that can be effected electronically. As a result, charge certificates will become redundant.

8.11.5.2   Land certificates
Because of the way e-conveyancing works under the Act there will no longer be a requirement for the registered proprietor to produce the land certificate to the Registry on a disposition of a registered estate or when applying to register a notice or restriction. This is because it is incompatible with the system of e-conveyancing. Instead there are special procedures to enable the registered proprietor to secure the cancellation of a notice (s 36) and object to the entry of a restriction (s 45). The Act says very little about land certificates at all. The only provision is in Sch 10, para 4 in which there is a power by rules to make provision about:

(a)   when a certificate of registration of title may be issued;
(b)   the form and content of such a certificate; and
(c)   when such a certificate must be produced or surrendered to the registrar.

As the register alone is conclusive as to the state of the title, the entries in the land certificate may be out of date. Because of this, the Law Commission envisage that a land certificate will probably in future no longer contain a copy of the register. It will merely certify the registration of a parcel of land and identify the name of the registered proprietor.

8.12   KEY POINTS FOR THE PRACTITIONER

- Under the proposed system of e-conveyancing, the register should be a complete and accurate reflection of the state of the title of the land at any given time, so that it is possible to investigate title to land on-line, with the absolute minimum of additional enquiries and inspections.
- The Land Registry will control permitted access to the e-conveyancing network. This means that conveyancers will in practice need the continued approval of the Registry to be able to effect e-conveyances.
- It is intended that the Registry will also provide a means of managing a chain of transactions by monitoring them electronically, by using an on-line chain matrix for inspection by the parties involved.

- Conveyancing practitioners will need to reconsider their procedures for taking instructions from their clients to make quite sure that they are properly authorized to effect electronic signatures on behalf of clients. The client needs to give their informed consent to this.
- Draft e-contracts and e-transfers must be approved by the Land Registry before they can be ready to be made effective.
- The beneficial effect of e-conveyancing is that the time lag between completion and registration that arises in the paper-based system will be eradicated. Changes to the register will be made automatically as a consequence of electronic deeds and documents and applications created by conveyancing practitioners on behalf of their client sellers and buyers.
- The Inland Revenue has indicated that there will be legislation to extend the stamp duty regime to cover transfers of land that are made electronically, by e-conveyancing. A detailed set of proposals, containing drafts of any necessary paragraphs and regulations, is to be published in due course.
- Conveyancing practitioners will need to be sure that they have taken all reasonable steps to protect their IT systems from third-party attack and misuse of their digital signatures.
- Access to the Land Registry network can only be allowed by means of an agreement with the registrar. The agreement is called in the Act a 'network access agreement' and it will authorize access for most if not all aspects of conveyancing when conducted electronically.
- Different levels of access might be given to different types of users of the e-conveyancing system, depending on the part they play in the conveyancing transaction. There could be different levels of access for estate agents, mortgage lenders and conveyancing practitioners.
- Schedule 5, para 2 of the Act covers terms of access and states that the terms shall be such as the registrar thinks fit, but importantly this includes charging for access to the network.
- Network transaction rules, as yet unmade, will be of considerable practical importance, as they will in effect detail how e-conveyancing is to be conducted or performed.
- Schedule 5, para 6 of the Act makes it clear that network access agreement obligations prevail where there may be a conflict of obligations, eg professional conduct.
- The registrar has a duty to provide such assistance as he or she thinks appropriate for the purpose of enabling persons who wish to do their own conveyancing to do so by means of the Land Registry network.
- Where a practitioner/user of the Land Registry network purports to sign an agreement on behalf of their client then the conveyancer shall be deemed to have authority to sign on behalf of their client in favour of any other party to the transaction.

Chapter 9
Adverse Possession

9.1   INTRODUCTION

The established law of adverse possession is based on limitation. Section 15 of the Limitation Act 1980 bars an action for the recovery of land 12 years after the cause of action to recover the land arises. Time starts to run when:

(a)   the legal owner of the land has discontinued possession or has been dispossessed; and
(b)   the squatter has taken adverse possession.

To show adverse possession the squatter must enjoy:

(a)   factual possession of the land; and
(b)   an intention to possess the land to the exclusion of others including the paper title owner.

The Act does not interfere with the substantive law as it relates to the twin concepts of discontinuance/dispossession and adverse possession. What it changes is when and how the squatter can take advantage of the fact that the owner is no longer in possession and he or she is in adverse possession. The fundamental principle of the new law is that adverse possession, for however long, will not extinguish title to a registered estate.

The case for reform of the law of adverse possession has been argued strongly for many years (eg by the Law Commission and the Land Registry in the 1998 Report). In *J A Pye (Oxford) Holdings Ltd v Graham* [2000] Ch 676 Neuberger J reluctantly gave judgment in favour of squatters entitled to 25 hectares of land in Berkshire (since reversed by the Court of Appeal). He commented that:

A frequent justification for limitation periods generally is that people should not be able to sit on their rights indefinitely . . . However, if as in the present case the owner of land has no immediate use for it and is content to let another person trespass on the land for the time being, it is hard to see what principle of justice entitles the trespasser to acquire the land for nothing from the owner simply because he has been permitted to remain there for 12 years. To say that in such circumstances the owner who has sat on his rights should therefore be deprived of his land appears to me to be both illogical and disproportionate.

Other recent high profile cases have caused public disquiet, namely those involving squatters successfully acquiring parts of an inner London borough's housing supply. Moreover a common perception exists that in depriving an owner of recovering his or her land the doctrine of adverse possession is incompatible with human rights. Up to 20,000 applications a year are made by squatters to the Land Registry, roughly 75 per cent of which are successful. In making matters harder for the squatter the 2002 Act aims to strike a fairer balance between landowner and adverse possessor.

9.2   NO CHANGE TO UNREGISTERED LAND

It is important to appreciate that the law of adverse possession as it relates to unregistered land remains unaffected by the 2002 Act. The Law Commission's justification for this appears to be that title to unregistered land is relative and rests essentially on possession. Indeed gaps in an unregistered paper title are often remedied by showing possession of land for the limitation period. With registered land however title is based on registration — it is the fact of registration that confers title and the doctrine of adverse possession runs contrary to the fundamental concept of registered title, namely, that title is indefeasible through registration. It is only where the register is not conclusive, eg in relation to boundaries and short leases that are not registrable, that the justification for adverse possession should be the same as it is for unregistered land.

It follows that owners of unregistered land should consider applying for voluntary first registration. This would be a sensible course of action given that the changes made under the Act make life harder for the squatter of registered land. This would be particularly the case for someone who owns vacant land which is not regularly inspected, or where there have been previous acts of trespass.

9.3   THE NEW LAW

The provisions of the 2002 Act relating to adverse possession are contained in ss 96–98 and Sch 6. In short, the fundamentals of the new law are as follows:

(a)   adverse possession of itself and for however long, will not bar the owner's title to a registered estate;

(b)   a squatter can apply to be registered as proprietor after ten years' adverse possession;

(c)   the registered proprietor, any registered chargee, and certain other persons interested in the land will be notified of the squatter's application;

(d)   if the application is not opposed by any of those notified, the squatter will be registered as proprietor of the land;

(e)   if any of those notified oppose the squatter's application it will be refused, unless the squatter can bring himself or herself within one of three limited exceptions;

(f)   if the application for registration is refused but the squatter remains in adverse possession for a further two years, he or she will be entitled to apply once again to be registered. This time the squatter will be registered as proprietor whether or not the registered proprietor objects;

(g)   where the registered proprietor brings proceedings to recover possession from a squatter, the action will succeed unless the squatter can establish certain limited exceptions consistent with those in (e) and (f) above.

It will be seen from the above that the new scheme produces a decisive outcome. Either the squatter is evicted or otherwise ceases to be in adverse possession, or the squatter is registered as proprietor of the land.

There are particular rules for special cases and transitional provisions are included to protect the rights of squatters who have barred the rights of the registered proprietor prior to the Act coming into force. These are considered further at 9.6 below.

The fundamental aspects of the new law are now considered.

9.3.1   Adverse possession of itself and for however long, will not bar the owner's title to a registered estate

The governing principle of the new scheme is contained in s 96. It provides that in relation to a registered estate in land or registered rentcharge, no period of limitation runs in relation to:

(a)   actions for the recovery of land (except in favour of a chargee); and

(b)   actions for redemption.

In other words, title to such an estate or rentcharge cannot be extinguished under the Limitation Act 1980, s 17. This is based on the fact that the register is conclusive as to ownership.

In certain situations the owner who seeks to recover land will not have a registered estate even though the land is registered title. Such persons would include lessees under leases for 21 years or less (whose lease was granted before the Act came into force), licensees and tenants at will. For these 'owners' the Limitation Act 1980 will continue to apply and, potentially, they could still be time barred from recovering possession from a squatter.

9.3.2   The squatter's right to apply for registration after ten years' adverse possession

Subject to certain exceptions considered below, a person may apply to the registrar to become a proprietor of a registered estate if he or she has been in adverse possession of that estate for an unbroken period of ten years ending on the date of the application (Sch 6, para 1(1)). The squatter must prove to the registrar that he or she has been in adverse possession for the relevant period (as was the case under the Land Registration Act 1925, s 75). The estate need not have been registered throughout the period of adverse possession; so when the squatter entered the land it may have been unregistered but then later became registered land.

To satisfy the ten-year requirement the squatter need not show that he or she has personally been in adverse possession for that period. The squatter may add to his or her period of possession an earlier squatter's period in possession provided he or she did not evict the earlier squatter (on the basis that he or she would not then be the earlier squatter's successor in title). Even if the squatter is evicted by the registered proprietor (other than pursuant to a judgment for possession) the squatter can still apply within six months of being evicted (Sch 6, para 1(2)). The basis for this is that it would be wrong in principle for a registered proprietor to deny a squatter's right to apply by having resorted to self-help.

Under the Act adverse possession has the same meaning as it does for the purposes of the Limitation Act 1980, s 15, ie when time would have started running under the 1980 Act (see Sch 6, para 11(1)). The Act qualifies this in two respects. First, it disapplies a technical rule about the adverse possession of a reversion which is not needed under the scheme which the Act introduces. Secondly, and more significantly, the commencement of proceedings asserting a right to possession is to be disregarded. Such proceedings would of course have stopped time running under the old law but this principle has no relevance to the new law because a right of recovery is never barred by lapse of time alone.

9.3.2.1   Exceptions to the squatter's rights
In the following situations the squatter cannot make a valid application to be registered even though he or she may have been in possession for at least ten years:

(a)   where there are possession proceedings against the squatter that are still current;

(b)   if judgment is given against the squatter in those proceedings, within two years of the judgment (after which the judgment ceases to be enforceable);

(c)   where for the purposes of the Limitation (Enemies and War Prisoners) Act 1945 the proprietor is either an enemy or held in enemy territory;

(d)   where the registered proprietor is suffering from mental disability so as to be unable to make decisions about an application or is unable to communicate such decisions because of mental disability or physical impairment.

The effect of exceptions (a) and (b) is that the registered proprietor can take proceedings against the squatter without fear of having to fend off an application for registration by the squatter at the same time. There is power for the registrar to enter a note on the register to indicate that the registered proprietor falls within exceptions (c) or (d). Exception (d) is designed to cover the situation where the registered proprietor or the person looking after his or her affairs, eg an attorney, fails to receive any notice served under the Act. It goes beyond the protection afforded under the Limitation Act 1980 because the disability merely has to be suffered at the time of the squatter's application, rather than earlier when adverse possession began. It also includes an inability to communicate through physical impairment as well, eg loss of speech.

9.3.3   The registered proprietor, any registered chargee, and certain other persons interested in the land will be notified of the squatter's application

Once a squatter's valid application to be registered has been received, the registrar must serve notice on all those who would be prejudiced if the squatter's application were successful. By receiving such notice these persons will then have an opportunity of opposing the squatter's application. The persons who are entitled to receive notice are:

(a)   the registered proprietor;

(b)   the proprietor of any registered charge;

(c)   in the case of a leasehold estate, the proprietor of any superior registered estate(s);

(d)   any person who, on application to the registrar, is registered in accordance with land registration rules as a person who is to be notified, eg an equitable chargee under a charging order or a rentcharge owner;

(e)   such other persons as land registration rules may provide. This is likely to include a trustee in bankruptcy where the proprietor has been made bankrupt, the Charity Commission in respect of land held under charitable trusts and the Church Commissioners as regards benefices.

The registrar's notice must inform the person:

(a)   of the application for registration;

(b)   that the person may serve a counter-notice on the registrar within a period prescribed by land registration rules (likely to be three months);

(c)   that if such a counter-notice is not served by at least one of those notified, the registrar must enter the applicant/squatter as the new proprietor of the estate.

9.3.4   If the application is not opposed by any of those notified the squatter will be registered as proprietor of the land

Where the registrar serves a notice and no counter-notice is served on him or her within the prescribed time, the registrar *must* approve the squatter's application to be registered as proprietor of the land in place of the existing proprietor (Sch 6, para 4). See 9.4 below for the effect of such registration. An obvious but important point to be made here is that the registered proprietor and any registered chargee should keep their address for service with the Land Registry up to date. Otherwise, they risk not receiving the registrar's notice and not appreciating the need to serve a counter-notice. As a result, their land would be lost to the squatter.

9.3.5   If any of those notified oppose the squatter's application it will be refused, unless the squatter can bring himself or herself within one of three limited exceptions

If a counter-notice is served on the registrar, he or she must reject the squatter's application unless the squatter can establish one of three exceptions described below, which will entitle the squatter to be registered (Sch 6, para 5(1)). (However all is not lost because even if the squatter's application is rejected, the squatter can re-apply to be registered if he she remains in adverse possession for a further two years (see 9.3.6 below).) The three exceptions are set out below and then explained in more detail:

(a)   where, under the principles of proprietary estoppel, it would be unconscionable for the registered proprietor to object to the squatter's application to be registered;

(b)   where the squatter was otherwise entitled to the land;

(c)   boundaries: where the squatter is the owner of adjacent property and has been in adverse possession of the land in question under the mistaken but reasonable belief that he or she was the owner of it.

The exceptions at (a) and (b) are available to the squatter under the present law but a different approach is adopted by the Act. Under the present law, to time bar the paper owner the squatter need only show that he or she has been in adverse possession for 12 years; there is no need to take costly legal proceedings to prove estoppel. However under the new law, in addition to showing ten years' adverse possession the squatter must, if a counter-notice is served, establish one of these exceptions as well.

If agreement cannot be reached entitling the squatter to be registered under one of the three exceptions, the registrar must refer the matter to the adjudicator for resolution (see chapter 11 for further discussion of the adjudicator's powers).

The three exceptions enabling a squatter to be registered as proprietor are now considered:

9.3.5.1 Estoppel
To fall within this exception the squatter must show:

(a)   that it is unconscionable to dispossess him or her; and

(b)   that the circumstances are such that he or she ought to be registered as the proprietor.

To establish that an 'equity' has arisen in the squatter's favour he or she will have to show that:

(a)   in some way, the registered proprietor encouraged or allowed the squatter to believe that he or she owned the parcel of land in question;

(b)   in this belief, the squatter acted to his or her detriment to the knowledge of the proprietor; and

(c)   it would be unconscionable for the proprietor to deny the squatter the rights which he or she believed he or she had.

A case in which the estoppel exception may arise is where a squatter has built on the owner's land in the mistaken belief that he or she was the owner of it and the owner has knowingly acquiesced in the mistake. Another might be where a purchaser has paid for the land and moved in, but there is no binding contract and the purchaser has not perfected his or her title by registration.

Under general equitable principles, once the equity has arisen a court has a discretion as to how to give effect to the equity. It will ascertain 'the minimum equity' to do justice to the claimant (*Crabb v Arun DC* [1976] Ch 179, 198 *per* Scarman LJ). This could range from an order for the transfer of the fee simple (as in *Pascoe v Turner* [1979] 1 WLR 431); the grant of some right over the land (eg an easement in *Crabb v Arun DC* above); or simply an order for compensation for loss suffered (*Baker v Baker* [1993] 2 FLR 247). Under the Act it is envisaged that the adjudicator will resolve disputed claims based on these principles. There is a right of appeal from an adjudicator's decision (see chapter 11).

9.3.5.2 Some other right to the land
The Law Commission has given two examples of where it thinks this exception might apply:

(a)   where the claimant is entitled to the land under the will or intestacy of the deceased proprietor; and

(b)   where the claimant contracted to buy the land and paid the purchase price, but the legal estate was never transferred to the buyer. The squatter/buyer is thus a beneficiary under a bare trust and may be in adverse possession (see *Bridges v Mees* [1957] Ch 475).

As far as these first two exceptions are concerned we think it is questionable how relevant they will be in the context of adverse possession — the point being that the claimant may have difficulty in proving he or she is in adverse possession in the first place. This is because if the squatter is occupying by permission or licence of the owner then his or her possession would not be adverse. However, presumably the squatter's argument would be based on the fact that he or she is entitled to be registered, regardless of his or her adverse possession.

9.3.5.3   Reasonable mistake as to boundary

The third and most radical exception applies where the land being claimed by the squatter is adjacent to land which the squatter already owns. In addition the boundary between the two properties must be a general boundary, ie not fixed. (Boundaries are rarely 'fixed', as this is a costly procedure — if they are fixed, a note to this effect will be made in the Property Register; see also 6.3.)

To fall within the exception the squatter must prove that:

(a)   there has been a period of adverse possession of at least ten years by the squatter or the squatter's predecessor in title ending on the date of the application;

(b)   for at least ten years of that period, the squatter or the squatter's predecessor in title reasonably believed that the land to which the application relates belonged to him or her; and

(c)   the estate to which the land relates was registered more than one year prior to the date of the application.

The reason for requirement (c) is because of the 12-year limitation period in unregistered land. It is conceivable that a squatter may have been in adverse possession of unregistered land for more than ten years but less than 12 years. If the title were then registered while requirements (a) and (b) were otherwise met, the squatter could apply to be registered as proprietor immediately the owner registered his or her title. If this occurred the owner would have no opportunity to evict the squatter. Requirement (c) resolves the difficulty by giving the registered proprietor time to seek that eviction. The Law Commission has recommended that the limitation period for unregistered land be reduced from 12 to ten years. If this change were introduced, requirement (c) would no longer be needed and could be repealed. As squatters can only use the 'reasonable boundary mistake' exception once land has been registered for at least one year, it follows that owners of recently registered land have one year to see off 'boundary creepers'. If necessary, owners should consider issuing possession proceedings against creepers immediately following first registration.

Typically, the 'reasonable boundary mistake' exception will arise where the boundaries as they appear on the filed plan of the register do not correspond with the boundaries on the ground. This may be because dividing walls or fences were erected in the wrong place and not in accordance with the plan lodged at the Land Registry. It might also be the case that physical features, such as trees, suggest that the boundary is in one place but, according to the filed plan, it is in another.

9.3.6 The right for the squatter to make a further application for registration after two more years' adverse possession

The Law Commission has determined that two years is a reasonable time to allow the registered proprietor or other interested person, eg a chargee, to either start proceedings to evict the squatter or to regularize the squatter's possession by negotiating a tenancy or licence agreement. As the 1998 Report explained:

> It is important that the marketability of land should be upheld, and if a registered proprietor fails to take steps to vindicate his or her title within two years of being given a clear warning to do so, we consider that it should be extinguished and that the squatter should obtain the land. Were this not so, possession and title could remain permanently out of kilter.

Accordingly the Act allows the squatter a second bite of the cherry. The squatter may reapply to become the registered proprietor in three situations:

(a) Where the squatter remains in adverse possession two years after the rejection of his or her application to be registered, eg the registered proprietor or other interested person has failed to take steps to evict the squatter or regularize the squatter's possession. This is likely to be the commonest situation. However, we think it may also pose evidential difficulties in a situation where a proprietor is required to prove an informal 'agreement' with the squatter.

(b) Where the squatter remains in adverse possession and the proprietor or other interested person obtains a judgment for possession against the squatter but fails to enforce it within two years. In these circumstances the judgment for possession becomes unenforceable.

(c) Where the squatter remains in adverse possession and proceedings against the squatter are discontinued or struck out more than two years after the squatter's application was rejected. (Note: if they are struck out or discontinued before two years has passed then situation (a) will apply.)

Importantly, if any of these three circumstances are established the registrar *must* register the applicant as proprietor in place of the existing proprietor (Sch 6, para 7). So this time the squatter will be registered as proprietor whether or not the registered proprietor objects.

9.3.7 Where the registered proprietor brings proceedings to recover possession from a squatter, the action will succeed unless the squatter can establish certain limited defences

The general rule is that the registered proprietor or chargee is entitled to possession as against the squatter regardless of how long the squatter has been in adverse possession, ie limitation is no longer a bar in registered land. However, there are exceptions to this rule in which the squatter will be able to successfully defend the possession proceedings.

These defences mirror the squatter's entitlement to apply for registration under 9.3.5 and 9.3.6 above. It follows that a statutory defence will exist if the squatter has been in adverse possession for ten years and could insist on being registered by virtue of the one of the three exceptions listed above, eg a reasonable mistake as to boundary. Similarly a defence will exist where the registered proprietor has previously failed to take steps to evict the squatter or regularize the squatter's possession within two years from the squatter's original rejected application (the first situation under 9.3.6 above). Equally a defence will exist where the squatter has some independent right to possession, eg an equity arising by virtue of proprietary estoppel. Thus the squatter's position in defending possession proceedings reflects that which applies in relation to a squatter's application for registration outlined above.

9.4   THE EFFECT OF A SQUATTER'S REGISTRATION

9.4.1   Successor in title

Under the old law, where a squatter had been in adverse possession of registered land for the limitation period, the registered proprietor held the estate on a bare trust for the squatter (Land Registration Act 1925, s 75). The concept of trust is now abandoned and instead, where a squatter's application for registration is successful, the squatter will become entitled to be registered as the new proprietor as of right. The squatter will thus become the successor in title to the previous registered proprietor. Any claims that the former registered proprietor may have had against the squatter for damages for trespass or to recover rent are extinguished (according with the position under the Limitation Act 1980, s 17). Where the property is a lease granted after 1995, the squatter's registration will operate as an 'excluded assignment' under the Landlord and Tenant (Covenants) Act 1995, s 11. In this way the previous registered proprietor, ie the former tenant, will remain liable on the lease covenants.

9.4.2   Registered charges

As a general principle, the registration of the squatter as proprietor will not affect the priority of any interest affecting the registered estate (Sch 6, para 9(2)). Thus, the land will be taken by the squatter subject to the same estates, rights, and interests that bound the previous proprietor. There is one significant exception to this principle. The squatter will not normally be bound by an existing registered charge. This is because the owner of the charge has the same opportunity as the owner of the land to object to the squatter's application. If the chargee fails to do so, then it follows that the squatter should take free of the charge as well (see Sch 6, para 9(3)).

There are two rare cases where a squatter may be bound by an existing charge. The first is where the squatter is registered notwithstanding that the registered chargee objects, because the facts fall within one of the three 'exceptions'. (Note that here the squatter may not necessarily be bound by the charge, eg if the squatter's independent right preceded the charge and took priority over it, perhaps as an overriding interest.) The second situation is where the charge is not a registered charge but is, for example, a charging order (although as before, the squatter may not necessarily be bound if the squatter's right preceded it).

The squatter may have acquired land, which is part of a larger estate, the whole of which is charged. In this case, if the squatter is bound by the charge, he or she may require the chargee to apportion the charge (see Sch 6, para 10). This means that part of the debt is assigned to the squatter's land and part to the remainder of the mortgagor's land. The apportionment is made on the basis of the respective values of the parcels of land subject to the charge and the amount of the mortgage debt when the squatter requires the apportionment to be made. By paying the apportioned amount to the chargee (plus the chargee's costs of making the apportionment) the squatter is entitled to have his or her estate discharged from the charge and can proceed to sell the land if he or she wishes. (The mortgagor's liability under the charge is also reduced.) This principle of apportionment is in line with the Law Commission's aim of keeping land 'in commerce', ie more easily saleable.

9.5   SPECIAL CASES OF ADVERSE POSSESSION

The three special cases of adverse possession provided for in the 2002 Act are in respect of rentcharges, trusts and Crown foreshore. These are now considered.

9.5.1   Rentcharges

Under the Limitation Act 1980, s 38(8), the rights of a rentcharge owner are barred in two situations:

(a)   where no rent is paid for 12 years (thus extinguishing the rentcharge);
(b)   where rent is paid to a third party for 12 years (entitling the third party to the rentcharge).

Under the Act, it is intended that land registration rules will be passed at a later date to deal with rentcharges, with some modifications and exceptions to the existing law. The Law Commission's reasons for postponing this are threefold. First, that the rules 'are likely to be technical and of a length that is disproportionate to their comparative unimportance'. Secondly, that the incidence of rentcharges tends to be rather localized (they are most commonly found in Greater Manchester, Lancashire, Sunderland, and Bristol); and, thirdly, that most rentcharges will terminate in 2037 in any event (see Rentcharges Act 1977, ss 2, 3).

9.5.2   Trusts — adverse possession by a stranger of land held in trust

Under the Act, when a registered estate is held in trust (ie a trust of land or a settlement under the Settled Land Act 1925) the squatter will not be regarded as being in adverse possession, as long as there are successive interests in the land. Thus, a squatter can only commence adverse possession where the interest of each of the beneficiaries in the estate is an interest in possession (Sch 6, para 12). This principle accords with the same objectives as the Limitation Act 1980, namely that a squatter's adverse possession should not prejudice the rights of beneficiaries who are not yet entitled in possession. Essentially, those with future interests must be protected against squatters.

An example of how this applies would be as follows. Assume land is held on trust for A for life and thereafter for B absolutely. S, a squatter, takes adverse possession of the land during A's lifetime. As long as A is alive, S will be unable to apply to be registered as proprietor. It is only ten years after B's interest has fallen into possession when A dies that S can make an application to be registered.

9.5.3   Trusts — adverse possession by a trustee or beneficiary of land held in trust

Neither a trustee nor a beneficiary (other than a beneficiary who is absolutely entitled) can be in adverse possession for the purposes of the Act (see Sch 6, para 11(1) and the Limitation Act 1980, s 21(1)(b)). It follows that neither can apply to be registered as proprietor under Sch 6, para 1 or resist proceedings to recover possession.

9.5.4   Foreshore

'Foreshore' is defined by the Act as 'the shore and bed of the sea and of any tidal water, below the line of the medium high tide between the spring and neap tides' (Sch 6, para 13(3)). Foreshore belongs to the Crown. Most of it is not held for an estate in fee simple but held by the Crown in demesne, ie in its capacity as paramount feudal lord. Section 79(1) of the Act allows the Crown to grant itself a fee simple out of land held in demesne in order to register it. In this way the Crown is able to register its foreshore and protect vulnerable areas from the intrusion of squatters. We understand that this is something the Crown Estate will be likely to do.

In respect of foreshore the limitation period for adverse possession under the Limitation Act 1980 is 60 years. This reflects the difficulty the Crown has in monitoring the foreshore to ensure that no one is in adverse possession. Similarly, under the Act a squatter must be in adverse possession of foreshore for at least 60 years (instead of ten) before he or she can apply to be registered as proprietor (Sch 6, para 13(1)). Where land has ceased to be foreshore the period is either 60 years, or ten years from the time when the land ceased to be foreshore, whichever is the shorter (Sch 6, para 13(2)). So even where the foreshore is adjacent to the squatter's land and the squatter reasonably believes that the foreshore belongs to him or her, the squatter will still have to wait 60 years from taking possession before making an application to be registered as proprietor.

9.6   TRANSITIONAL PROVISIONS

9.6.1   Delayed introduction of Sch 6, para 5(4)

In one situation the provisions of the 2002 Act, when they come into force, could prejudice the rights of a registered proprietor. This is where a squatter applies to be registered on the basis that he or she reasonably but mistakenly believed himself or herself to be the owner of the land under Sch 6, para 5(4). Theoretically, on the day the legislation is brought into force, a squatter could use this exception (provided he or she had been in adverse possession for ten years) even though the proprietor could have commenced possession proceedings against the squatter the day before. To protect the proprietor in this situation it is intended to bring Sch 6, para 5(4) into force one year after the rest of Sch 6. This will give the proprietor one year either to take proceedings against the squatter or regularize the position so that the squatter is no longer in adverse possession, eg by agreeing a licence to occupy.

9.6.2   Preserving vested rights

The Act contains provisions to protect the rights of a squatter who, prior to the coming into force of the Act, had become entitled to be registered as proprietor under the Land Registration Act 1925, s 75, but who had not been registered. In this case, immediately before the coming into force of the Act the registered proprietor would hold the estate on bare trust for the squatter. Section 75 of the Land Registration Act 1925 is repealed but the Act protects squatters in this position by entitling them to be registered (Sch 12, para 18(1)). The entitlement is also a defence to any possession proceedings (Sch 12, para 18(2)). The entitlement also gives the squatter a proprietary right and, if in actual occupation, the squatter will have an overriding interest against third parties (Sch 12, paras 7, 11; see 12.4). Transitional provisions for rentcharges held in trust under the Land Registration Act 1925, s 75 will be made by land registration rules.

9.7   KEY POINTS FOR THE PRACTITIONER

- The changes to the law of adverse possession affect only registered land.
- The substantive law regarding what constitutes adverse possession has not been changed (eg factual possession and the intention to possess).
- Owners of unregistered land should consider applying for first registration. This would be sensible given that the changes to adverse possession in registered land make life harder for the squatter.

- Squatters can only use the 'reasonable boundary mistake' exception once land has been registered for at least one year. Owners of recently registered land therefore have one year to see off boundary creepers and should consider issuing possession proceedings immediately following first registration.
- The new law places the onus on the squatter to take the initiative. If the squatter wants to acquire the land, he or she must apply to be made the registered proprietor. The registered proprietor's title will not be barred by mere lapse of time.
- Squatters can apply to become registered proprietors after ten years' adverse possession (60 years for Crown foreshore).
- Advise clients to keep their addresses for service at the Land Registry up to date. This includes chargees as well as landowners. If clients' addresses are not up to date there is a risk that clients will not receive a Land Registry notice advising them of a squatter's application for registration.
- Remember that unless the registered proprietor serves a counter-notice within a prescribed period (to be determined) objecting to the squatter's application, the squatter will automatically become the registered proprietor.
- Even if the squatter's application is opposed by the registered proprietor or chargee, the squatter will still succeed if he or she can bring himself or herself within one of the three exceptions in Sch 6, para 5.
- The most radical of these exceptions is the right for 'boundary mistake' trespassers to become registered.
- The boundary mistake exception will not come into force until one year after the other provisions. Owners therefore have one year to see off boundary creepers (unless 12 years' adverse possession has already been clocked up).
- If an owner serves a successful counter-notice, consider commencing proceedings for possession immediately and, in any event, within two years. Alternatively consider regularizing the position, eg by granting a licence, so that the squatter is not in adverse possession.
- Remember that after two years, the squatter has a second bite of the cherry and can apply again. This time the registrar *must* register the squatter as proprietor, whether or not the owner objects.

Chapter 10
Land Registry Administration and Practice

10.1 INTRODUCTION

The 2002 Act has made some adjustments to the way the Land Registry is managed and administered. In particular it has made extensive changes to the way disputes are handled with the appointment of an 'Adjudicator to Her Majesty's Land Registry' as more particularly set out in Part 11 of the Act and considered in chapter 11 of this book. More mundane yet important administrative matters are covered by ss 99–106 of the Act and cover topics such as general administration, fees, indemnities and other miscellaneous items affecting the Land Registry. Each will now be considered below.

10.2 THE LAND REGISTRY

Section 99(1) makes it clear that there is to continue to be an office called Her Majesty's Land Registry which is to deal with the business of registration in all its detail under the provisions of the 2002 Act. Section 99(3) states that the Lord Chancellor shall appoint a person to be the Chief Land Registrar. Section 99(2) stipulates that the Land Registry is to consist of the Chief Land Registrar (who is its head) and the staff appointed by him or her. Section 99(4) then announces that Sch 7 has effect, which makes further provision about the running of the Land Registry. The contents of Sch 7 will now be considered.

10.2.1   Schedule 7 — running the Land Registry

Paragraph 1 of the schedule covers the office of the Chief Land Registrar and sets out very basic employment details. For example, these include the provisions in para 1(2) which state that the Lord Chancellor may remove the registrar from office if the registrar is unable or unfit to discharge the functions required of this office. Paragraph 2 covers the remuneration and other benefits accruing to the post including pension provisions. They will all be paid as the Lord Chancellor may determine. There is also a specific provision (para 2(3)), allowing the Lord Chancellor to pay compensation to a former Chief Land Registrar after presumably early determination of his or her employment.

Paragraph 3 allows the registrar to appoint such staff as he or she thinks fit. Paragraph 4 provides an indemnity (albeit a qualified one, as set out below) for registry staff. No member of the Land Registry is to be liable in damages for anything done or omitted to be done in the discharge or purported discharge of any function relating to land registration. However, there is one qualification to this indemnity. It will not apply if it is shown that the act or omission was in bad faith. (This follows the same arrangement on the Land Registration Act 1925, s 131.) Finally one change of a political nature in the schedule is that para 7 makes the office of Chief Land Registrar a disqualifying office for the purposes of membership of the House of Commons. Previously this was not the case and so the Act makes appropriate amendments to the Commons Disqualification Act 1975.

10.3   CONDUCT OF BUSINESS

The conduct of the business of the land registry will be governed by s 100(1)–(4) of the 2002 Act but will inevitably rely upon regulations yet to be made by the Lord Chancellor. For example, as in s 126(6) of the Land Registration Act 1925, s 100(2) permits the Lord Chancellor to make regulations that make provision about the carrying out of functions during any vacancy in the office of registrar.

Section 100(1) provides that any member of the land registry who is authorized for the purpose by the registrar may carry out any function of the registrar. As a consequence of s 100(3) the Lord Chancellor may also by order designate a particular office of the Land Registry as the appropriate office for the receipt of applications or alternatively a specified description of application. The current order is the Land Registration (District Registries) Order 2000 and there are currently 24 district offices around England and Wales. (The regulations mentioned in relation to s 100(2) and this order under s 100(3) must by reason of s 128(3) of the Act be made by statutory instrument to be laid before Parliament.) The current practice of the Land Registry is to divide up the country by local government regions and allocate a district registry to be responsible for particular regions. However, the possible future departure from this current practice would be to designate a district registry as being responsible for particular types of application. The Law Commission cites the possibility of one registry being empowered to handle applications by the Crown for the first registration of demesne land under Pt 7 of the Act.

Section 100(4) authorizes the registrar to prepare and publish such forms and directions as he or she considers necessary or desirable for facilitating the conduct of the business of registration under the terms of the Act. This follows very much what was in the Land Registration Act 1925, s 127. This power has been used by the Registry in assisting the public and conveyancing practitioners in such diverse matters as how to complete official Land Registry search applications and the conditions of use for the direct access computer service to access the register.

10.4 THE ANNUAL REPORT

Each year the registry issues a comprehensive report on the conduct and performance of the Registry for the previous year. It is a revealing and detailed analysis of the work and finances of the Registry that tries to show how the Registry has met (or failed to meet), targets for the year under scrutiny. The 2002 Act makes provision for the continuation of this practice. Section 101(1)–(3) is concerned with the Registry annual report. Section 101(1) requires the registrar to make an annual report on the business of the Land Registry to the Lord Chancellor. Section 101(2) provides that the registrar must publish every report under this section and may do so in such manner as he or she thinks fit. Currently the annual report can be accessed over the internet at the Land Registry web-site, < www.landreg.gov.uk >. Section 101(3) requires the Lord Chancellor to lay copies of every annual report before Parliament.

10.5 FEES AND INDEMNITIES

This section deals with the fee income paid by Land Registry applicants or customers when making applications to the Registry. It also deals with the payments by the Registry by way of the statutory indemnity available when a party suffers loss as a result of an error or omission at or by the Registry.

10.5.1 Fees

Section 102 allows the Registry to receive fees for the services it provides. The Lord Chancellor may, with the advice of the Rule Committee, defined by s 127(2) of the 2002 Act, and with the consent of the Treasury, prescribe fees to be paid for dealings with the Land Registry. (There are two exemptions. The first is under s 69(3)(b) regarding the access of historical information relating to a registered title. The second relates to possible consultancy and advisory services that the Registry may provide under s 105 of the Act. This is considered below in 10.6.) Provision can also be made about how the fees are to be paid, eg to allow credit accounts, etc.

10.5.2 Indemnities

If a person is registered as a proprietor of a registered title then the state guarantees that the legal estate is indeed vested in the registered proprietor. Moreover, if that is proved to be wrong, ie that the registers are wrong, then any innocent party suffering loss will be compensated for the loss of any estate or interest in a registered title. As a consequence the Land Registry are most careful in vetting titles submitted for first registration. Rectification can occur and would involve an amendment to the registers or filed plan to put right a substantive error or any claim that has been given legal recognition. The court will make rectification although the Chief Land Registrar will in effect deal with it. Before the Act, s 82 of the Land Registration Act 1925 listed various cases where rectification may be claimed. The Act now covers indemnity by s 103 which states that Sch 8 of the Act has effect and makes provision for the payment of indemnities by the registrar. (See 6.11 concerning alteration of the register generally.)

Schedule 8, para 1 lists the circumstances in which a person may suffer loss and, as a result, be entitled to be indemnified by the registrar. The system of registered land is predicated upon the concept that a person who suffers loss as a result of an error or omission in the register will be compensated by the state. Schedule 8, referred from s 103 of Act, provides the right of indemnity. This follows the changes made to the 1925 provisions that were substituted by s 2 of the Land Registration Act 1997. Because of the effects of the substituted provisions of the Land Registration Act 1997, now followed in the Act, the indemnity rules were revised as from 27 April 1997. An indemnity will now be paid to a claimant who has suffered loss as a result of an error or omission in the register whether or not the register is in fact rectified. This is of course subject to the proper care provisions, etc mentioned below. No indemnity will be paid for costs and expenses without the registrar's prior approval. This will be available if there is loss suffered as a result of rectification or indeed non-rectification. An indemnity payment may also be available as a result of an error made by the Registry, for example in an official search result or as a result of the Registry losing a deed or document. The full list of those entitled is set out in para 1(1)(a)–(h).

The indemnity will only be available if the claimant has suffered actual loss. For example, if rectification is ordered so that an overriding interest can be recognized, then the court has held that there is no loss for indemnity purposes, see *Re Chowood's Registered Land* [1933] Ch 574. (This example should now fall within the indemnity provisions set out in Sch 8.)

There is one particularly important exclusion affecting the right to indemnity. Paragraph 5 of Sch 8 stipulates that no indemnity is available where the applicant has caused or substantially contributed to the loss by fraud or lack of proper care. This will also be true if the applicant derives title through a person who contributed to the loss by fraud or lack of proper care unless the applicant was entitled by reason of a disposition for valuable consideration which has been registered or is protected by an entry within the registers.

The amount of the indemnity will depend upon the nature of the case and will fit one of two templates. First, if rectification is not ordered, the amount of the indemnity will not exceed the value of the claimed estate, charge or interest at the time of making the error or omission. Secondly, if rectification is ordered, the amount of the indemnity will not exceed the value of the claimed estate, charge or interest at the time just before rectification took place.

Paragraph 10 of Sch 8 allows the registrar to seek recovery of all or part of any indemnity paid out from any person who caused or substantially contributed to the loss by his or her fraud. The registrar can also assume any right of action the claimant would have been entitled to had the indemnity not been paid. Furthermore, where the register has been rectified, the registrar may enforce any right of action which the persons in whose favour the register was rectified would have been entitled to enforce if the register had not been rectified.

There are time limits for indemnity claims. For the purposes of the Limitation Act 1980 a liability to pay an indemnity under this schedule is a simple contract debt. The claim will therefore be barred six years after the cause of action arose. Furthermore, the cause of action arises at the time when the claimant knows, or but for his or her own default might have known, of the existence of the claim (see Sch 8, para 8). The schedule does extend the current practice by including new arrangements for the making of provisions for possible interest payments. Schedule 8, para 9 of the schedule states that rules may make provision about the payment of interest on an indemnity under this schedule. These rules may cover the circumstances in which interest is payable as well as the periods for and the rates at which it is payable.

10.6   MISCELLANEOUS MATTERS

This part of Land Registry administration is concerned with three elements. First, it covers in s 104 general information about land, secondly, it covers consultancy and advisory services in s 105, and thirdly it covers in s 106 incidental powers especially relating to companies. Each will be considered below.

10.6.1   General information about land

Section 103 gives the registrar power to publish information about land in England and Wales if it appears to the registrar to be information in which there is a legitimate public interest. Each quarter the Registry issue property price information that regularly features in the national and local press. This information is gleaned from the many transfers that are lodged at the Land Registry and which include a consideration in many cases that represents the market value of the property transferred. It is from these figures that the quarterly figures are compiled and it is just this kind of data or information that would be covered by this section. Indeed as the 2002 Act will expand the number of registrable leases, with leases of more than seven years to run being compulsorily registrable, this data or information will be even more comprehensive.

10.6.2   Consultancy and advisory services

Section 105 allows the registrar to provide or arrange the provision of consultancy or advisory services about the registration of land in England and Wales or elsewhere. The terms on which such matters are provided under this section by the registrar, in particular terms as to payment, shall be as the registrar thinks fit. This frees up the registrar to strike commercial deals and to seek fees for which there will be no statutory fetter. We assume this will enable the registrar to offer consultancy and advisory services abroad, especially in relation to the creation and maintenance of a proposed system of e-conveyancing such as that contemplated by the Act.

10.6.3   Incidental powers: companies

Section 106 allows the registrar, if he or she considers it expedient so to do, to form or participate in the formation of a company, limited or otherwise under the Companies Act 1985, or to purchase or invest in a company. This is in particular with regard to access to historical data regarding registered titles, the land registry e-conveyancing network, electronic financial settlement, education, and training in relation to the Land Registry network and the consultancy and advisory services mentioned in 10.6.2 above. This will allow the registrar to create business ventures with a view to maximizing the revenue stream of the Registry, especially with regard to the topics listed. This includes joint ventures where necessary to achieve the aims and objectives of the Act and the system of land registration.

10.7   KEY POINTS FOR THE PRACTITIONER

- The Land Registry is to consist of the Chief Land Registrar (who is its head) and the staff appointed by him or her. The office of Chief Land Registrar is a disqualifying office for the purposes of membership of the House of Commons.
- The Lord Chancellor may also by order designate a particular office of the Land Registry as the appropriate office for the receipt of applications or alternatively a specified description of application.
- Schedule 8, para 1 of the Act lists matters in respect of which a person is entitled to be indemnified by the registrar if he or she suffers loss by reason of them. The full list is set out in para 1(1)(a)–(h).
- No indemnity will be paid for costs and expenses without the registrar's prior approval. This will be available if there is loss suffered as a result of rectification or indeed non-rectification. An indemnity payment may also be available as a result of an error made by the Registry.
- No indemnity is available where the applicant has caused or substantially contributed to the loss by fraud or lack of proper care.
- Schedule 8, para 10 allows the registrar to seek recovery of all or part of any indemnity paid out from any person who caused or substantially contributed to the loss by his or her fraud.

- There are time limits for indemnity claims. For the purposes of the Limitation Act 1980 a liability to pay an indemnity under this schedule is a simple contract debt. The claim will therefore be barred six years after the cause of action arose.
- The registrar has the power to publish information about land in England and Wales if it appears to the registrar to be information in which there is a legitimate public interest, such as the quarterly property price information.
- The Act allows the registrar to provide or arrange the provision of consultancy or advisory services about the registration of land in England and Wales or elsewhere.

Chapter 11
Adjudication and Other Judicial Provisions

11.1   ADJUDICATION

Article 6.1 of the European Convention on Human Rights (ECHR) provides that, 'In the determination of his civil rights and obligations . . . everyone is entitled to a fair and public hearing within a reasonable time by an independent and impartial tribunal established by law.' One of the significant new provisions of the 2002 Act is the creation of the adjudicator — an independent officer whose role is to deal with contested applications that cannot be resolved by agreement between the parties. Previously this function was performed by the Solicitor to HM Land Registry but, in the light of Art 6 of the ECHR, it was perceived that the Solicitor was not sufficiently independent of the Land Registry. Hence we now have the new adjudicator and the adjudication provisions under Part 11 of the Act (ss 107–114). Apart from an apparent independence, the principal benefit of adjudication is that it obviates the need for expensive court proceedings.

Within the relevant administrative provisions in Sch 9 the Act allows for the appointment of the adjudicator by the Lord Chancellor and the delegation of staff to assist in the adjudicator's functions. In practice, there will be too many applications for one person to deal with so the adjudicator's powers will be entrusted to appropriately qualified Land Registry staff. However, non-administrative functions may only be delegated to staff who have a ten-year general qualification within the meaning of s 71 of the Courts and Legal Services Act 1990 (Sch 9, para 4(2)). Likewise, the adjudicator must have this minimum ten-year general qualification (s 107(2)). Under the Courts and Legal Services Act 1990, s 71(3)(c), a person has a 'general qualification' if 'he has a right of audience in relation to any class of proceedings in any part of the Supreme Court, or all proceedings in county courts or magistrates' courts'. The adjudicator is under the supervision of the Council on Tribunals and is thus subject to the requirements of the Council in the Tribunals and Inquiries Act 1992. This requires the adjudicator to give reasons for his or her decisions, if requested. Previously, the Solicitor to the Land Registry was not obliged to give reasons (although in practice he or she usually did).

11.2   THE ADJUDICATOR'S JURISDICTION

The adjudicator's two main functions are laid down in s 108(1) of the 2002 Act. They are:

(a)   To determine matters referred to him or her under the 'right to object' provisions of s 73(7), ie disputes between a person who has made an application to the registrar and some other person. Anyone may object to an application that has been made to the registrar except in two situations. These are:

(i)   Cautions against first registration. Only the person who lodged the caution (or that person's personal representative) may object to an application for the cancellation of it (see 3.5 and s 18)).
(ii)   Unilateral notice. Only the person shown in the register as the beneficiary of the notice may object to an application to cancel it (see 3.5 and s 36).

Under s 73(7), where an objection to an application is made, unless the registrar considers the objection to be groundless or agreement can be reached, he or she must refer the matter to the adjudicator. This may not necessarily be the whole application but merely one or more of the issues raised by it.

(b)   To hear appeals by a person who is aggrieved by a decision of the registrar concerning entry into or termination of a network access agreement for e-conveyancing (Sch 5, para 4). This is a vital role for the future. It is the one way in which a conveyancer can appeal against a decision by the registrar to stop a conveyancer making a living by e-conveyancing. (Importantly, the adjudicator cannot hear other disputes that an applicant may have with the registrar. For these, the applicant should consider an application for judicial review or, in respect of an order to produce a document or to pay costs, an appeal to the county court: see below and ss 75(4) and 76(5).)

The other functions of the adjudicator include:

(a)   Giving effect to an equity by estoppel on a squatter's application to be registered as proprietor. As explained in chapter 9, the claimant may prove that it is unconscionable to dispossess him or her and that circumstances are such that the claimant ought to be registered as the proprietor of the land. In this case, the adjudicator will determine the extent of the relief that will be granted to him or her, ie the 'minimum equity' to do justice in the case (see 9.3 and chapter 9 generally on adverse possession).

(b) A power (on direct application to the adjudicator) to rectify or set aside a conveyancing document (s 108(2)). This is an important new function as previously the registrar could only refer such matters to the High Court, which inevitably resulted in delay and further costs. This power applies only in relation to a document which does any one of the following:

(i) effects a qualifying disposition of a registered estate or charge where that disposition is either a registrable disposition or one which creates an interest which may be protected by a notice, eg a transfer, grant of a lease or a deed creating a restrictive covenant; or

(ii) is a contract to do the above; or

(iii) effects a transfer of an interest which is the subject of a notice in the register, eg a conveyance of a profit *à prendre* that was noted on the register but not registered with its own title, and there was an error in that conveyance.

The general law about the effect of a High Court order for rectification or setting aside a document applies to an order made under this power (s 108(4)). Thus, rectification will relate back to the time when the document was executed (*Earl of Malmsbury v Countess of Malmsbury* (1862) 31 Beav 407) and the document is to be read as if drawn up in its rectified form (*Craddock Bros v Hunt* [1923] 2 Ch 136).

11.3   PROCEEDINGS BEFORE THE ADJUDICATOR

When an application is made to the adjudicator for the rectification or setting aside of a document, or a matter is referred to the adjudicator under s 73(7) of the 2002 Act, the adjudicator can either determine the matter from the papers submitted to him or her, or hold a hearing. The adjudicator's determination is enforceable as an order of the court (s 112). This means that a court can deal with non-compliance as contempt.

Hearings are held in public unless the adjudicator is satisfied that it is just and reasonable to exclude the public (s 109(1)). Land registration rules will regulate the practice and procedure to be followed in the proceedings and matters incidental and consequential on them. Section 109(3) lists the likely areas that the rules will cover. They are:

(a) when hearings are to be held;

(b) requiring persons to attend hearings to give evidence or to produce documents;

(c) the form in which any decision of the adjudicator is to be given;

(d) payment of costs of a party to the proceedings by another party to the proceedings; and

(e)   wasted costs order, ie liability for costs thrown away as a result of neglect or delay by a party's legal representative.

In respect of a s 73(7) referral, s 110(1) permits the adjudicator to direct a party to the proceedings before him or her to commence proceedings in court within a specified time. This may be appropriate where the application raises an important or difficult point of law, or where substantial or complex disputes of fact exist, or where other issues are already before the court (such as matrimonial proceedings between the parties). The court also has powers not available to the adjudicator, eg to award damages. The adjudicator can refer to court the whole of the proceedings before him or her, or specific issues within those proceedings. Land registration rules will make further provision about references to the court (s 110(2)).

A right of appeal to the High Court exists from a decision of the adjudicator (s 111(1)). In respect of an adjudicator's decision concerning entry into or termination of an e-conveyancing network access agreement, the right of appeal is on a point of law only (s 111(2)). This is because it effectively amounts to a second appeal, the original decision having been taken by the registrar. Yet perhaps the point should be made that in restricting an appeal to a point of law only, the state is exercising a measure of control over conveyancers and conveyancing. As far as s 73(7) referral decisions are concerned, the right of appeal is allowed on a point of law or fact.

11.4   PROCEEDINGS BEFORE THE REGISTRAR

Under the 2002 Act the land registrar is given similar powers to those given under the Land Registration Act 1925. Subject to rules to be made, the registrar may:

(a)   Require a person to produce a document for the purposes of the proceedings before the registrar (s 75(1)). This is enforceable as an order of the court, so a court can deal with non-compliance as contempt.

(b)   Make an order for costs in relation to proceedings before the registrar (s 76(1)). The rules may make provision about who may be required to pay costs, whose costs a person may be required to pay, the kind of costs payable and the assessment of costs (s 76(2)). The rules may also include provision about costs incurred by the registrar and liability for wasted costs arising from the neglect or delay of legal representatives (s 76(3)).

A person aggrieved by either of these two orders may appeal to a county court, which may make any order which appears appropriate (ss 75(4), 76(5)). However, a person seeking to challenge any other decision of the registrar would need to seek judicial review in the High Court, eg a challenge to the registrar's decision to enter (or not to enter) a restriction under s 42 (see 5.5.3).

11.5 CRIMINAL OFFENCES

The 2002 Act creates new offences to replace similar offences under the Land Registration Act 1925. They relate to suppression of information and improper alteration of the registers and are now considered below.

11.5.1 Suppression of information

Here a person commits an offence if in the course of proceedings relating to registration under the Act that person suppresses information with the intention of concealing a person's right or claim, or substantiating a false claim (s 123(1)). The word 'proceedings' is to be construed widely so that it includes not only proceedings before the adjudicator but also any procedure in connection with an application to the registrar under the Act. The offence may be tried on indictment or summarily. A person convicted on indictment is liable to imprisonment for a term not exceeding two years or to an unlimited fine. A summary conviction will lead to imprisonment for a term not exceeding six months or to a fine not exceeding the statutory maximum, or to both.

11.5.2 Improper alteration of the registers

Under s 124(1) a person commits an offence if he or she dishonestly induces another to:

(a) change the register of title or cautions register; or
(b) to authorize the making of such a change.

A change to the register includes a change to a document referred to in it (s 124(4)).

An example of offence (a) would be where someone deliberately makes a false statement in an application for registration. Offence (b) is new and is designed to cover a situation that could arise in e-conveyancing. As we explained in chapter 8, those who enter into network access agreements, eg solicitors and licensed conveyancers, may be authorized to change the register once those changes have been authorized by the registrar. The offence in (b) will cover the situation where a party to a network access agreement dishonestly induces the Land Registry to agree to a particular change in the register and the party then makes the change. Moreover under s 124(2) a person commits an offence if he or she intentionally or recklessly makes an unauthorized change in the register of title or cautions register (including a change to a document referred to in it). Thus, parties to network access agreements who intend to change the register must first check that they are authorized and also the extent of their authorization. Penalties for the offences under s 124 are the same as for the suppression of information offence (see above).

11.5.3   Privilege against self-incrimination

The 2002 Act replicates the Land Registration Act 1925 by providing that the privilege against self-incrimination (so far as relating to offences under the Act) does not entitle a person to refuse to answer any question or produce any document or thing in any legal proceedings other than criminal proceedings (s 125(1)). However, in line with other statutes, no evidence so obtained is admissible in any criminal proceedings under the Act against either the person from whom it was obtained or that person's spouse (s 125(2)).

11.6   KEY POINTS FOR THE PRACTITIONER

- The adjudicator is an independent officer whose role is to deal with contested applications that cannot be resolved by agreement between the parties.
- This avoids the need to take expensive court proceedings.
- The adjudicator is required to give reasons for his or her decisions, if requested.
- The adjudicator's two main functions are:
  - to determine matters referred to him or her under the 'right to object' provisions of s 73(7), ie disputes between a person who has made an application to the registrar and some other person;
  - to hear appeals by a person who is aggrieved by a decision of the registrar concerning entry into or termination of a network access agreement for e-conveyancing.
- The adjudicator's other functions include giving effect to an equity by estoppel on a squatter's application to be registered as proprietor and a power (on direct application) to rectify or set aside conveyancing documents.
- The adjudicator can either determine the matter from the papers submitted to him or her, or hold a hearing.
- The adjudicator's decision is enforceable as an order of the court.
- Land registration rules will regulate the practice and procedure to be followed in adjudication proceedings and matters incidental and consequential on them.
- The adjudicator can refer the matter to the court, eg on an important or difficult point of law or on substantial or complex disputes of fact.
- A right of appeal from an adjudicator's decision lies to the High Court.
- The land registrar may require a person to produce a document for the purposes of the proceedings before him or her, and can make an order for costs.
- The Act creates criminal offences relating to suppression of information and improper alteration of the registers.
- This includes a new offence where a party to a network access agreement dishonestly induces the Land Registry to agree to a particular change in the register and the party then makes the change.
- Another new offence is where such a person intentionally or recklessly makes an unauthorized change in the register of title or cautions register.

Chapter 12
Overriding Interests

12.1 INTRODUCTION

Overriding interests are one of a number of interests in land that bind a proprietor of registered land but they differ in a substantial way from the other categories of interests in that they bind the owner of the legal estate regardless of whether they are entered on the register. It is for this reason that they have caused uncertainty and have been the subject of several reports that have attempted to deal with the problems, culminating in the Land Registration Act 2002.

We have explained that the Act aims to create an electronically based conveyancing system under which it will be possible to investigate title on-line with the minimum of additional enquiries. However, a major obstacle to achieving that goal is the existence of overriding interests which are not entered on the register but still bind a person who acquires the subject property. Accordingly, the Act has reduced the circumstances in which overriding interests can exist. The policy behind the Act is that interests should only have overriding status where protection against buyers is needed, but where it is neither reasonable to expect nor sensible to require any entry on the register. With the advent of electronic conveyancing the circumstances in which overriding interests can arise will be reduced. This is because, in future, expressly created rights will only be created through simultaneous registration.

In addition to electronic conveyancing, the Act adopts four approaches for dealing with the problems associated with overriding interests, which are explained in this chapter. In brief they are:

(a)   the abolition of certain rights which can exist as overriding interests. These include the liability to repair the chancel of a church and the rights of those acquired by squatters under adverse possession (see chapter 9 regarding the reform of adverse possession generally);

(b)   the phasing out after ten years of several existing categories of overriding interest, including the ancient rights of franchises, manorial rights, Crown rents, rights concerning embankments and sea walls, and corn rents;

 (c)   the narrowing down and clarification of the scope of some previous categories that remain as overriding interests. The most important of these are easements and profits under the old s 70(1)(a) of the Land Registration Act 1925 and the rights of persons in actual occupation or in receipt of rents and profits under the old s 70(1)(g) of the 1925 Act;

(d)   a requirement that when overriding interests come to light they are, as far as possible, entered on the register. In addition, a new requirement exists in which a person applying for registration must disclose any overriding interests known to them.

The Act provides for the continued existence of 14 categories of overriding interest and creates one new category, the Public-Private Partnership (PPP) lease. PPP leases are considered at 7.4.3. Five of the 14 categories will disappear after ten years. For three categories (legal easements and profits, the rights of persons in actual occupation and short leases, ie for seven years or less), the substantive requirements for what amounts to an overriding interest will be different depending on whether it is a first registration or a subsequent registrable disposition for valuable consideration. The Act recognizes this distinction by listing those interests which override first registration in Sch 1 and those interests which override registered dispositions in Sch 3. These two categories of interests are now considered.

12.2   UNREGISTERED INTERESTS WHICH OVERRIDE FIRST REGISTRATION

These are set out in Sch 1 to the 2002 Act. When a person becomes the first registered proprietor of land on first registration he or she takes the estate subject to certain interests, including interests the burden of which is entered on the register (s 11(4)(a)) and interests the burden of which is not so entered but which fall within any of the paragraphs of Sch 1 (ie overriding interests) (s 11(4)(b)). The 14 interests in Sch 1 are considered below. There is also a fifteenth interest provided for in s 90. This is the PPP lease which takes effect as if it were included in Sch 1.

12.2.1   Short leases

Subject to the exceptions discussed below, a leasehold estate granted for a term not exceeding seven years from the date of the grant, overrides first registration

(Sch 1, para 1). This replicates the position under the Land Registration Act 1925, s 70(1)(k) save for the reduction in the duration of short leases from 21 years to seven. In future it is likely that the Lord Chancellor will reduce the period still further to three years. The policy behind excluding short leases from having their own registered titles is to prevent the register from becoming cluttered up with leases which will soon expire. A notice of the short lease should be entered on the register of the title out of which it has been granted.

The following three types of leases cannot be overriding interests even if they are for seven years or less; instead they must be registered with their own titles:

(a)   a reversionary lease granted out of unregistered land to take effect in possession more than three months after the date of the grant of the lease (this is new — they are excluded because they may be difficult to discover, see 3.2.1 and 3.3.4);

(b)   a lease granted out of an unregistered legal estate under the right to buy provisions of Pt V of the Housing Act 1985 (no change from the previous law, see 3.3.5); and

(c)   a lease granted by a private sector landlord out of an unregistered legal estate to a person who was formerly a secure tenant and has a preserved right to buy under the Housing Act 1985 (no change from the previous law).

12.2.2   Interests of persons in actual occupation

It should be emphasized that this section of the book deals with the overriding status of occupier's rights on *first registration*. For an examination of occupier's rights in relation to registered dispositions, see 12.3.2 below. Historically the interests of persons in actual occupation have been the most problematic of overriding interests and this has resulted in considerable amounts of litigation. The pre-Act equivalent statutory provision was s 70(1)(g) of the Land Registration Act 1925 which read, 'The rights of every person in actual occupation of the land or in receipt of rents or profits thereof, save where enquiry is made of such person and the rights are not disclosed.'

As far as the Act is concerned in relation to unregistered interests which override first registration, Sch 1, para 2 defines the interests of persons in actual occupation as, 'An interest belonging to a person in actual occupation, so far as relating to land of which he is in actual occupation, except for an interest under a settlement under the Settled Land Act 1925.'

The Law Commission concluded that there was a continued need to protect the rights of those in actual occupation. This is predicated on the assumption that such persons will often not have appreciated the need to take further steps to protect their rights against purchasers by lodging a caution against first registration. This is especially so for informally created rights (cf where the interest can be protected by a land charge registration, eg Class F matrimonial homes right of occupation; if this is possible then the interest ought to be registered).

Unlike the current law it should be noted that the Act does not give overriding status to persons who are merely in receipt of rents and profits, ie not in actual occupation. This is a change from s 70(1)(g). It is often very difficult for a buyer to discover the existence of an intermediate landlord from an inspection of the property. The Law Commission therefore concluded that persons in receipt of rents and profits should no longer have overriding status (although transitional provisions exist in relation to registered dispositions, see 12.3.2 below).

The new law retains the exception that a beneficiary under a settlement under the Settled Land Act 1925 is excluded from overriding status. Although this goes against the Law Commission's original recommendation, it was ultimately decided that the exception was sensible given that, since the Trusts of Land and Appointment of Trustees Act 1996 came into force, such settlements can no longer be created.

Another point to note concerning the new law is the wording in Sch 1, para 2 'so far as relating to land of which he is in actual occupation'. Again this is new. It means that where someone is in actual occupation of part of the land but they have rights over the whole of the land purchased, their rights protected by actual occupation are confined to the part which they occupy.

A further change in the law, in relation to occupier's rights on first registration, is the absence of the qualification in s 70(1)(g) which says, 'save where enquiry is made of such person and the rights are not disclosed'. These words are excluded because they can have no relevance to overriding interests on first registration. Whether a purchaser has made enquiries of a person in actual occupation is irrelevant on first registration because the question of whether or not the first registered proprietor is bound by the rights of an occupier will have been decided at an earlier stage under the unregistered conveyancing rules. That is to say, on completion when the legal title became vested in the purchaser. However, it should be noted that the qualification is retained for registered dispositions, for the reasons explained at 12.3.2.1 below.

12.2.3   Legal easements and profits *à prendre*

Here there is an important change. Under the previous law, *equitable* easements that were openly exercised and enjoyed by the dominant owner as appurtenant to his or her land could take effect, on first registration, as overriding interests (see Land Registration Act, s 70(1)(a); *Celsteel Ltd v Alton House Holdings Ltd* [1985] 1 WLR 204; *Thatcher v Douglas* (1996) 146 NLJ 282). Under the new law, only *legal* easements and profits *à prendre* can do so (Sch 1, para 3). Thus, in preventing unregistered equitable easements from acquiring overriding status the decision in the *Celsteel* case is reversed. This is in line with the general principle underlying the Act that rights which are expressly created over land should be completed by registration. It also reflects the established view in unregistered land that equitable easements should only bind a purchaser if they are registered as Class D(iii) land charges under the Land Charges Act 1972. It is hoped in future that few legal easements and profits will qualify as overriding interests in any event. This is because the Act contains rule-making powers to ensure that, as far as possible, overriding interests are disclosed to the registrar on first registration to enable them to be noted on the register (see s 71(a) and 12.5 below). The change in the law restricting easements as overriding interests also affects registered dispositions (see 12.3.3 below).

12.2.4   Customary and public rights

Both customary and public rights remain as overriding interests under the Act (Sch 1, paras 4, 5; previously Land Registration Act 1925, s 70(1)(a)). Public rights are those which are exercisable by anyone, whether they own land or not, by virtue of the general law. They can be quite extensive and have been held to include a freehold vested in a highway authority in respect of a dedicated highway (*Secretary of State for the Environment, Transport and the Regions v Baylis (Gloucester) Ltd* (2000) 80 P & CR 324). Customary rights on the other hand are those which were enjoyed by inhabitants of a particular locality, many of which still survive today. Examples of customary rights being upheld include holding a fair or wake on waste land in Wraysbury (*Wyld v Silver* [1963] Ch 243), fishing for oysters in Saltash (*Goodman v Mayor of Saltash* (1882) 7 App Cas 633) and grazing beasts on common land in Huntingdon (*Peggs v Lamb* [1994] Ch 172). Customary rights are similar to public rights except that they benefit a more limited class of persons.

12.2.5   Local land charges

There is no change for this category of overriding interest. Schedule 1, para 6 of the Act replicates s 70(1)(i) of the Land Registration Act 1925 by allowing a local land charge to override first registration. They are governed by the Local Land Charges Act 1975 and are being computerized together with other local searches as part of the National Land Information Service. It should be noted that a local land charge secured by the payment of money cannot be realized unless it is registered as a registered charge (see s 55 and 5.6.1).

12.2.6   Mines and minerals

There is no change to these categories of overriding interest. The overriding status of certain mining and mineral rights previously found in s 70(1)(l) and (m) of the Land Registration Act 1925 are preserved in Sch 1, paras 7–9 of the Act. Many of these rights would prove impossible to register given their extent and complexity and the prohibitive cost of preparing plans for them. Accordingly it was thought best to preserve their overriding status. The rights are:

(a)   an interest in any coal or coal mine, the rights attached to any such interest and the rights of any person under s 38, 49 or 51 of the Coal Industry Act 1994;

(b)   in the case of land to which title was registered before 1898, rights to mines and minerals (and incidental rights) created before 1898; and

(c)   in the case of land to which title was registered between 1898 and 1925 inclusive, rights to mines and minerals (and incidental rights) created before the date of registration of the title.

12.2.7   Miscellaneous interests

Lastly, five categories of overriding interest are grouped together under a miscellaneous heading (Sch 1, paras 10–14). Often onerous, they are rare, of ancient origin and sometimes very difficult to discover. They all had overriding status under the Land Registration Act 1925 and are:

(a)   a franchise;

(b)   a manorial right;

(c)   a right to rent which was reserved to the Crown on the granting of any freehold estate (whether or not the right is still vested in the Crown) ('Crown rents');

(d)   a non-statutory right in respect of an embankment or sea or river wall; and

(e)   a right to payment in lieu of tithe ('corn rents').

Following consultation, the retention of these miscellaneous items as overriding interests was unpopular, but the Law Commission concluded that to abolish their overriding status immediately might risk a contravention of the right to property under the European Convention on Human Rights (Art 1, First Protocol). Accordingly the Act provides that these rights will cease to have overriding status ten years after the Act comes into force. In the meantime, s 117 of the Act allows persons with the benefit of these rights to protect them during the ten-year period without charge (those who have the benefit of such rights should probably be aware of them). This can be achieved by entering a caution against first registration (for unregistered land) or an entry on the register (for registered land). If the interests are protected in this way, an intending buyer of the subject property will of course be made aware of them.

 ## 12.3   UNREGISTERED INTERESTS WHICH OVERRIDE REGISTERED DISPOSITIONS

As we explained in relation to ss 29 and 30 of the 2002 Act (see 4.4.1), a registered disposition for valuable consideration of a registered estate or a registered charge takes subject to those overriding interests affecting the estate or charge that are listed in Sch 3 (together with any PPP lease which is also classified as an overriding interest (see 7.4.3)). Twelve of these 15 interests are identical to those which override first registration and have been considered above at 12.2. The three categories of overriding interest that differ from those that apply on first registration are short leases, interests of persons in actual occupation and easements and profits. These are now considered.

12.3.1 Short leases

In 12.2.1 we mentioned three exceptions in which short leases, ie those granted for a term not exceeding seven years, are not classified as overriding interests. In respect of registered dispositions there are five further exceptions. These are all registrable dispositions granted out of a registered estate and therefore cannot be overriding interests because they must be registered in their own right. They are:

(a) a reversionary lease granted to take effect in possession more than three months after the date of the grant of the lease;

(b) a lease under which the right to possession is discontinuous;

(c) a lease granted in pursuance of the right-to-buy provisions of Pt V of the Housing Act 1985;

(d) a lease granted by a private sector landlord to a person who was formerly a secure tenant and has a preserved right to buy; and

(e) a lease of a franchise or a manor.

12.3.1.1 Transitional arrangements

Transitional arrangements are in place for existing short leases that are overriding interests under the old law (ie not more than 21 years in duration). Schedule 12, para 12 provides, in effect, that leases that were previously granted for a term of more than seven but not more than 21 years will remain as overriding interests after the Act comes into force. However, any assignment of such leases will trigger compulsory registration if the term has more than seven years to run at the time of the assignment (s 4(1)(a), (2)(b)).

12.3.2 Interests of persons in actual occupation

This is an important area of registered land law with very real practical significance. As we have seen, a guiding principle of the reforms in this area is that expressly created rights which are substantively registrable should be registered and no longer enjoy the protection of being an overriding interest. However, in this case we are essentially concerned with rights which arise informally in favour of those who may not appreciate the need to register them. In this respect we think it is worth quoting from the Consultative Document, *Land Registration for the 21st Century* (Law Com No 254) para 5.61:

> . . . it is unreasonable to expect all encumbrancers to register their rights, particularly where those rights arise informally, under (say) a constructive trust or by estoppel. The law pragmatically recognises that some rights can be created informally, and to require their registration would defeat the sound policy that

underlies their recognition. Furthermore, when people occupy land they are often unlikely to appreciate the need to take the formal step of registering any rights that they have in it. They will probably regard their occupation as the only necessary protection. The retention of this category of overriding interest is justified . . . because this a very clear case where protection against purchasers is needed but where it is not reasonable to expect or not sensible to require any entry on the register.

Schedule 3, para 2 provides that an interest belonging at the time of a registered disposition to a person in actual occupation is an overriding interest, so far as it relates to land of which he or she is in actual occupation. To this general principle, there is an important qualification. This is that actual occupation only protects a person's occupation so far as it relates to land of which that person is in actual occupation. Any rights that person has over *other* registered land must be protected by an appropriate entry in the register for that title. This reverses the Court of Appeal decision in *Ferrishurst Ltd v Wallcite Ltd* [1999] Ch 355 in which an overriding interest was held to extend to the whole of a registered title, not merely the part in occupation.

12.3.2.1   Exceptions to the general rule

There are four exceptions to the general principle that an interest belonging at the time of a registered disposition to a person in actual occupation is an overriding interest, so far as it relates to land of which he or she is in actual occupation. They are:

(a)   An interest under a settlement under the Settled Land Act 1925 (see explanation above at 12.2.2).

(b)   An interest of a person of whom inquiry was made before the disposition and who failed to disclose the right when he or she could reasonably have been expected to do so. This is very similar to the wording of s 70(1)(g) of the Land Registration Act 1925 ('. . . save where enquiry is made of such person and the rights are not disclosed'). The exception operates as a form of estoppel.

(c)   This is new and important — the rights of persons whose occupation is not apparent. An interest will not be protected as an overriding interest if:

(i)   it belongs to a person whose occupation would not have been obvious on a reasonably careful inspection of the land at the time of the disposition; and

(ii)   the person to whom the disposition is made does not have actual knowledge at that time.

The Law Commission emphasised three important points concerning this new exception:

(i)   it is the occupier's *occupation* that must be apparent, not the occupier's interest;

- (ii)   the test is not one of constructive notice of the occupation. It is the less exacting one applicable to an intending purchaser, namely that it should be *obvious* on a reasonably careful inspection of the land; and

- (iii)   even if the person's occupation is not apparent, the exception does not apply where a purchaser has *actual* knowledge of the occupation.

(d)   A lease granted to take effect in possession more than three months after the grant and which has not taken effect in possession at the time of the disposition. This would be rare and is a corollary of the requirement to register reversionary leases that are to take effect in possession more than three months after their grant (s 4(1)(d) compulsory first registration; s 27(2)(b)(ii) registrable dispositions).

As previously mentioned, persons who are not in actual occupation but in receipt of rents and profits are no longer afforded overriding status (see 12.2.2 above). However, a transitional provision provides that an interest which, immediately before the coming into force of the Act, was an overriding interest under s 70(1)(g) of the Land Registration Act 1925 by virtue of a person's receipt of rent and profits, continues to be so for the purposes of Sch 3 (Sch 12, para 8). However, if thereafter the person ceases to be in receipt of rent and profits (eg because the lease ends), the interest will cease to be overriding. Thus, if another lease were granted and new rents received, the overriding interest could not be revived.

12.3.3   Legal easements and profits *à prendre*

Easements and profits were a major source of concern to the Law Commission who were determined to restrict the circumstances in which easements and profits could acquire overriding status. The problem, as commonly perceived, is that a purchaser of registered land will often find it very difficult to discover easements and profits that are not otherwise noted on the register. This is compounded by the fact that non-user of an easement or profit, even for many years, will fail to raise any presumption of abandonment (*Benn v Hardinge* (1992) 66 P & CR 246). The Law Commission considered it wrong in principle that easements and profits created expressly should take effect as overriding interests; they ought properly to be completed by registration.

As a result, the reforms in this area are extensive. The Act effectively provides that no easements or profits expressly granted or reserved out of registered land after the Act comes into force can take effect as overriding interests. This is because such rights will not take effect at law until they are registered, ie they are registrable dispositions (s 27(1), see 4.3.2.4). This is in line with a principal aim of the Act, which is to ensure that it is possible to investigate title to land almost entirely on-line with the minimum of additional enquiries.

In addition, no equitable easements or profits, however created, are capable of overriding a registered disposition (reversing the decision in *Celsteel Ltd v Alton House Holdings Ltd* [1985] 1 WLR 204). It follows that only a *legal* easement or profit can be overriding in relation to a registered disposition (Sch 3, para 3(1)). Moreover, once the Act is in force the only legal easements and profits that will be capable of being overriding interests are:

(a)   those already in existence when the Act comes into force (that have not been registered);

(b)   those arising by prescription (which is not reformed by the Act); and

(c)   those arising by implied grant or reservation, eg under s 62 of the Law of Property Act 1925.

Moreover, to circumvent the non-abandonment presumption, under Sch 3, para 3(1) certain categories of legal easement and profit are excluded from overriding status altogether. These cannot be overriding interests unless they have either been registered under the Commons Registration Act 1965 or have been exercised within one year prior to the registered disposition in question. They are:

(a)   those that are not within the actual knowledge of the person to whom the disposition was made; and

(b)   those that would not have been obvious on a reasonably careful inspection of the land over which the easement or profit is exercisable.

Importantly it therefore follows that a buyer of registered land for valuable consideration will only be bound by an easement or profit that is an overriding interest if:

(a)   it is registered under the Commons Registration Act 1965; or

(b)   the buyer actually knows about it; or

(c)   it is patent, ie obvious from a reasonable inspection of the land over which the easement or profit is exercisable, so that no seller would be obliged to disclose it; or

(d)   it has been exercised within one year before the date of purchase.

As a result of the above, buyers' pre-contract enquiries should request sellers to disclose:

(a)   any unregistered easements and profits affecting the land of which they are aware; and

(b)   any easements or profits that have been exercised in the previous 12 months.

This makes good practical sense for all conveyancers. There will be those with the benefit of unregistered easements and profits that have not been exercised for more than a year. These persons should immediately protect their rights either by lodging a caution against first registration if the servient land is unregistered or by registering them if the servient land is registered. These are important practical steps of which conveyancers should be aware.

12.3.3.1   *Transitional arrangements*
The Act contains a transitional provision to allow existing easements or profits which are overriding interests at the time the Act comes into force but which would not qualify under the new provisions to retain their overriding status (Sch 12, para 9). This is something that buyers should be made aware of and appropriate inquiry made of the seller at the pre-contract stage.

A second transitional provision states that for three years after the Act comes into force *any* legal easement or profit that is not registered will be an overriding interest (Sch 12, para 10). An example of this would be an implied grant under s 62 of the Law of Property Act 1925. The intention is to strike a fair balance between buyers and those with the benefit of these rights and to allow time for the latter to register them. For three years therefore, prudent buyers will continue to make the same enquiries as they would have done before the Act came into force. It should be noted however that *equitable* easements and profits are not protected by the three-year concessionary period. Thus, any equitable easements and profits created after the Act comes into force must be protected by registration if they are to be binding on a buyer of the servient land.

12.4   OVERRIDING INTERESTS ABOLISHED BY THE ACT

The overriding interests that are abolished by the 2002 Act are:

(a)   'Liability to repair the chancel of any church' (Land Registration Act 1925, s 70(1)(c)). Abolition follows from the Court of Appeal decision in *Aston Cantlow Parochial Church Council v Wallbank* [2001] EWCA Civ 713 which held that chancel repair liability contravenes the European Convention on Human Rights and is therefore unenforceable.

(b)   'Rights acquired or in course of being acquired under the Limitation Acts' (s 70(1)(f) of the 1925 Act). As we explained in chapter 9, the Act introduces an entirely new scheme of adverse possession for registered land. There are, however, limited transitional provisions to protect squatters' vested rights. For three years after the Act comes into force, a squatter who had already extinguished the owner's title before the Act came into force (ie the 12-year limitation period had expired) will continue to have an overriding interest even if he or she is not in actual occupation (Sch 12, paras 7, 11). The squatter will have three years to protect his or her position by registering his or her rights. In addition, on first registration, the legal estate is vested in the first registered proprietor subject to interests acquired under the Limitation Act 1980 of which he or she has notice at the time of registration (ss 11(4)(c), 12(4)(d); see 3.4).

(c) 'In the case of a possessory qualified or good leasehold title, all estates rights interests and powers excepted from the effect of registration' (s 70(1)(h) of the 1925 Act). The Act already protects the priority of an interest that appears from the register to be excepted from the effect of registration (ss 29(2)(a)(iii), 30(2)(a)(iii)). Further, the court or registrar may alter the register to give effect to any estate, right or interest excepted from the effect of registration (Sch 4, paras 2(1)(c), 5(c)).

12.5   REGISTRATION OF OVERRIDING INTERESTS THAT COME TO LIGHT

The 2002 Act contains provisions which are designed to ensure that, when overriding interests come to light, they are protected on the register:

(a)   On a first registration application or on an application to register a registered disposition the applicant must provide to the registrar such information as rules may provide concerning overriding interests affecting the estate (s 71). This is to enable such overriding interests to be entered on the register. The rules should provide guidance as to exactly what information the registrar will require.

(b)   If it appears to the registrar that a registered estate is subject to an overriding interest that falls within Sch 1, he or she may enter a notice of it in the register (s 37). However the registrar will not do so in respect of three categories of overriding interest which cannot be entered on the register:

(i)   a lease granted for a term of three years or less from the date of the grant which is not required to be registered (s 33(b));

(ii)   a PPP lease; and

(iii) any interest in any coal or coal mine and certain other rights in relation to coal (s 33(e)).

(c)   If an overriding interest has been protected by an entry of a notice on the register, it can never again become an overriding interest. This is the case even if the notice were removed from the register by mistake. Any person suffering loss as a result of such an error could, however, seek an indemnity (see Sch 8, para 1(1)(b)).

12.6   KEY POINTS FOR THE PRACTITIONER

- The policy of the Act is that interests should only have overriding status where protection against buyers is needed, but where it is neither reasonable to expect nor sensible to require any entry on the register.
- Those interests which override first registration are set out in Sch 1; the most important of these are short leases (seven years or less), the rights of persons in actual occupation and legal easements and profits.

- The rights of persons merely in receipt of rents and profits no longer enjoy overriding status.
- Where someone is in actual occupation of part of land but they have rights over the whole of the land, their rights protected by actual occupation are confined only to the part they occupy.
- The decision in *Celsteel Ltd v Alton House Holdings Ltd* [1985] 1 WLR 204 is reversed so that only legal easements and profits can be overriding interests, not equitable ones.
- There is to be a phasing out of certain miscellaneous overriding interests after ten years; those persons with the benefit of these interests may protect them by registration within the ten-year period without charge.
- Leases that were previously granted for a term of more than seven but not more than 21 years will remain as overriding interests after the Act comes into force.
- There are exceptions in which persons in actual occupation will not have overriding status (see 12.3.2.1 above).
- In this respect there is one new important exception — the rights of persons whose occupation is not apparent. An interest will not be protected as an overriding interest if (a) it belongs to a person whose occupation would not have been obvious on a reasonably careful inspection of the land at the time of the disposition, and (b) the person to whom the disposition is made does not have actual knowledge at that time.
- No easements or profits expressly granted or reserved out of registered land after the Act comes into force can take effect as overriding interests.
- A buyer of registered land for valuable consideration will only be bound by an easement or profit that is an overriding interest if:
  - it is registered under the Commons Registration Act 1965; or
  - the buyer actually knows about it; or
  - it is obvious from a reasonable inspection of the land; or
  - it has been exercised within one year before the date of purchase.
- Buyers' pre-contract enquiries should therefore request sellers to disclose (a) any unregistered easements and profits affecting the land of which they are aware, and (b) any easements or profits that have been exercised in the previous 12 months.
- A transitional arrangement provides that for three years after the Act comes into force any legal easement or profit that is not registered will be an overriding interest.
- When overriding interests come to light they are, as far as possible, to be entered on the register. A person applying for registration must disclose any overriding interests known to them.
- Once an overriding interest has been protected by an entry of a notice on the register, it can never again become an overriding interest.
- After ten years the likely categories of overriding interest that will bind a registered disponee of registered land will be:
  - most leases granted for three years or less;

- the interests of persons in actual occupation where that actual occupation is apparent and the interest is either a beneficial interest under a trust or arose informally (eg equity arising by estoppel);
- legal easements and profits that have arisen by implied grant or reservation or by prescription;
- customary and public rights;
- local land charges;
- certain mineral rights.
- The justification for keeping the overriding status of the above interests will be the guiding principle that protection against buyers is needed and that it would be unreasonable to expect them to be entered on the register.

Land Registration Act 2002

2002 CHAPTER 9
ARRANGEMENT OF SECTIONS

CONTENTS

PART 1
PRELIMINARY

PART 2
FIRST REGISTRATION OF TITLE

CHAPTER 1
FIRST REGISTRATION

Voluntary registration

Compulsory registration

Classes of title

Effect of first registration

Dependent estates

Supplementary

CHAPTER 2
CAUTIONS AGAINST FIRST REGISTRATION

PART 3
DISPOSITIONS OF REGISTERED LAND

Powers of disposition

Registrable dispositions

Effect of dispositions on priority

PART 4
NOTICES AND RESTRICTIONS

Notices

Restrictions

PART 5
CHARGES

PART 6
REGISTRATION: GENERAL

Contents

SCHEDULES:

Land Registration Act 2002

2002 CHAPTER 9

An Act to make provision about land registration; and for connected purposes.

[26th February 2002]

BE IT ENACTED by the Queen's most Excellent Majesty, by and with the advice and consent of the Lords Spiritual and Temporal, and Commons, in this present Parliament assembled, and by the authority of the same, as follows:—

PART 1
PRELIMINARY

1. Register of title

(1) There is to continue to be a register of title kept by the registrar.

(2) Rules may make provision about how the register is to be kept and may, in particular, make provision about—

    (a) the information to be included in the register,

    (b) the form in which information included in the register is to be kept, and

    (c) the arrangement of that information.

2. Scope of title registration

This Act makes provision about the registration of title to—

    (a) unregistered legal estates which are interests of any of the following kinds—

        (i) an estate in land,

        (ii) a rentcharge,

        (iii) a franchise,

        (iv) a profit a prendre in gross, and

        (v) any other interest or charge which subsists for the benefit of, or is a charge on, an interest the title to which is registered; and

    (b) interests capable of subsisting at law which are created by a disposition of an interest the title to which is registered.

PART 2

FIRST REGISTRATION OF TITLE

CHAPTER 1

FIRST REGISTRATION

Voluntary registration

3. When title may be registered

(1) This section applies to any unregistered legal estate which is an interest of any of the following kinds—

    (a)   an estate in land,

    (b)   a rentcharge,

    (c)   a franchise, and

    (d)   a profit a prendre in gross.

(2) Subject to the following provisions, a person may apply to the registrar to be registered as the proprietor of an unregistered legal estate to which this section applies if—

    (a)   the estate is vested in him, or

    (b)   he is entitled to require the estate to be vested in him.

(3) Subject to subsection (4), an application under subsection (2) in respect of a leasehold estate may only be made if the estate was granted for a term of which more than seven years are unexpired.

(4) In the case of an estate in land, subsection (3) does not apply if the right to possession under the lease is discontinuous.

(5) A person may not make an application under subsection (2)(a) in respect of a leasehold estate vested in him as a mortgagee where there is a subsisting right of redemption.

(6) A person may not make an application under subsection (2)(b) if his entitlement is as a person who has contracted to buy under a contract.

(7) If a person holds in the same right both—

    (a)   a lease in possession, and

    (b)   a lease to take effect in possession on, or within a month of, the end of the lease in possession,

then, to the extent that they relate to the same land, they are to be treated for the purposes of this section as creating one continuous term.

Compulsory registration

4. When title must be registered

(1) The requirement of registration applies on the occurrence of any of the following events—

    (a)   the transfer of a qualifying estate—

        (i)   for valuable or other consideration, by way of gift or in pursuance of an order of any court, or

        (ii)   by means of an assent (including a vesting assent);

    (b)   the transfer of an unregistered legal estate in land in circumstances where section 171A of the Housing Act 1985 (c. 68) applies (disposal by landlord which leads to a person no longer being a secure tenant);

    (c)   the grant out of a qualifying estate of an estate in land—

        (i)   for a term of years absolute of more than seven years from the date of the grant, and

(ii)   for valuable or other consideration, by way of gift or in pursuance of an order
         of any court;

(d)   the grant out of a qualifying estate of an estate in land for a term of years absolute
      to take effect in possession after the end of the period of three months beginning
      with the date of the grant;

(e)   the grant of a lease in pursuance of Part 5 of the Housing Act 1985 (the right to
      buy) out of an unregistered legal estate in land;

(f)   the grant of a lease out of an unregistered legal estate in land in such
      circumstances as are mentioned in paragraph (b);

(g)   the creation of a protected first legal mortgage of a qualifying estate.

(2)   For the purposes of subsection (1), a qualifying estate is an unregistered legal estate
which is—

(a)   a freehold estate in land, or

(b)   a leasehold estate in land for a term which, at the time of the transfer, grant or
      creation, has more than seven years to run.

(3)   In subsection (1)(a), the reference to transfer does not include transfer by operation
of law.

(4)   Subsection (1)(a) does not apply to—

(a)   the assignment of a mortgage term, or

(b)   the assignment or surrender of a lease to the owner of the immediate reversion
      where the term is to merge in that reversion.

(5)   Subsection (1)(c) does not apply to the grant of an estate to a person as a mortgagee.

(6)   For the purposes of subsection (1)(a) and (c), if the estate transferred or granted has
a negative value, it is to be regarded as transferred or granted for valuable or other
consideration.

(7)   In subsection (1)(a) and (c), references to transfer or grant by way of gift include
transfer or grant for the purpose of—

(a)   constituting a trust under which the settlor does not retain the whole of the
      beneficial interest, or

(b)   uniting the bare legal title and the beneficial interest in property held under a trust
      under which the settlor did not, on constitution, retain the whole of the beneficial
      interest.

(8)   For the purposes of subsection (1)(g)—

(a)   a legal mortgage is protected if it takes effect on its creation as a mortgage to be
      protected by the deposit of documents relating to the mortgaged estate, and

(b)   a first legal mortgage is one which, on its creation, ranks in priority ahead of any
      other mortgages then affecting the mortgaged estate.

(9)   In this section—

'land' does not include mines and minerals held apart from the surface;

'vesting assent' has the same meaning as in the Settled Land Act 1925 (c. 18).

5. Power to extend section 4

(1)   The Lord Chancellor may by order—

(a)   amend section 4 so as to add to the events on the occurrence of which the
      requirement of registration applies such relevant event as he may specify in the
      order, and

(b)   make such consequential amendments of any provision of, or having effect under,
      any Act as he thinks appropriate.

(2)   For the purposes of subsection (1)(a), a relevant event is an event relating to an unregistered legal estate which is an interest of any of the following kinds—

    (a)   an estate in land,

    (b)   a rentcharge,

    (c)   a franchise, and

    (d)   a profit a prendre in gross.

(3)   The power conferred by subsection (1) may not be exercised so as to require the title to an estate granted to a person as a mortgagee to be registered.

(4)   Before making an order under this section the Lord Chancellor must consult such persons as he considers appropriate.

6.   Duty to apply for registration of title

(1)   If the requirement of registration applies, the responsible estate owner, or his successor in title, must, before the end of the period for registration, apply to the registrar to be registered as the proprietor of the registrable estate.

(2)   If the requirement of registration applies because of section 4(1)(g)—

    (a)   the registrable estate is the estate charged by the mortgage, and

    (b)   the responsible estate owner is the owner of that estate.

(3)   If the requirement of registration applies otherwise than because of section 4(1)(g)—

    (a)   the registrable estate is the estate which is transferred or granted, and

    (b)   the responsible estate owner is the transferee or grantee of that estate.

(4)   The period for registration is 2 months beginning with the date on which the relevant event occurs, or such longer period as the registrar may provide under subsection (5).

(5)   If on the application of any interested person the registrar is satisfied that there is good reason for doing so, he may by order provide that the period for registration ends on such later date as he may specify in the order.

(6)   Rules may make provision enabling the mortgagee under any mortgage falling within section 4(1)(g) to require the estate charged by the mortgage to be registered whether or not the mortgagor consents.

7.   Effect of non-compliance with section 6

(1)   If the requirement of registration is not complied with, the transfer, grant or creation becomes void as regards the transfer, grant or creation of a legal estate.

(2)   On the application of subsection (1)—

    (a)   in a case falling within section 4(1)(a) or (b), the title to the legal estate reverts to the transferor who holds it on a bare trust for the transferee, and

    (b)   in a case falling within section 4(1)(c) to (g), the grant or creation has effect as a contract made for valuable consideration to grant or create the legal estate concerned.

(3)   If an order under section 6(5) is made in a case where subsection (1) has already applied, that application of the subsection is to be treated as not having occurred.

(4)   The possibility of reverter under subsection (1) is to be disregarded for the purposes of determining whether a fee simple is a fee simple absolute.

8.   Liability for making good void transfers etc

If a legal estate is retransferred, regranted or recreated because of a failure to comply with the requirement of registration, the transferee, grantee or, as the case may be, the mortgagor—

    (a)   is liable to the other party for all the proper costs of and incidental to the retransfer, regrant or recreation of the legal estate, and

(b) is liable to indemnify the other party in respect of any other liability reasonably incurred by him because of the failure to comply with the requirement of registration.

Classes of title

9. Titles to freehold estates

(1) In the case of an application for registration under this Chapter of a freehold estate, the classes of title with which the applicant may be registered as proprietor are—

(a) absolute title,

(b) qualified title, and

(c) possessory title;

and the following provisions deal with when each of the classes of title is available.

(2) A person may be registered with absolute title if the registrar is of the opinion that the person's title to the estate is such as a willing buyer could properly be advised by a competent professional adviser to accept.

(3) In applying subsection (2), the registrar may disregard the fact that a person's title appears to him to be open to objection if he is of the opinion that the defect will not cause the holding under the title to be disturbed.

(4) A person may be registered with qualified title if the registrar is of the opinion that the person's title to the estate has been established only for a limited period or subject to certain reservations which cannot be disregarded under subsection (3).

(5) A person may be registered with possessory title if the registrar is of the opinion—

(a) that the person is in actual possession of the land, or in receipt of the rents and profits of the land, by virtue of the estate, and

(b) that there is no other class of title with which he may be registered.

10. Titles to leasehold estates

(1) In the case of an application for registration under this Chapter of a leasehold estate, the classes of title with which the applicant may be registered as proprietor are—

(a) absolute title,

(b) good leasehold title,

(c) qualified title, and

(d) possessory title;

and the following provisions deal with when each of the classes of title is available.

(2) A person may be registered with absolute title if—

(a) the registrar is of the opinion that the person's title to the estate is such as a willing buyer could properly be advised by a competent professional adviser to accept, and

(b) the registrar approves the lessor's title to grant the lease.

(3) A person may be registered with good leasehold title if the registrar is of the opinion that the person's title to the estate is such as a willing buyer could properly be advised by a competent professional adviser to accept.

(4) In applying subsection (2) or (3), the registrar may disregard the fact that a person's title appears to him to be open to objection if he is of the opinion that the defect will not cause the holding under the title to be disturbed.

(5) A person may be registered with qualified title if the registrar is of the opinion that the person's title to the estate, or the lessor's title to the reversion, has been established only for a limited period or subject to certain reservations which cannot be disregarded under subsection (4).

(6)   A person may be registered with possessory title if the registrar is of the opinion—

  (a)   that the person is in actual possession of the land, or in receipt of the rents and profits of the land, by virtue of the estate, and

  (b)   that there is no other class of title with which he may be registered.

Effect of first registration

11.   Freehold estates

(1)   This section is concerned with the registration of a person under this Chapter as the proprietor of a freehold estate.

(2)   Registration with absolute title has the effect described in subsections (3) to (5).

(3)   The estate is vested in the proprietor together with all interests subsisting for the benefit of the estate.

(4)   The estate is vested in the proprietor subject only to the following interests affecting the estate at the time of registration—

  (a)   interests which are the subject of an entry in the register in relation to the estate,

  (b)   unregistered interests which fall within any of the paragraphs of Schedule 1, and

  (c)   interests acquired under the Limitation Act 1980 (c. 58) of which the proprietor has notice.

(5)   If the proprietor is not entitled to the estate for his own benefit, or not entitled solely for his own benefit, then, as between himself and the persons beneficially entitled to the estate, the estate is vested in him subject to such of their interests as he has notice of.

(6)   Registration with qualified title has the same effect as registration with absolute title, except that it does not affect the enforcement of any estate, right or interest which appears from the register to be excepted from the effect of registration.

(7)   Registration with possessory title has the same effect as registration with absolute title, except that it does not affect the enforcement of any estate, right or interest adverse to, or in derogation of, the proprietor's title subsisting at the time of registration or then capable of arising.

12.   Leasehold estates

(1)   This section is concerned with the registration of a person under this Chapter as the proprietor of a leasehold estate.

(2)   Registration with absolute title has the effect described in subsections (3) to (5).

(3)   The estate is vested in the proprietor together with all interests subsisting for the benefit of the estate.

(4)   The estate is vested subject only to the following interests affecting the estate at the time of registration—

  (a)   implied and express covenants, obligations and liabilities incident to the estate,

  (b)   interests which are the subject of an entry in the register in relation to the estate,

  (c)   unregistered interests which fall within any of the paragraphs of Schedule 1, and

  (d)   interests acquired under the Limitation Act 1980 (c. 58) of which the proprietor has notice.

(5)   If the proprietor is not entitled to the estate for his own benefit, or not entitled solely for his own benefit, then, as between himself and the persons beneficially entitled to the estate, the estate is vested in him subject to such of their interests as he has notice of.

(6)   Registration with good leasehold title has the same effect as registration with absolute title, except that it does not affect the enforcement of any estate, right or interest affecting, or in derogation of, the title of the lessor to grant the lease.

(7) Registration with qualified title has the same effect as registration with absolute title except that it does not affect the enforcement of any estate, right or interest which appears from the register to be excepted from the effect of registration.

(8) Registration with possessory title has the same effect as registration with absolute title, except that it does not affect the enforcement of any estate, right or interest adverse to, or in derogation of, the proprietor's title subsisting at the time of registration or then capable of arising.

Dependent estates

13. Appurtenant rights and charges

Rules may—

(a) make provision for the registration of the proprietor of a registered estate as the proprietor of an unregistered legal estate which subsists for the benefit of the registered estate;

(b) make provision for the registration of a person as the proprietor of an unregistered legal estate which is a charge on a registered estate.

Supplementary

14. Rules about first registration

Rules may—

(a) make provision about the making of applications for registration under this Chapter;

(b) make provision about the functions of the registrar following the making of such an application, including provision about—

(i) the examination of title, and

(ii) the entries to be made in the register where such an application is approved;

(c) make provision about the effect of any entry made in the register in pursuance of such an application.

CHAPTER 2
CAUTIONS AGAINST FIRST REGISTRATION

15. Right to lodge

(1) Subject to subsection (3), a person may lodge a caution against the registration of title to an unregistered legal estate if he claims to be—

(a) the owner of a qualifying estate, or

(b) entitled to an interest affecting a qualifying estate.

(2) For the purposes of subsection (1), a qualifying estate is a legal estate which—

(a) relates to land to which the caution relates, and

(b) is an interest of any of the following kinds—

(i) an estate in land,

(ii) a rentcharge,

(iii) a franchise, and

(iv) a profit a prendre in gross.

(3) No caution may be lodged under subsection (1)—

(a) in the case of paragraph (a), by virtue of ownership of—

(i) a freehold estate in land, or

(ii) a leasehold estate in land granted for a term of which more than seven years are unexpired;

(b) in the case of paragraph (b), by virtue of entitlement to such a leasehold estate as is mentioned in paragraph (a)(ii) of this subsection.

(4)   The right under subsection (1) is exercisable by application to the registrar.

16.   Effect

(1)   Where an application for registration under this Part relates to a legal estate which is the subject of a caution against first registration, the registrar must give the cautioner notice of the application and of his right to object to it.

(2)   The registrar may not determine an application to which subsection (1) applies before the end of such period as rules may provide, unless the cautioner has exercised his right to object to the application or given the registrar notice that he does not intend to do so.

(3)   Except as provided by this section, a caution against first registration has no effect and, in particular, has no effect on the validity or priority of any interest of the cautioner in the legal estate to which the caution relates.

(4)   For the purposes of subsection (1), notice given by a person acting on behalf of an applicant for registration under this Part is to be treated as given by the registrar if—

(a)   the person is of a description provided by rules, and

(b)   notice is given in such circumstances as rules may provide.

17.   Withdrawal

The cautioner may withdraw a caution against first registration by application to the registrar.

18.   Cancellation

(1)   A person may apply to the registrar for cancellation of a caution against first registration if he is—

(a)   the owner of the legal estate to which the caution relates, or

(b)   a person of such other description as rules may provide.

(2)   Subject to rules, no application under subsection (1)(a) may be made by a person who—

(a)   consented in such manner as rules may provide to the lodging of the caution, or

(b)   derives title to the legal estate by operation of law from a person who did so.

(3)   Where an application is made under subsection (1), the registrar must give the cautioner notice of the application and of the effect of subsection (4).

(4)   If the cautioner does not exercise his right to object to the application before the end of such period as rules may provide, the registrar must cancel the caution.

19.   Cautions register

(1)   The registrar must keep a register of cautions against first registration.

(2)   Rules may make provision about how the cautions register is to be kept and may, in particular, make provision about—

(a)   the information to be included in the register,

(b)   the form in which information included in the register is to be kept, and

(c)   the arrangement of that information.

20.   Alteration of register by court

(1)   The court may make an order for alteration of the cautions register for the purpose of—

(a)   correcting a mistake, or

(b)   bringing the register up to date.

(2)   An order under subsection (1) has effect when served on the registrar to impose a duty on him to give effect to it.

(3) Rules may make provision about—
- (a) the circumstances in which there is a duty to exercise the power under subsection (1),
- (b) the form of an order under that subsection, and
- (c) service of such an order.

21. Alteration of register by registrar

(1) The registrar may alter the cautions register for the purpose of—
- (a) correcting a mistake, or
- (b) bringing the register up to date.

(2) Rules may make provision about—
- (a) the circumstances in which there is a duty to exercise the power under subsection (1),
- (b) how the cautions register is to be altered in exercise of that power,
- (c) applications for the exercise of that power, and
- (d) procedure in relation to the exercise of that power, whether on application or otherwise.

(3) Where an alteration is made under this section, the registrar may pay such amount as he thinks fit in respect of any costs reasonably incurred by a person in connection with the alteration.

22. Supplementary

In this Chapter, 'the cautioner', in relation to a caution against first registration, means the person who lodged the caution, or such other person as rules may provide.

PART 3
DISPOSITIONS OF REGISTERED LAND

Powers of disposition

23. Owner's powers

(1) Owner's powers in relation to a registered estate consist of—
- (a) power to make a disposition of any kind permitted by the general law in relation to an interest of that description, other than a mortgage by demise or sub-demise, and
- (b) power to charge the estate at law with the payment of money.

(2) Owner's powers in relation to a registered charge consist of—
- (a) power to make a disposition of any kind permitted by the general law in relation to an interest of that description, other than a legal sub-mortgage, and
- (b) power to charge at law with the payment of money indebtedness secured by the registered charge.

(3) In subsection (2)(a), 'legal sub-mortgage' means—
- (a) a transfer by way of mortgage,
- (b) a sub-mortgage by sub-demise, and
- (c) a charge by way of legal mortgage.

24. Right to exercise owner's powers

A person is entitled to exercise owner's powers in relation to a registered estate or charge if he is—
- (a) the registered proprietor, or
- (b) entitled to be registered as the proprietor.

25. Mode of exercise

(1) A registrable disposition of a registered estate or charge only has effect if it complies with such requirements as to form and content as rules may provide.

(2) Rules may apply subsection (1) to any other kind of disposition which depends for its effect on registration.

26. Protection of disponees

(1) Subject to subsection (2), a person's right to exercise owner's powers in relation to a registered estate or charge is to be taken to be free from any limitation affecting the validity of a disposition.

(2) Subsection (1) does not apply to a limitation—

    (a) reflected by an entry in the register, or

    (b) imposed by, or under, this Act.

(3) This section has effect only for the purpose of preventing the title of a disponee being questioned (and so does not affect the lawfulness of a disposition).

Registrable dispositions

27. Dispositions required to be registered

(1) If a disposition of a registered estate or registered charge is required to be completed by registration, it does not operate at law until the relevant registration requirements are met.

(2) In the case of a registered estate, the following are the dispositions which are required to be completed by registration—

    (a) a transfer,

    (b) where the registered estate is an estate in land, the grant of a term of years absolute—

        (i) for a term of more than seven years from the date of the grant,

        (ii) to take effect in possession after the end of the period of three months beginning with the date of the grant,

        (iii) under which the right to possession is discontinuous,

        (iv) in pursuance of Part 5 of the Housing Act 1985 (c. 68) (the right to buy), or

        (v) in circumstances where section 171A of that Act applies (disposal by landlord which leads to a person no longer being a secure tenant),

    (c) where the registered estate is a franchise or manor, the grant of a lease,

    (d) the express grant or reservation of an interest of a kind falling within section 1(2)(a) of the Law of Property Act 1925 (c. 20), other than one which is capable of being registered under the Commons Registration Act 1965 (c. 64),

    (e) the express grant or reservation of an interest of a kind falling within section 1(2)(b) or (e) of the Law of Property Act 1925, and

    (f) the grant of a legal charge.

(3) In the case of a registered charge, the following are the dispositions which are required to be completed by registration—

    (a) a transfer, and

    (b) the grant of a sub-charge.

(4) Schedule 2 to this Act (which deals with the relevant registration requirements) has effect.

(5) This section applies to dispositions by operation of law as it applies to other dispositions, but with the exception of the following—

    (a) a transfer on the death or bankruptcy of an individual proprietor,

(b)   a transfer on the dissolution of a corporate proprietor, and

(c)   the creation of a legal charge which is a local land charge.

(6)   Rules may make provision about applications to the registrar for the purpose of meeting registration requirements under this section.

(7)   In subsection (2)(d), the reference to express grant does not include grant as a result of the operation of section 62 of the Law of Property Act 1925 (c. 20).

Effect of dispositions on priority

28.   Basic rule

(1)   Except as provided by sections 29 and 30, the priority of an interest affecting a registered estate or charge is not affected by a disposition of the estate or charge.

(2)   It makes no difference for the purposes of this section whether the interest or disposition is registered.

29.   Effect of registered dispositions: estates

(1)   If a registrable disposition of a registered estate is made for valuable consideration, completion of the disposition by registration has the effect of postponing to the interest under the disposition any interest affecting the estate immediately before the disposition whose priority is not protected at the time of registration.

(2)   For the purposes of subsection (1), the priority of an interest is protected—

    (a)   in any case, if the interest—

        (i)   is a registered charge or the subject of a notice in the register,

        (ii)   falls within any of the paragraphs of Schedule 3, or

        (iii)   appears from the register to be excepted from the effect of registration, and

    (b)   in the case of a disposition of a leasehold estate, if the burden of the interest is incident to the estate.

(3)   Subsection (2)(a)(ii) does not apply to an interest which has been the subject of a notice in the register at any time since the coming into force of this section.

(4)   Where the grant of a leasehold estate in land out of a registered estate does not involve a registrable disposition, this section has effect as if—

    (a)   the grant involved such a disposition, and

    (b)   the disposition were registered at the time of the grant.

30.   Effect of registered dispositions: charges

(1)   If a registrable disposition of a registered charge is made for valuable consideration, completion of the disposition by registration has the effect of postponing to the interest under the disposition any interest affecting the charge immediately before the disposition whose priority is not protected at the time of registration.

(2)   For the purposes of subsection (1), the priority of an interest is protected—

    (a)   in any case, if the interest—

        (i)   is a registered charge or the subject of a notice in the register,

        (ii)   falls within any of the paragraphs of Schedule 3, or

        (iii)   appears from the register to be excepted from the effect of registration, and

    (b)   in the case of a disposition of a charge which relates to a leasehold estate, if the burden of the interest is incident to the estate.

(3)   Subsection (2)(a)(ii) does not apply to an interest which has been the subject of a notice in the register at any time since the coming into force of this section.

31. Inland Revenue charges

The effect of a disposition of a registered estate or charge on a charge under section 237 of the Inheritance Tax Act 1984 (c. 51) (charge for unpaid tax) is to be determined, not in accordance with sections 28 to 30 above, but in accordance with sections 237(6) and 238 of that Act (under which a purchaser in good faith for money or money's worth takes free from the charge in the absence of registration).

PART 4

NOTICES AND RESTRICTIONS

Notices

32. Nature and effect

(1) A notice is an entry in the register in respect of the burden of an interest affecting a registered estate or charge.

(2) The entry of a notice is to be made in relation to the registered estate or charge affected by the interest concerned.

(3) The fact that an interest is the subject of a notice does not necessarily mean that the interest is valid, but does mean that the priority of the interest, if valid, is protected for the purposes of sections 29 and 30.

33. Excluded interests

No notice may be entered in the register in respect of any of the following—

(a) an interest under—
   (i) a trust of land, or
   (ii) a settlement under the Settled Land Act 1925 (c. 18),
(b) a leasehold estate in land which—
   (i) is granted for a term of years of three years or less from the date of the grant, and
   (ii) is not required to be registered,
(c) a restrictive covenant made between a lessor and lessee, so far as relating to the demised premises,
(d) an interest which is capable of being registered under the Commons Registration Act 1965 (c. 64), and
(e) an interest in any coal or coal mine, the rights attached to any such interest and the rights of any person under section 38, 49 or 51 of the Coal Industry Act 1994 (c. 21).

34. Entry on application

(1) A person who claims to be entitled to the benefit of an interest affecting a registered estate or charge may, if the interest is not excluded by section 33, apply to the registrar for the entry in the register of a notice in respect of the interest.

(2) Subject to rules, an application under this section may be for—

(a) an agreed notice, or
(b) a unilateral notice.

(3) The registrar may only approve an application for an agreed notice if—

(a) the applicant is the relevant registered proprietor, or a person entitled to be registered as such proprietor,
(b) the relevant registered proprietor, or a person entitled to be registered as such proprietor, consents to the entry of the notice, or

(c) the registrar is satisfied as to the validity of the applicant's claim.

(4) In subsection (3), references to the relevant registered proprietor are to the proprietor of the registered estate or charge affected by the interest to which the application relates.

35. Unilateral notices

(1) If the registrar enters a notice in the register in pursuance of an application under section 34(2)(b) ('a unilateral notice'), he must give notice of the entry to—

(a) the proprietor of the registered estate or charge to which it relates, and

(b) such other persons as rules may provide.

(2) A unilateral notice must—

(a) indicate that it is such a notice, and

(b) identify who is the beneficiary of the notice.

(3) The person shown in the register as the beneficiary of a unilateral notice, or such other person as rules may provide, may apply to the registrar for the removal of the notice from the register.

36. Cancellation of unilateral notices

(1) A person may apply to the registrar for the cancellation of a unilateral notice if he is—

(a) the registered proprietor of the estate or charge to which the notice relates, or

(b) a person entitled to be registered as the proprietor of that estate or charge.

(2) Where an application is made under subsection (1), the registrar must give the beneficiary of the notice notice of the application and of the effect of subsection (3).

(3) If the beneficiary of the notice does not exercise his right to object to the application before the end of such period as rules may provide, the registrar must cancel the notice.

(4) In this section—

'beneficiary', in relation to a unilateral notice, means the person shown in the register as the beneficiary of the notice, or such other person as rules may provide;

'unilateral notice' means a notice entered in the register in pursuance of an application under section 34(2)(b).

37. Unregistered interests

(1) If it appears to the registrar that a registered estate is subject to an unregistered interest which—

(a) falls within any of the paragraphs of Schedule 1, and

(b) is not excluded by section 33,

he may enter a notice in the register in respect of the interest.

(2) The registrar must give notice of an entry under this section to such persons as rules may provide.

38. Registrable dispositions

Where a person is entered in the register as the proprietor of an interest under a disposition falling within section 27(2)(b) to (e), the registrar must also enter a notice in the register in respect of that interest.

39. Supplementary

Rules may make provision about the form and content of notices in the register.

Restrictions

40. Nature

(1) A restriction is an entry in the register regulating the circumstances in which a disposition of a registered estate or charge may be the subject of an entry in the register.

(2)   A restriction may, in particular—

    (a)   prohibit the making of an entry in respect of any disposition, or a disposition of a kind specified in the restriction;

    (b)   prohibit the making of an entry—

       (i)   indefinitely,

      (ii)   for a period specified in the restriction, or

     (iii)   until the occurrence of an event so specified.

(3)   Without prejudice to the generality of subsection (2)(b)(iii), the events which may be specified include—

    (a)   the giving of notice,

    (b)   the obtaining of consent, and

    (c)   the making of an order by the court or registrar.

(4)   The entry of a restriction is to be made in relation to the registered estate or charge to which it relates.

41.   Effect

(1)   Where a restriction is entered in the register, no entry in respect of a disposition to which the restriction applies may be made in the register otherwise than in accordance with the terms of the restriction, subject to any order under subsection (2).

(2)   The registrar may by order—

    (a)   disapply a restriction in relation to a disposition specified in the order or dispositions of a kind so specified, or

    (b)   provide that a restriction has effect, in relation to a disposition specified in the order or dispositions of a kind so specified, with modifications so specified.

(3)   The power under subsection (2) is exercisable only on the application of a person who appears to the registrar to have a sufficient interest in the restriction.

42.   Power of registrar to enter

(1)   The registrar may enter a restriction in the register if it appears to him that it is necessary or desirable to do so for the purpose of—

    (a)   preventing invalidity or unlawfulness in relation to dispositions of a registered estate or charge,

    (b)   securing that interests which are capable of being overreached on a disposition of a registered estate or charge are overreached, or

    (c)   protecting a right or claim in relation to a registered estate or charge.

(2)   No restriction may be entered under subsection (1)(c) for the purpose of protecting the priority of an interest which is, or could be, the subject of a notice.

(3)   The registrar must give notice of any entry made under this section to the proprietor of the registered estate or charge concerned, except where the entry is made in pursuance of an application under section 43.

(4)   For the purposes of subsection (1)(c), a person entitled to the benefit of a charging order relating to an interest under a trust shall be treated as having a right or claim in relation to the trust property.

43.   Applications

(1)   A person may apply to the registrar for the entry of a restriction under section 42(1) if—

    (a)   he is the relevant registered proprietor, or a person entitled to be registered as such proprietor,

(b)   the relevant registered proprietor, or a person entitled to be registered as such proprietor, consents to the application, or

(c)   he otherwise has a sufficient interest in the making of the entry.

(2)   Rules may—

(a)   require the making of an application under subsection (1) in such circumstances, and by such person, as the rules may provide;

(b)   make provision about the form of consent for the purposes of subsection (1)(b);

(c)   provide for classes of person to be regarded as included in subsection (1)(c);

(d)   specify standard forms of restriction.

(3)   If an application under subsection (1) is made for the entry of a restriction which is not in a form specified under subsection (2)(d), the registrar may only approve the application if it appears to him—

(a)   that the terms of the proposed restriction are reasonable, and

(b)   that applying the proposed restriction would—

(i)   be straightforward, and

(ii)   not place an unreasonable burden on him.

(4)   In subsection (1), references to the relevant registered proprietor are to the proprietor of the registered estate or charge to which the application relates.

44.   Obligatory restrictions

(1)   If the registrar enters two or more persons in the register as the proprietor of a registered estate in land, he must also enter in the register such restrictions as rules may provide for the purpose of securing that interests which are capable of being overreached on a disposition of the estate are overreached.

(2)   Where under any enactment the registrar is required to enter a restriction without application, the form of the restriction shall be such as rules may provide.

45.   Notifiable applications

(1)   Where an application under section 43(1) is notifiable, the registrar must give notice of the application, and of the right to object to it, to—

(a)   the proprietor of the registered estate or charge to which it relates, and

(b)   such other persons as rules may provide.

(2)   The registrar may not determine an application to which subsection (1) applies before the end of such period as rules may provide, unless the person, or each of the persons, notified under that subsection has exercised his right to object to the application or given the registrar notice that he does not intend to do so.

(3)   For the purposes of this section, an application under section 43(1) is notifiable unless it is—

(a)   made by or with the consent of the proprietor of the registered estate or charge to which the application relates, or a person entitled to be registered as such proprietor,

(b)   made in pursuance of rules under section 43(2)(a), or

(c)   an application for the entry of a restriction reflecting a limitation under an order of the court or registrar, or an undertaking given in place of such an order.

46.   Power of court to order entry

(1)   If it appears to the court that it is necessary or desirable to do so for the purpose of protecting a right or claim in relation to a registered estate or charge, it may make an order requiring the registrar to enter a restriction in the register.

(2)   No order under this section may be made for the purpose of protecting the priority of an interest which is, or could be, the subject of a notice.

(3)   The court may include in an order under this section a direction that an entry made in pursuance of the order is to have overriding priority.

(4)   If an order under this section includes a direction under subsection (3), the registrar must make such entry in the register as rules may provide.

(5)   The court may make the exercise of its power under subsection (3) subject to such terms and conditions as it thinks fit.

47.   Withdrawal

A person may apply to the registrar for the withdrawal of a restriction if—

    (a)   the restriction was entered in such circumstances as rules may provide, and

    (b)   he is of such a description as rules may provide.

PART 5

CHARGES

Relative priority

48.   Registered charges

(1)   Registered charges on the same registered estate, or on the same registered charge, are to be taken to rank as between themselves in the order shown in the register.

(2)   Rules may make provision about—

    (a)   how the priority of registered charges as between themselves is to be shown in the register, and

    (b)   applications for registration of the priority of registered charges as between themselves.

49.   Tacking and further advances

(1)   The proprietor of a registered charge may make a further advance on the security of the charge ranking in priority to a subsequent charge if he has not received from the subsequent chargee notice of the creation of the subsequent charge.

(2)   Notice given for the purposes of subsection (1) shall be treated as received at the time when, in accordance with rules, it ought to have been received.

(3)   The proprietor of a registered charge may also make a further advance on the security of the charge ranking in priority to a subsequent charge if—

    (a)   the advance is made in pursuance of an obligation, and

    (b)   at the time of the creation of the subsequent charge the obligation was entered in the register in accordance with rules.

(4)   The proprietor of a registered charge may also make a further advance on the security of the charge ranking in priority to a subsequent charge if—

    (a)   the parties to the prior charge have agreed a maximum amount for which the charge is security, and

    (b)   at the time of the creation of the subsequent charge the agreement was entered in the register in accordance with rules.

(5)   Rules may—

    (a)   disapply subsection (4) in relation to charges of a description specified in the rules, or

    (b)   provide for the application of that subsection to be subject, in the case of charges of a description so specified, to compliance with such conditions as may be so specified.

(6) Except as provided by this section, tacking in relation to a charge over registered land is only possible with the agreement of the subsequent chargee.

50. Overriding statutory charges: duty of notification

If the registrar enters a person in the register as the proprietor of a charge which—

(a) is created by or under an enactment, and

(b) has effect to postpone a charge which at the time of registration of the statutory charge is—

(i) entered in the register, or

(ii) the basis for an entry in the register,

he must in accordance with rules give notice of the creation of the statutory charge to such person as rules may provide.

Powers as chargee

51. Effect of completion by registration

On completion of the relevant registration requirements, a charge created by means of a registrable disposition of a registered estate has effect, if it would not otherwise do so, as a charge by deed by way of legal mortgage.

52. Protection of disponees

(1) Subject to any entry in the register to the contrary, the proprietor of a registered charge is to be taken to have, in relation to the property subject to the charge, the powers of disposition conferred by law on the owner of a legal mortgage.

(2) Subsection (1) has effect only for the purpose of preventing the title of a disponee being questioned (and so does not affect the lawfulness of a disposition).

53. Powers as sub-chargee

The registered proprietor of a sub-charge has, in relation to the property subject to the principal charge or any intermediate charge, the same powers as the sub-chargor.

Realisation of security

54. Proceeds of sale: chargee's duty

For the purposes of section 105 of the Law of Property Act 1925 (c. 20) (mortgagee's duties in relation to application of proceeds of sale), in its application to the proceeds of sale of registered land, a person shall be taken to have notice of anything in the register immediately before the disposition on sale.

55. Local land charges

A charge over registered land which is a local land charge may only be realised if the title to the charge is registered.

Miscellaneous

56. Receipt in case of joint proprietors

Where a charge is registered in the name of two or more proprietors, a valid receipt for the money secured by the charge may be given by—

(a) the registered proprietors,

(b) the survivors or survivor of the registered proprietors, or

(c) the personal representative of the last survivor of the registered proprietors.

57. Entry of right of consolidation

Rules may make provision about entry in the register of a right of consolidation in relation to a registered charge.

PART 6
REGISTRATION: GENERAL

Registration as proprietor

58. Conclusiveness

(1) If, on the entry of a person in the register as the proprietor of a legal estate, the legal estate would not otherwise be vested in him, it shall be deemed to be vested in him as a result of the registration.

(2) Subsection (1) does not apply where the entry is made in pursuance of a registrable disposition in relation to which some other registration requirement remains to be met.

59. Dependent estates

(1) The entry of a person in the register as the proprietor of a legal estate which subsists for the benefit of a registered estate must be made in relation to the registered estate.

(2) The entry of a person in the register as the proprietor of a charge on a registered estate must be made in relation to that estate.

(3) The entry of a person in the register as the proprietor of a sub-charge on a registered charge must be made in relation to that charge.

Boundaries

60. Boundaries

(1) The boundary of a registered estate as shown for the purposes of the register is a general boundary, unless shown as determined under this section.

(2) A general boundary does not determine the exact line of the boundary.

(3) Rules may make provision enabling or requiring the exact line of the boundary of a registered estate to be determined and may, in particular, make provision about—

    (a) the circumstances in which the exact line of a boundary may or must be determined,

    (b) how the exact line of a boundary may be determined,

    (c) procedure in relation to applications for determination, and

    (d) the recording of the fact of determination in the register or the index maintained under section 68.

(4) Rules under this section must provide for applications for determination to be made to the registrar.

61. Accretion and diluvion

(1) The fact that a registered estate in land is shown in the register as having a particular boundary does not affect the operation of accretion or diluvion.

(2) An agreement about the operation of accretion or diluvion in relation to a registered estate in land has effect only if registered in accordance with rules.

Quality of title

62. Power to upgrade title

(1) Where the title to a freehold estate is entered in the register as possessory or qualified, the registrar may enter it as absolute if he is satisfied as to the title to the estate.

(2) Where the title to a leasehold estate is entered in the register as good leasehold, the registrar may enter it as absolute if he is satisfied as to the superior title.

(3)   Where the title to a leasehold estate is entered in the register as possessory or qualified the registrar may—

(a)   enter it as good leasehold if he is satisfied as to the title to the estate, and

(b)   enter it as absolute if he is satisfied both as to the title to the estate and as to the superior title.

(4)   Where the title to a freehold estate in land has been entered in the register as possessory for at least twelve years, the registrar may enter it as absolute if he is satisfied that the proprietor is in possession of the land.

(5)   Where the title to a leasehold estate in land has been entered in the register as possessory for at least twelve years, the registrar may enter it as good leasehold if he is satisfied that the proprietor is in possession of the land.

(6)   None of the powers under subsections (1) to (5) is exercisable if there is outstanding any claim adverse to the title of the registered proprietor which is made by virtue of an estate, right or interest whose enforceability is preserved by virtue of the existing entry about the class of title.

(7)   The only persons who may apply to the registrar for the exercise of any of the powers under subsections (1) to (5) are—

(a)   the proprietor of the estate to which the application relates,

(b)   a person entitled to be registered as the proprietor of that estate,

(c)   the proprietor of a registered charge affecting that estate, and

(d)   a person interested in a registered estate which derives from that estate.

(8)   In determining for the purposes of this section whether he is satisfied as to any title, the registrar is to apply the same standards as those which apply under section 9 or 10 to first registration of title.

(9)   The Lord Chancellor may by order amend subsection (4) or (5) by substituting for the number of years for the time being specified in that subsection such number of years as the order may provide.

63.   Effect of upgrading title

(1)   On the title to a registered freehold or leasehold estate being entered under section 62 as absolute, the proprietor ceases to hold the estate subject to any estate, right or interest whose enforceability was preserved by virtue of the previous entry about the class of title.

(2)   Subsection (1) also applies on the title to a registered leasehold estate being entered under section 62 as good leasehold, except that the entry does not affect or prejudice the enforcement of any estate, right or interest affecting, or in derogation of, the title of the lessor to grant the lease.

64.   Use of register to record defects in title

(1)   If it appears to the registrar that a right to determine a registered estate in land is exercisable, he may enter the fact in the register.

(2)   Rules may make provision about entries under subsection (1) and may, in particular, make provision about—

(a)   the circumstances in which there is a duty to exercise the power conferred by that subsection,

(b)   how entries under that subsection are to be made, and

(c)   the removal of such entries.

Alteration of register

65.   Alteration of register

Schedule 4 (which makes provision about alteration of the register) has effect.

Information etc.

66. Inspection of the registers etc

(1) Any person may inspect and make copies of, or of any part of—

    (a) the register of title,

    (b) any document kept by the registrar which is referred to in the register of title,

    (c) any other document kept by the registrar which relates to an application to him, or

    (d) the register of cautions against first registration.

(2) The right under subsection (1) is subject to rules which may, in particular—

    (a) provide for exceptions to the right, and

    (b) impose conditions on its exercise, including conditions requiring the payment of fees.

67. Official copies of the registers etc

(1) An official copy of, or of a part of—

    (a) the register of title,

    (b) any document which is referred to in the register of title and kept by the registrar,

    (c) any other document kept by the registrar which relates to an application to him, or

    (d) the register of cautions against first registration,

is admissible in evidence to the same extent as the original.

(2) A person who relies on an official copy in which there is a mistake is not liable for loss suffered by another by reason of the mistake.

(3) Rules may make provision for the issue of official copies and may, in particular, make provision about—

    (a) the form of official copies,

    (b) who may issue official copies,

    (c) applications for official copies, and

    (d) the conditions to be met by applicants for official copies, including conditions requiring the payment of fees.

68. Index

(1) The registrar must keep an index for the purpose of enabling the following matters to be ascertained in relation to any parcel of land—

    (a) whether any registered estate relates to the land,

    (b) how any registered estate which relates to the land is identified for the purposes of the register,

    (c) whether the land is affected by any, and, if so what, caution against first registration, and

    (d) such other matters as rules may provide.

(2) Rules may—

    (a) make provision about how the index is to be kept and may, in particular, make provision about—

        (i) the information to be included in the index,

        (ii) the form in which information included in the index is to be kept, and

        (iii) the arrangement of that information;

    (b) make provision about official searches of the index.

69. Historical information

(1) The registrar may on application provide information about the history of a registered title.

(2) Rules may make provision about applications for the exercise of the power conferred by subsection (1).

(3) The registrar may—

   (a) arrange for the provision of information about the history of registered titles, and
   (b) authorise anyone who has the function of providing information under paragraph (a) to have access on such terms as the registrar thinks fit to any relevant information kept by him.

70. Official searches

Rules may make provision for official searches of the register, including searches of pending applications for first registration, and may, in particular, make provision about—

   (a) the form of applications for searches,
   (b) the manner in which such applications may be made,
   (c) the form of official search certificates, and
   (d) the manner in which such certificates may be issued.

Applications

71. Duty to disclose unregistered interests

Where rules so provide—

   (a) a person applying for registration under Chapter 1 of Part 2 must provide to the registrar such information as the rules may provide about any interest affecting the estate to which the application relates which—
      (i)   falls within any of the paragraphs of Schedule 1, and
      (ii) is of a description specified by the rules;
   (b) a person applying to register a registrable disposition of a registered estate must provide to the registrar such information as the rules may provide about any unregistered interest affecting the estate which—
      (i)   falls within any of the paragraphs of Schedule 3, and
      (ii) is of description specified by the rules.

72. Priority protection

(1) For the purposes of this section, an application for an entry in the register is protected if—

   (a) it is one to which a priority period relates, and
   (b) it is made before the end of that period.

(2) Where an application for an entry in the register is protected, any entry made in the register during the priority period relating to the application is postponed to any entry made in pursuance of it.

(3) Subsection (2) does not apply if—

   (a) the earlier entry was made in pursuance of a protected application, and
   (b) the priority period relating to that application ranks ahead of the one relating to the application for the other entry.

(4) Subsection (2) does not apply if the earlier entry is one to which a direction under section 46(3) applies.

(5) The registrar may defer dealing with an application for an entry in the register if it appears to him that subsection (2) might apply to the entry were he to make it.

(6) Rules may—

   (a) make provision for priority periods in connection with—

(i) official searches of the register, including searches of pending applications for first registration, or

(ii) the noting in the register of a contract for the making of a registrable disposition of a registered estate or charge;

(b) make provision for the keeping of records in relation to priority periods and the inspection of such records.

(7) Rules under subsection (6)(a) may, in particular, make provision about—

(a) the commencement and length of a priority period,

(b) the applications for registration to which such a period relates,

(c) the order in which competing priority periods rank, and

(d) the application of subsections (2) and (3) in cases where more than one priority period relates to the same application.

73. Objections

(1) Subject to subsections (2) and (3), anyone may object to an application to the registrar.

(2) In the case of an application under section 18, only the person who lodged the caution to which the application relates, or such other person as rules may provide, may object.

(3) In the case of an application under section 36, only the person shown in the register as the beneficiary of the notice to which the application relates, or such other person as rules may provide, may object.

(4) The right to object under this section is subject to rules.

(5) Where an objection is made under this section, the registrar—

(a) must give notice of the objection to the applicant, and

(b) may not determine the application until the objection has been disposed of.

(6) Subsection (5) does not apply if the objection is one which the registrar is satisfied is groundless.

(7) If it is not possible to dispose by agreement of an objection to which subsection (5) applies, the registrar must refer the matter to the adjudicator.

(8) Rules may make provision about references under subsection (7).

74. Effective date of registration

An entry made in the register in pursuance of—

(a) an application for registration of an unregistered legal estate, or

(b) an application for registration in relation to a disposition required to be completed by registration,

has effect from the time of the making of the application.

Proceedings before the registrar

75. Production of documents

(1) The registrar may require a person to produce a document for the purposes of proceedings before him.

(2) The power under subsection (1) is subject to rules.

(3) A requirement under subsection (1) shall be enforceable as an order of the court.

(4) A person aggrieved by a requirement under subsection (1) may appeal to a county court, which may make any order which appears appropriate.

76. Costs

(1)   The registrar may make orders about costs in relation to proceedings before him.

(2)   The power under subsection (1) is subject to rules which may, in particular, make provision about—

(a)   who may be required to pay costs,

(b)   whose costs a person may be required to pay,

(c)   the kind of costs which a person may be required to pay, and

(d)   the assessment of costs.

(3)   Without prejudice to the generality of subsection (2), rules under that subsection may include provision about—

(a)   costs of the registrar, and

(b)   liability for costs thrown away as the result of neglect or delay by a legal representative of a party to proceedings.

(4)   An order under subsection (1) shall be enforceable as an order of the court.

(5)   A person aggrieved by an order under subsection (1) may appeal to a county court, which may make any order which appears appropriate.

Miscellaneous

77.   Duty to act reasonably

(1)   A person must not exercise any of the following rights without reasonable cause—

(a)   the right to lodge a caution under section 15,

(b)   the right to apply for the entry of a notice or restriction, and

(c)   the right to object to an application to the registrar.

(2)   The duty under this section is owed to any person who suffers damage in consequence of its breach.

78.   Notice of trust not to affect registrar

The registrar shall not be affected with notice of a trust.

PART 7
SPECIAL CASES

The Crown

79.   Voluntary registration of demesne land

(1)   Her Majesty may grant an estate in fee simple absolute in possession out of demesne land to Herself.

(2)   The grant of an estate under subsection (1) is to be regarded as not having been made unless an application under section 3 is made in respect of the estate before the end of the period for registration.

(3)   The period for registration is two months beginning with the date of the grant, or such longer period as the registrar may provide under subsection (4).

(4)   If on the application of Her Majesty the registrar is satisfied that there is a good reason for doing so, he may by order provide that the period for registration ends on such later date as he may specify in the order.

(5)   If an order under subsection (4) is made in a case where subsection (2) has already applied, that application of the subsection is to be treated as not having occurred.

80.   Compulsory registration of grants out of demesne land

(1)   Section 4(1) shall apply as if the following were included among the events listed—

    (a)   the grant by Her Majesty out of demesne land of an estate in fee simple absolute in possession, otherwise than under section 79;

    (b)   the grant by Her Majesty out of demesne land of an estate in land—

        (i)   for a term of years absolute of more than seven years from the date of the grant, and

        (ii)   for valuable or other consideration, by way of gift or in pursuance of an order of any court.

(2)   In subsection (1)(b)(ii), the reference to grant by way of gift includes grant for the purpose of constituting a trust under which Her Majesty does not retain the whole of the beneficial interest.

(3)   Subsection (1) does not apply to the grant of an estate in mines and minerals held apart from the surface.

(4)   The Lord Chancellor may by order—

    (a)   amend this section so as to add to the events in subsection (1) such events relating to demesne land as he may specify in the order, and

    (b)   make such consequential amendments of any provision of, or having effect under, any Act as he thinks appropriate.

(5)   In its application by virtue of subsection (1), section 7 has effect with the substitution for subsection (2) of—

     '(2)   On the application of subsection (1), the grant has effect as a contract made for valuable consideration to grant the legal estate concerned.'

81.   Demesne land: cautions against first registration

(1)   Section 15 shall apply as if demesne land were held by Her Majesty for an unregistered estate in fee simple absolute in possession.

(2)   The provisions of this Act relating to cautions against first registration shall, in relation to cautions lodged by virtue of subsection (1), have effect subject to such modifications as rules may provide.

82.   Escheat etc

(1)   Rules may make provision about—

    (a)   the determination of a registered freehold estate in land, and

    (b)   the registration of an unregistered freehold legal estate in land in respect of land to which a former registered freehold estate in land related.

(2)   Rules under this section may, in particular—

    (a)   make provision for determination to be dependent on the meeting of such registration requirements as the rules may specify;

    (b)   make provision for entries relating to a freehold estate in land to continue in the register, notwithstanding determination, for such time as the rules may provide;

    (c)   make provision for the making in the register in relation to a former freehold estate in land of such entries as the rules may provide;

    (d)   make provision imposing requirements to be met in connection with an application for the registration of such an unregistered estate as is mentioned in subsection (1)(b).

83.   Crown and Duchy land: representation

(1)   With respect to a Crown or Duchy interest, the appropriate authority—

    (a)   may represent the owner of the interest for all purposes of this Act,

    (b)   is entitled to receive such notice as that person is entitled to receive under this Act, and

(c) may make such applications and do such other acts as that person is entitled to make or do under this Act.

(2) In this section—

'the appropriate authority' means—

(a) in relation to an interest belonging to Her Majesty in right of the Crown and forming part of the Crown Estate, the Crown Estate Commissioners;

(b) in relation to any other interest belonging to Her Majesty in right of the Crown, the government department having the management of the interest or, if there is no such department, such person as Her Majesty may appoint in writing under the Royal Sign Manual;

(c) in relation to an interest belonging to Her Majesty in right of the Duchy of Lancaster, the Chancellor of the Duchy;

(d) in relation to an interest belonging to the Duchy of Cornwall, such person as the Duke of Cornwall, or the possessor for the time being of the Duchy of Cornwall, appoints;

(e) in relation to an interest belonging to a government department, or held in trust for Her Majesty for the purposes of a government department, that department;

'Crown interest' means an interest belonging to Her Majesty in right of the Crown, or belonging to a government department, or held in trust for Her Majesty for the purposes of a government department;

'Duchy interest' means an interest belonging to Her Majesty in right of the Duchy of Lancaster, or belonging to the Duchy of Cornwall;

'interest' means any estate, interest or charge in or over land and any right or claim in relation to land.

84. Disapplication of requirements relating to Duchy land

Nothing in any enactment relating to the Duchy of Lancaster or the Duchy of Cornwall shall have effect to impose any requirement with respect to formalities or enrolment in relation to a disposition by a registered proprietor.

85. Bona vacantia

Rules may make provision about how the passing of a registered estate or charge as bona vacantia is to be dealt with for the purposes of this Act.

Pending actions etc

86. Bankruptcy

(1) In this Act, references to an interest affecting an estate or charge do not include a petition in bankruptcy or bankruptcy order.

(2) As soon as practicable after registration of a petition in bankruptcy as a pending action under the Land Charges Act 1972 (c. 61), the registrar must enter in the register in relation to any registered estate or charge which appears to him to be affected a notice in respect of the pending action.

(3) Unless cancelled by the registrar in such manner as rules may provide, a notice entered under subsection (2) continues in force until—

(a) a restriction is entered in the register under subsection (4), or

(b) the trustee in bankruptcy is registered as proprietor.

(4) As soon as practicable after registration of a bankruptcy order under the Land Charges Act 1972, the registrar must, in relation to any registered estate or charge which

appears to him to be affected by the order, enter in the register a restriction reflecting the effect of the Insolvency Act 1986 (c. 45).

(5)   Where the proprietor of a registered estate or charge is adjudged bankrupt, the title of his trustee in bankruptcy is void as against a person to whom a registrable disposition of the estate or charge is made if—

    (a)   the disposition is made for valuable consideration,

    (b)   the person to whom the disposition is made acts in good faith, and

    (c)   at the time of the disposition—

        (i)   no notice or restriction is entered under this section in relation to the registered estate or charge, and

       (ii)   the person to whom the disposition is made has no notice of the bankruptcy petition or the adjudication.

(6)   Subsection (5) only applies if the relevant registration requirements are met in relation to the disposition, but, when they are met, has effect as from the date of the disposition.

(7)   Nothing in this section requires a person to whom a registrable disposition is made to make any search under the Land Charges Act 1972.

87.   Pending land actions, writs, orders and deeds of arrangement

(1)   Subject to the following provisions, references in this Act to an interest affecting an estate or charge include—

    (a)   a pending land action within the meaning of the Land Charges Act 1972,

    (b)   a writ or order of the kind mentioned in section 6(1)(a) of that Act (writ or order affecting land issued or made by any court for the purposes of enforcing a judgment or recognisance),

    (c)   an order appointing a receiver or sequestrator, and

    (d)   a deed of arrangement.

(2)   No notice may be entered in the register in respect of—

    (a)   an order appointing a receiver or sequestrator, or

    (b)   a deed of arrangement.

(3)   None of the matters mentioned in subsection (1) shall be capable of falling within paragraph 2 of Schedule 1 or 3.

(4)   In its application to any of the matters mentioned in subsection (1), this Act shall have effect subject to such modifications as rules may provide.

(5)   In this section, 'deed of arrangement' has the same meaning as in the Deeds of Arrangement Act 1914 (c. 47).

Miscellaneous

88.   Incorporeal hereditaments

In its application to—

    (a)   rentcharges,

    (b)   franchises,

    (c)   profits a prendre in gross, or

    (d)   manors,

this Act shall have effect subject to such modification as rules may provide.

89.   Settlements

(1)   Rules may make provision for the purposes of this Act in relation to the application to registered land of the enactments relating to settlements under the Settled Land Act 1925 (c. 18).

(2)   Rules under this section may include provision modifying any of those enactments in its application to registered land.

(3)   In this section, 'registered land' means an interest the title to which is, or is required to be, registered.

90.   PPP leases relating to transport in London

(1)   No application for registration under section 3 may be made in respect of a leasehold estate in land under a PPP lease.

(2)   The requirement of registration does not apply on the grant or transfer of a leasehold estate in land under a PPP lease.

(3)   For the purposes of section 27, the following are not dispositions requiring to be completed by registration—

(a)   the grant of a term of years absolute under a PPP lease;

(b)   the express grant of an interest falling within section 1(2) of the Law of Property Act 1925 (c. 20), where the interest is created for the benefit of a leasehold estate in land under a PPP lease.

(4)   No notice may be entered in the register in respect of an interest under a PPP lease.

(5)   Schedules 1 and 3 have effect as if they included a paragraph referring to a PPP lease.

(6)   In this section, 'PPP lease' has the meaning given by section 218 of the Greater London Authority Act 1999 (c. 29) (which makes provision about leases created for public-private partnerships relating to transport in London).

PART 8
ELECTRONIC CONVEYANCING

91.   Electronic dispositions: formalities

(1)   This section applies to a document in electronic form where—

(a)   the document purports to effect a disposition which falls within subsection (2), and

(b)   the conditions in subsection (3) are met.

(2)   A disposition falls within this subsection if it is—

(a)   a disposition of a registered estate or charge,

(b)   a disposition of an interest which is the subject of a notice in the register, or

(c)   a disposition which triggers the requirement of registration,

which is of a kind specified by rules.

(3)   The conditions referred to above are that—

(a)   the document makes provision for the time and date when it takes effect,

(b)   the document has the electronic signature of each person by whom it purports to be authenticated,

(c)   each electronic signature is certified, and

(d)   such other conditions as rules may provide are met.

(4)   A document to which this section applies is to be regarded as—

(a)   in writing, and

(b)   signed by each individual, and sealed by each corporation, whose electronic signature it has.

(5)   A document to which this section applies is to be regarded for the purposes of any enactment as a deed.

(6)   If a document to which this section applies is authenticated by a person as agent, it is to be regarded for the purposes of any enactment as authenticated by him under the written authority of his principal.

(7)   If notice of an assignment made by means of a document to which this section applies is given in electronic form in accordance with rules, it is to be regarded for the purposes of any enactment as given in writing.

(8)   The right conferred by section 75 of the Law of Property Act 1925 (c. 20) (purchaser's right to have the execution of a conveyance attested) does not apply to a document to which this section applies.

(9)   If subsection (4) of section 36A of the Companies Act 1985 (c. 6) (execution of documents) applies to a document because of subsection (4) above, subsection (6) of that section (presumption of due execution) shall have effect in relation to the document with the substitution of 'authenticated' for 'signed'.

(10)   In this section, references to an electronic signature and to the certification of such a signature are to be read in accordance with section 7(2) and (3) of the Electronic Communications Act 2000 (c. 7).

92.   Land registry network

(1)   The registrar may provide, or arrange for the provision of, an electronic communications network for use for such purposes as he thinks fit relating to registration or the carrying on of transactions which—

(a)   involve registration, and

(b)   are capable of being effected electronically.

(2)   Schedule 5 (which makes provision in connection with a network provided under subsection (1) and transactions carried on by means of such a network) has effect.

93.   Power to require simultaneous registration

(1)   This section applies to a disposition of—

(a)   a registered estate or charge, or

(b)   an interest which is the subject of a notice in the register,

where the disposition is of a description specified by rules.

(2)   A disposition to which this section applies, or a contract to make such a disposition, only has effect if it is made by means of a document in electronic form and if, when the document purports to take effect—

(a)   it is electronically communicated to the registrar, and

(b)   the relevant registration requirements are met.

(3)   For the purposes of subsection (2)(b), the relevant registration requirements are—

(a)   in the case of a registrable disposition, the requirements under Schedule 2, and

(b)   in the case of any other disposition, or a contract, such requirements as rules may provide.

(4)   Section 27(1) does not apply to a disposition to which this section applies.

(5)   Before making rules under this section the Lord Chancellor must consult such persons as he considers appropriate.

(6)   In this section, 'disposition', in relation to a registered charge, includes postponement.

94.   Electronic settlement

The registrar may take such steps as he thinks fit for the purpose of securing the provision of a system of electronic settlement in relation to transactions involving registration.

95.   Supplementary

Rules may—

   (a)· make provision about the communication of documents in electronic form to the registrar;

   (b) make provision about the electronic storage of documents communicated to the registrar in electronic form.

PART 9
ADVERSE POSSESSION

96. Disapplication of periods of limitation

(1) No period of limitation under section 15 of the Limitation Act 1980 (c. 58) (time limits in relation to recovery of land) shall run against any person, other than a chargee, in relation to an estate in land or rentcharge the title to which is registered.

(2) No period of limitation under section 16 of that Act (time limits in relation to redemption of land) shall run against any person in relation to such an estate in land or rentcharge.

(3) Accordingly, section 17 of that Act (extinction of title on expiry of time limit) does not operate to extinguish the title of any person where, by virtue of this section, a period of limitation does not run against him.

97. Registration of adverse possessor

Schedule 6 (which makes provision about the registration of an adverse possessor of an estate in land or rentcharge) has effect.

98. Defences

(1) A person has a defence to an action for possession of land if—

   (a) on the day immediately preceding that on which the action was brought he was entitled to make an application under paragraph 1 of Schedule 6 to be registered as the proprietor of an estate in the land, and

   (b) had he made such an application on that day, the condition in paragraph 5(4) of that Schedule would have been satisfied.

(2) A judgment for possession of land ceases to be enforceable at the end of the period of two years beginning with the date of the judgment if the proceedings in which the judgment is given were commenced against a person who was at that time entitled to make an application under paragraph 1 of Schedule 6.

(3) A person has a defence to an action for possession of land if on the day immediately preceding that on which the action was brought he was entitled to make an application under paragraph 6 of Schedule 6 to be registered as the proprietor of an estate in the land.

(4) A judgment for possession of land ceases to be enforceable at the end of the period of two years beginning with the date of the judgment if, at the end of that period, the person against whom the judgment was given is entitled to make an application under paragraph 6 of Schedule 6 to be registered as the proprietor of an estate in the land.

(5) Where in any proceedings a court determines that—

   (a) a person is entitled to a defence under this section, or

   (b) a judgment for possession has ceased to be enforceable against a person by virtue of subsection (4),

the court must order the registrar to register him as the proprietor of the estate in relation to which he is entitled to make an application under Schedule 6.

(6) The defences under this section are additional to any other defences a person may have.

(7) Rules may make provision to prohibit the recovery of rent due under a rentcharge from a person who has been in adverse possession of the rentcharge.

PART 10

LAND REGISTRY

Administration

99. The land registry

(1)   There is to continue to be an office called Her Majesty's Land Registry which is to deal with the business of registration under this Act.

(2)   The land registry is to consist of—

  (a)   the Chief Land Registrar, who is its head, and

  (b)   the staff appointed by him;

and references in this Act to a member of the land registry are to be read accordingly.

(3)   The Lord Chancellor shall appoint a person to be the Chief Land Registrar.

(4)   Schedule 7 (which makes further provision about the land registry) has effect.

100.   Conduct of business

(1)   Any function of the registrar may be carried out by any member of the land registry who is authorised for the purpose by the registrar.

(2)   The Lord Chancellor may by regulations make provision about the carrying out of functions during any vacancy in the office of registrar.

(3)   The Lord Chancellor may by order designate a particular office of the land registry as the proper office for the receipt of applications or a specified description of application.

(4)   The registrar may prepare and publish such forms and directions as he considers necessary or desirable for facilitating the conduct of the business of registration under this Act.

101.   Annual report

(1)   The registrar must make an annual report on the business of the land registry to the Lord Chancellor.

(2)   The registrar must publish every report under this section and may do so in such manner as he thinks fit.

(3)   The Lord Chancellor must lay copies of every report under this section before Parliament.

Fees and indemnities

102.   Fee orders

The Lord Chancellor may with the advice and assistance of the body referred to in section 127(2) (the Rule Committee), and the consent of the Treasury, by order—

  (a)   prescribe fees to be paid in respect of dealings with the land registry, except under section 69(3)(b) or 105;

  (b)   make provision about the payment of prescribed fees.

103.   Indemnities

Schedule 8 (which makes provision for the payment of indemnities by the registrar) has effect.

Miscellaneous

104.   General information about land

The registrar may publish information about land in England and Wales if it appears to him to be information in which there is legitimate public interest.

105. Consultancy and advisory services

(1)   The registrar may provide, or arrange for the provision of, consultancy or advisory services about the registration of land in England and Wales or elsewhere.

(2)   The terms on which services are provided under this section by the registrar, in particular terms as to payment, shall be such as he thinks fit.

106. Incidental powers: companies

(1)   If the registrar considers it expedient to do so in connection with his functions under section 69(3)(a), 92(1), 94 or 105(1) or paragraph 10 of Schedule 5, he may—

(a)   form, or participate in the formation of, a company, or

(b)   purchase, or invest in, a company.

(2)   In this section—

'company' means a company within the meaning of the Companies Act 1985 (c. 6);

'invest' means invest in any way (whether by acquiring assets, securities or rights or otherwise).

(3)   This section is without prejudice to any powers of the registrar exercisable otherwise than by virtue of this section.

PART 11
ADJUDICATION

107. The adjudicator

(1)   The Lord Chancellor shall appoint a person to be the Adjudicator to Her Majesty's Land Registry.

(2)   To be qualified for appointment under subsection (1), a person must have a 10 year general qualification (within the meaning of section 71 of the Courts and Legal Services Act 1990 (c. 41)).

(3)   Schedule 9 (which makes further provision about the adjudicator) has effect.

108. Jurisdiction

(1)   The adjudicator has the following functions—

(a)   determining matters referred to him under section 73(7), and

(b)   determining appeals under paragraph 4 of Schedule 5.

(2)   Also, the adjudicator may, on application, make any order which the High Court could make for the rectification or setting aside of a document which—

(a)   effects a qualifying disposition of a registered estate or charge,

(b)   is a contract to make such a disposition, or

(c)   effects a transfer of an interest which is the subject of a notice in the register.

(3)   For the purposes of subsection (2)(a), a qualifying disposition is—

(a)   a registrable disposition, or

(b)   a disposition which creates an interest which may be the subject of a notice in the register.

(4)   The general law about the effect of an order of the High Court for the rectification or setting aside of a document shall apply to an order under this section.

109. Procedure

(1)   Hearings before the adjudicator shall be held in public, except where he is satisfied that exclusion of the public is just and reasonable.

(2)   Subject to that, rules may regulate the practice and procedure to be followed with respect to proceedings before the adjudicator and matters incidental to or consequential on such proceedings.

(3)   Rules under subsection (2) may, in particular, make provision about—

    (a)   when hearings are to be held,

    (b)   requiring persons to attend hearings to give evidence or to produce documents,

    (c)   the form in which any decision of the adjudicator is to be given,

    (d)   payment of costs of a party to proceedings by another party to the proceedings, and

    (e)   liability for costs thrown away as the result of neglect or delay by a legal representative of a party to proceedings.

110.   Functions in relation to disputes

(1)   In proceedings on a reference under section 73(7), the adjudicator may, instead of deciding a matter himself, direct a party to the proceedings to commence proceedings within a specified time in the court for the purpose of obtaining the court's decision on the matter.

(2)   Rules may make provision about the reference under subsection (1) of matters to the court and may, in particular, make provision about—

    (a)   adjournment of the proceedings before the adjudicator pending the outcome of the proceedings before the court, and

    (b)   the powers of the adjudicator in the event of failure to comply with a direction under subsection (1).

(3)   Rules may make provision about the functions of the adjudicator in consequence of a decision on a reference under section 73(7) and may, in particular, make provision enabling the adjudicator to determine, or give directions about the determination of—

    (a)   the application to which the reference relates, or

    (b)   such other present or future application to the registrar as the rules may provide.

(4)   If, in the case of a reference under section 73(7) relating to an application under paragraph 1 of Schedule 6, the adjudicator determines that it would be unconscionable because of an equity by estoppel for the registered proprietor to seek to dispossess the applicant, but that the circumstances are not such that the applicant ought to be registered as proprietor, the adjudicator—

    (a)   must determine how the equity due to the applicant is to be satisfied, and

    (b)   may for that purpose make any order that the High Court could make in the exercise of its equitable jurisdiction.

111.   Appeals

(1)   Subject to subsection (2), a person aggrieved by a decision of the adjudicator may appeal to the High Court.

(2)   In the case of a decision on an appeal under paragraph 4 of Schedule 5, only appeal on a point of law is possible.

(3)   If on an appeal under this section relating to an application under paragraph 1 of Schedule 6 the court determines that it would be unconscionable because of an equity by estoppel for the registered proprietor to seek to dispossess the applicant, but that the circumstances are not such that the applicant ought to be registered as proprietor, the court must determine how the equity due to the applicant is to be satisfied.

112.   Enforcement of orders etc

A requirement of the adjudicator shall be enforceable as an order of the court.

113.   Fees

The Lord Chancellor may by order—

    (a)   prescribe fees to be paid in respect of proceedings before the adjudicator;

    (b)   make provision about the payment of prescribed fees.

114. Supplementary

Power to make rules under this Part is exercisable by the Lord Chancellor.

PART 12

MISCELLANEOUS AND GENERAL

Miscellaneous

115. Rights of pre-emption

(1) A right of pre-emption in relation to registered land has effect from the time of creation as an interest capable of binding successors in title (subject to the rules about the effect of dispositions on priority).

(2) This section has effect in relation to rights of pre-emption created on or after the day on which this section comes into force.

116. Proprietary estoppel and mere equities

It is hereby declared for the avoidance of doubt that, in relation to registered land, each of the following—

(a) an equity by estoppel, and

(b) a mere equity,

has effect from the time the equity arises as an interest capable of binding successors in title (subject to the rules about the effect of dispositions on priority).

117. Reduction in unregistered interests with automatic protection

(1) Paragraphs 10 to 14 of Schedules 1 and 3 shall cease to have effect at the end of the period of ten years beginning with the day on which those Schedules come into force.

(2) If made before the end of the period mentioned in subsection (1), no fee may be charged for—

(a) an application to lodge a caution against first registration by virtue of an interest falling within any of paragraphs 10 to 14 of Schedule 1, or

(b) an application for the entry in the register of a notice in respect of an interest falling within any of paragraphs 10 to 14 of Schedule 3.

118. Power to reduce qualifying term

(1) The Lord Chancellor may by order substitute for the term specified in any of the following provisions—

(a) section 3(3),

(b) section 4(1)(c)(i) and (2)(b),

(c) section 15(3)(a)(ii),

(d) section 27(2)(b)(i),

(e) section 80(1)(b)(i),

(f) paragraph 1 of Schedule 1,

(g) paragraphs 4(1), 5(1) and 6(1) of Schedule 2, and

(h) paragraph 1 of Schedule 3,

such shorter term as he thinks fit.

(2) An order under this section may contain such transitional provision as the Lord Chancellor thinks fit.

(3) Before making an order under this section, the Lord Chancellor must consult such persons as he considers appropriate.

119. Power to deregister manors

On the application of the proprietor of a registered manor, the registrar may remove the title to the manor from the register.

120. Conclusiveness of filed copies etc

(1) This section applies where—

    (a) a disposition relates to land to which a registered estate relates, and

    (b) an entry in the register relating to the registered estate refers to a document kept by the registrar which is not an original.

(2) As between the parties to the disposition, the document kept by the registrar is to be taken—

    (a) to be correct, and

    (b) to contain all the material parts of the original document.

(3) No party to the disposition may require production of the original document.

(4) No party to the disposition is to be affected by any provision of the original document which is not contained in the document kept by the registrar.

121. Forwarding of applications to registrar of companies

The Lord Chancellor may by rules make provision about the transmission by the registrar to the registrar of companies (within the meaning of the Companies Act 1985 (c. 6)) of applications under—

    (a) Part 12 of that Act (registration of charges), or

    (b) Chapter 3 of Part 23 of that Act (corresponding provision for oversea companies).

122. Repeal of Land Registry Act 1862

(1) The Land Registry Act 1862 (c. 53) shall cease to have effect.

(2) The registrar shall have custody of records of title made under that Act.

(3) The registrar may discharge his duty under subsection (2) by keeping the relevant information in electronic form.

(4) The registrar may on application provide a copy of any information included in a record of title made under that Act.

(5) Rules may make provision about applications for the exercise of the power conferred by subsection (4).

Offences etc

123. Suppression of information

(1) A person commits an offence if in the course of proceedings relating to registration under this Act he suppresses information with the intention of—

    (a) concealing a person's right or claim, or

    (b) substantiating a false claim.

(2) A person guilty of an offence under this section is liable—

    (a) on conviction on indictment, to imprisonment for a term not exceeding two years or to a fine;

    (b) on summary conviction, to imprisonment for a term not exceeding six months or to a fine not exceeding the statutory maximum, or to both.

124. Improper alteration of the registers

(1) A person commits an offence if he dishonestly induces another—

    (a) to change the register of title or cautions register, or

    (b) to authorise the making of such a change.

(2)   A person commits an offence if he intentionally or recklessly makes an unauthorised change in the register of title or cautions register.

(3)   A person guilty of an offence under this section is liable—

    (a)   on conviction on indictment, to imprisonment for a term not exceeding 2 years or to a fine;

    (b)   on summary conviction, to imprisonment for a term not exceeding six months or to a fine not exceeding the statutory maximum, or to both.

(4)   In this section, references to changing the register of title include changing a document referred to in it.

125.   Privilege against self-incrimination

(1)   The privilege against self-incrimination, so far as relating to offences under this Act, shall not entitle a person to refuse to answer any question or produce any document or thing in any legal proceedings other than criminal proceedings.

(2)   No evidence obtained under subsection (1) shall be admissible in any criminal proceedings under this Act against the person from whom it was obtained or that person's spouse.

Land registration rules

126.   Miscellaneous and general powers

Schedule 10 (which contains miscellaneous and general land registration rule-making powers) has effect.

127.   Exercise of powers

(1)   Power to make land registration rules is exercisable by the Lord Chancellor with the advice and assistance of the Rule Committee.

(2)   The Rule Committee is a body consisting of—

    (a)   a judge of the Chancery Division of the High Court nominated by the Lord Chancellor,

    (b)   the registrar,

    (c)   a person nominated by the General Council of the Bar,

    (d)   a person nominated by the Council of the Law Society,

    (e)   a person nominated by the Council of Mortgage Lenders,

    (f)   a person nominated by the Council of Licensed Conveyancers,

    (g)   a person nominated by the Royal Institution of Chartered Surveyors,

    (h)   a person with experience in, and knowledge of, consumer affairs, and

    (i)   any person nominated under subsection (3).

(3)   The Lord Chancellor may nominate to be a member of the Rule Committee any person who appears to him to have qualifications or experience which would be of value to the committee in considering any matter with which it is concerned.

Supplementary

128.   Rules, regulations and orders

(1)   Any power of the Lord Chancellor to make rules, regulations or orders under this Act includes power to make different provision for different cases.

(2)   Any power of the Lord Chancellor to make rules, regulations or orders under this Act is exercisable by statutory instrument.

(3)   A statutory instrument containing—

    (a)   regulations under section 100(2), or

(b)   an order under section 100(3), 102 or 113,
is to be laid before Parliament after being made.

(4)   A statutory instrument containing—

(a)   land registration rules,

(b)   rules under Part 11 or section 121,

(c)   regulations under paragraph 5 of Schedule 9, or

(d)   an order under section 5(1), 62(9), 80(4), 118(1) or 130,

is subject to annulment in pursuance of a resolution of either House of Parliament.

(5)   Rules under section 93 or paragraph 1, 2 or 3 of Schedule 5 shall not be made unless a draft of the rules has been laid before and approved by resolution of each House of Parliament.

129.   Crown application

This Act binds the Crown.

130.   Application to internal waters

This Act applies to land covered by internal waters of the United Kingdom which are—

(a)   within England or Wales, or

(b)   adjacent to England or Wales and specified for the purposes of this section by order made by the Lord Chancellor.

131.   'Proprietor in possession'

(1)   For the purposes of this Act, land is in the possession of the proprietor of a registered estate in land if it is physically in his possession, or in that of a person who is entitled to be registered as the proprietor of the registered estate.

(2)   In the case of the following relationships, land which is (or is treated as being) in the possession of the second-mentioned person is to be treated for the purposes of subsection (1) as in the possession of the first-mentioned person—

(a)   landlord and tenant;

(b)   mortgagor and mortgagee;

(c)   licensor and licensee;

(d)   trustee and beneficiary.

(3)   In subsection (1), the reference to entitlement does not include entitlement under Schedule 6.

132.   General interpretation

(1)   In this Act—

'adjudicator' means the Adjudicator to Her Majesty's Land Registry;

'caution against first registration' means a caution lodged under section 15;

'cautions register' means the register kept under section 19(1);

'charge' means any mortgage, charge or lien for securing money or money's worth;

'demesne land' means land belonging to Her Majesty in right of the Crown which is not held for an estate in fee simple absolute in possession;

'land' includes—

(a)   buildings and other structures,

(b)   land covered with water, and

(c)   mines and minerals, whether or not held with the surface;

'land registration rules' means any rules under this Act, other than rules under section 93, Part 11, section 121 or paragraph 1, 2 or 3 of Schedule 5;

'legal estate' has the same meaning as in the Law of Property Act 1925 (c. 20);

'legal mortgage' has the same meaning as in the Law of Property Act 1925;

'mines and minerals' includes any strata or seam of minerals or substances in or under any land, and powers of working and getting any such minerals or substances;

'registrar' means the Chief Land Registrar;

'register' means the register of title, except in the context of cautions against first registration;

'registered' means entered in the register;

'registered charge' means a charge the title to which is entered in the register;

'registered estate' means a legal estate the title to which is entered in the register, other than a registered charge;

'registered land' means a registered estate or registered charge;

'registrable disposition' means a disposition which is required to be completed by registration under section 27;

'requirement of registration' means the requirement of registration under section 4;

'sub-charge' means a charge under section 23(2)(b);

'term of years absolute' has the same meaning as in the Law of Property Act 1925 (c. 20);

'valuable consideration' does not include marriage consideration or a nominal consideration in money.

(2)   In subsection (1), in the definition of 'demesne land', the reference to land belonging to Her Majesty does not include land in relation to which a freehold estate in land has determined, but in relation to which there has been no act of entry or management by the Crown.

(3)   In this Act—

(a)   references to the court are to the High Court or a county court,

(b)   references to an interest affecting an estate or charge are to an adverse right affecting the title to the estate or charge, and

(c)   references to the right to object to an application to the registrar are to the right under section 73.

Final provisions

133.   Minor and consequential amendments

Schedule 11 (which makes minor and consequential amendments) has effect.

134.   Transition

(1)   The Lord Chancellor may by order make such transitional provisions and savings as he thinks fit in connection with the coming into force of any of the provisions of this Act.

(2)   Schedule 12 (which makes transitional provisions and savings) has effect.

(3)   Nothing in Schedule 12 affects the power to make transitional provisions and savings under subsection (1); and an order under that subsection may modify any provision made by that Schedule.

135.   Repeals

The enactments specified in Schedule 13 (which include certain provisions which are already spent) are hereby repealed to the extent specified there.

136.   Short title, commencement and extent

(1)   This Act may be cited as the Land Registration Act 2002.

(2)   This Act shall come into force on such day as the Lord Chancellor may by order appoint, and different days may be so appointed for different purposes.

(3)   Subject to subsection (4), this Act extends to England and Wales only.

(4)   Any amendment or repeal by this Act of an existing enactment, other than—

    (a)   section 37 of the Requisitioned Land and War Works Act 1945 (c. 43), and

    (b)   Schedule 2A to the Building Societies Act 1986 (c. 53),

has the same extent as the enactment amended or repealed.

SCHEDULES

Sections 11 and 12   SCHEDULE 1
UNREGISTERED INTERESTS WHICH OVERRIDE FIRST REGISTRATION

Leasehold estates in land

1.   A leasehold estate in land granted for a term not exceeding seven years from the date of the grant, except for a lease the grant of which falls within section 4(1) (d), (e) or (f).

Interests of persons in actual occupation

2.   An interest belonging to a person in actual occupation, so far as relating to land of which he is in actual occupation, except for an interest under a settlement under the Settled Land Act 1925 (c. 18).

Easements and profits a prendre

3.   A legal easement or profit a prendre.

Customary and public rights

4.   A customary right.

5.   A public right.

Local land charges

6.   A local land charge.

Mines and minerals

7.   An interest in any coal or coal mine, the rights attached to any such interest and the rights of any person under section 38, 49 or 51 of the Coal Industry Act 1994 (c. 21).

8.   In the case of land to which title was registered before 1898, rights to mines and minerals (and incidental rights) created before 1898.

9.   In the case of land to which title was registered between 1898 and 1925 inclusive, rights to mines and minerals (and incidental rights) created before the date of registration of the title.

Miscellaneous

10.   A franchise.

11.   A manorial right.

12.   A right to rent which was reserved to the Crown on the granting of any freehold estate (whether or not the right is still vested in the Crown).

13.   A non-statutory right in respect of an embankment or sea or river wall.

14.   A right to payment in lieu of tithe.

Section 27   SCHEDULE 2
          REGISTRABLE DISPOSITIONS: REGISTRATION REQUIREMENTS

PART 1
REGISTERED ESTATES

Introductory

1. This Part deals with the registration requirements relating to those dispositions of registered estates which are required to be completed by registration.

Transfer

2.—(1) In the case of a transfer of whole or part, the transferee, or his successor in title, must be entered in the register as the proprietor.

(2) In the case of a transfer of part, such details of the transfer as rules may provide must be entered in the register in relation to the registered estate out of which the transfer is made.

Lease of estate in land

3.—(1) This paragraph applies to a disposition consisting of the grant out of an estate in land of a term of years absolute.

(2) In the case of a disposition to which this paragraph applies—

 (a) the grantee, or his successor in title, must be entered in the register as the proprietor of the lease, and

 (b) a notice in respect of the lease must be entered in the register.

Lease of franchise or manor

4.—(1) This paragraph applies to a disposition consisting of the grant out of a franchise or manor of a lease for a term of more than seven years from the date of the grant.

(2) In the case of a disposition to which this paragraph applies—

 (a) the grantee, or his successor in title, must be entered in the register as the proprietor of the lease, and

 (b) a notice in respect of the lease must be entered in the register.

5.—(1) This paragraph applies to a disposition consisting of the grant out of a franchise or manor of a lease for a term not exceeding seven years from the date of the grant.

(2) In the case of a disposition to which this paragraph applies, a notice in respect of the lease must be entered in the register.

Creation of independently registrable legal interest

6.—(1) This paragraph applies to a disposition consisting of the creation of a legal rentcharge or profit a prendre in gross, other than one created for, or for an interest equivalent to, a term of years absolute not exceeding seven years from the date of creation.

(2) In the case of a disposition to which this paragraph applies—

 (a) the grantee, or his successor in title, must be entered in the register as the proprietor of the interest created, and

 (b) a notice in respect of the interest created must be entered in the register.

(3) In sub-paragraph (1), the reference to a legal rentcharge or profit a prendre in gross is to one falling within section 1(2) of the Law of Property Act 1925 (c. 20).

Creation of other legal interest

7.—(1)   This paragraph applies to a disposition which—

  (a)   consists of the creation of an interest of a kind falling within section 1(2)(a), (b) or (e) of the Law of Property Act 1925, and

  (b)   is not a disposition to which paragraph 4, 5 or 6 applies.

  (2)   In the case of a disposition to which this paragraph applies—

  (a)   a notice in respect of the interest created must be entered in the register, and

  (b)   if the interest is created for the benefit of a registered estate, the proprietor of the registered estate must be entered in the register as its proprietor.

  (3)   Rules may provide for sub-paragraph (2) to have effect with modifications in relation to a right of entry over or in respect of a term of years absolute.

Creation of legal charge

8.   In the case of the creation of a charge, the chargee, or his successor in title, must be entered in the register as the proprietor of the charge.

PART 2
REGISTERED CHARGES

Introductory

9.   This Part deals with the registration requirements relating to those dispositions of registered charges which are required to be completed by registration.

Transfer

10.   In the case of a transfer, the transferee, or his successor in title, must be entered in the register as the proprietor.

Creation of sub-charge

11.   In the case of the creation of a sub-charge, the sub-chargee, or his successor in title, must be entered in the register as the proprietor of the sub-charge.

Sections 29 and 30   SCHEDULE 3
UNREGISTERED INTERESTS WHICH OVERRIDE REGISTERED DISPOSITIONS

Leasehold estates in land

1.   A leasehold estate in land granted for a term not exceeding seven years from the date of the grant, except for—

  (a)   a lease the grant of which falls within section 4(1)(d), (e) or (f);

  (b)   a lease the grant of which constitutes a registrable disposition.

Interests of persons in actual occupation

2.   An interest belonging at the time of the disposition to a person in actual occupation, so far as relating to land of which he is in actual occupation, except for—

  (a)   an interest under a settlement under the Settled Land Act 1925 (c. 18);

  (b)   an interest of a person of whom inquiry was made before the disposition and who failed to disclose the right when he could reasonably have been expected to do so;

  (c)   an interest—

(i)   which belongs to a person whose occupation would not have been obvious on a reasonably careful inspection of the land at the time of the disposition, and

(ii)   of which the person to whom the disposition is made does not have actual knowledge at that time;

(d)   a leasehold estate in land granted to take effect in possession after the end of the period of three months beginning with the date of the grant and which has not taken effect in possession at the time of the disposition.

Easements and profits a prendre

3.—(1)   A legal easement or profit a prendre, except for an easement, or a profit a prendre which is not registered under the Commons Registration Act 1965 (c. 64), which at the time of the disposition—

(a)   is not within the actual knowledge of the person to whom the disposition is made, and

(b)   would not have been obvious on a reasonably careful inspection of the land over which the easement or profit is exercisable.

(2)   The exception in sub-paragraph (1) does not apply if the person entitled to the easement or profit proves that it has been exercised in the period of one year ending with the day of the disposition.

Customary and public rights

4.   A customary right.

5.   A public right.

Local land charges

6.   A local land charge.

Mines and minerals

7.   An interest in any coal or coal mine, the rights attached to any such interest and the rights of any person under section 38, 49 or 51 of the Coal Industry Act 1994 (c. 21).

8.   In the case of land to which title was registered before 1898, rights to mines and minerals (and incidental rights) created before 1898.

9.   In the case of land to which title was registered between 1898 and 1925 inclusive, rights to mines and minerals (and incidental rights) created before the date of registration of the title.

Miscellaneous

10.   A franchise.

11.   A manorial right.

12.   A right to rent which was reserved to the Crown on the granting of any freehold estate (whether or not the right is still vested in the Crown).

13.   A non-statutory right in respect of an embankment or sea or river wall.

14.   A right to payment in lieu of tithe.

Section 65

SCHEDULE 4
ALTERATION OF THE REGISTER

Introductory

1.   In this Schedule, references to rectification, in relation to alteration of the register, are to alteration which—

    (a)   involves the correction of a mistake, and

    (b)   prejudicially affects the title of a registered proprietor.

Alteration pursuant to a court order

2.—(1)   The court may make an order for alteration of the register for the purpose of—

    (a)   correcting a mistake,

    (b)   bringing the register up to date, or

    (c)   giving effect to any estate, right or interest excepted from the effect of registration.

    (2)   An order under this paragraph has effect when served on the registrar to impose a duty on him to give effect to it.

3.—(1)   This paragraph applies to the power under paragraph 2, so far as relating to rectification.

    (2)   If alteration affects the title of the proprietor of a registered estate in land, no order may be made under paragraph 2 without the proprietor's consent in relation to land in his possession unless—

    (a)   he has by fraud or lack of proper care caused or substantially contributed to the mistake, or

    (b)   it would for any other reason be unjust for the alteration not to be made.

    (3)   If in any proceedings the court has power to make an order under paragraph 2, it must do so, unless there are exceptional circumstances which justify its not doing so.

    (4)   In sub-paragraph (2), the reference to the title of the proprietor of a registered estate in land includes his title to any registered estate which subsists for the benefit of the estate in land.

4.   Rules may—

    (a)   make provision about the circumstances in which there is a duty to exercise the power under paragraph 2, so far as not relating to rectification;

    (b)   make provision about the form of an order under paragraph 2;

    (c)   make provision about service of such an order.

Alteration otherwise than pursuant to a court order

5.   The registrar may alter the register for the purpose of—

    (a)   correcting a mistake,

    (b)   bringing the register up to date,

    (c)   giving effect to any estate, right or interest excepted from the effect of registration, or

    (d)   removing a superfluous entry.

6.—(1)   This paragraph applies to the power under paragraph 5, so far as relating to rectification.

    (2)   No alteration affecting the title of the proprietor of a registered estate in land may be made under paragraph 5 without the proprietor's consent in relation to land in his possession unless—

(a) he has by fraud or lack of proper care caused or substantially contributed to the mistake, or

(b) it would for any other reason be unjust for the alteration not to be made.

(3) If on an application for alteration under paragraph 5 the registrar has power to make the alteration, the application must be approved, unless there are exceptional circumstances which justify not making the alteration.

(4) In sub-paragraph (2), the reference to the title of the proprietor of a registered estate in land includes his title to any registered estate which subsists for the benefit of the estate in land.

7. Rules may—
(a) make provision about the circumstances in which there is a duty to exercise the power under paragraph 5, so far as not relating to rectification;
(b) make provision about how the register is to be altered in exercise of that power;
(c) make provision about applications for alteration under that paragraph, including provision requiring the making of such applications;
(d) make provision about procedure in relation to the exercise of that power, whether on application or otherwise.

Rectification and derivative interests

8. The powers under this Schedule to alter the register, so far as relating to rectification, extend to changing for the future the priority of any interest affecting the registered estate or charge concerned.

Costs in non-rectification cases

9.—(1) If the register is altered under this Schedule in a case not involving rectification, the registrar may pay such amount as he thinks fit in respect of any costs or expenses reasonably incurred by a person in connection with the alteration which have been incurred with the consent of the registrar.

(2) The registrar may make a payment under sub-paragraph (1) notwithstanding the absence of consent if—
(a) it appears to him—
(i) that the costs or expenses had to be incurred urgently, and
(ii) that it was not reasonably practicable to apply for his consent, or
(b) he has subsequently approved the incurring of the costs or expenses.

Section 92   SCHEDULE 5
                          LAND REGISTRY NETWORK

Access to network

1.—(1) A person who is not a member of the land registry may only have access to a land registry network under authority conferred by means of an agreement with the registrar.

(2) An agreement for the purposes of sub-paragraph (1) ('network access agreement') may authorise access for—
(a) the communication, posting or retrieval of information,
(b) the making of changes to the register of title or cautions register,
(c) the issue of official search certificates,
(d) the issue of official copies, or
(e) such other conveyancing purposes as the registrar thinks fit.

(3)   Rules may regulate the use of network access agreements to confer authority to carry out functions of the registrar.

(4)   The registrar must, on application, enter into a network access agreement with the applicant if the applicant meets such criteria as rules may provide.

Terms of access

2.—(1)   The terms on which access to a land registry network is authorised shall be such as the registrar thinks fit, subject to sub-paragraphs (3) and (4), and may, in particular, include charges for access.

(2)   The power under sub-paragraph (1) may be used, not only for the purpose of regulating the use of the network, but also for—

(a)   securing that the person granted access uses the network to carry on such qualifying transactions as may be specified in, or under, the agreement,

(b)   such other purpose relating to the carrying on of qualifying transactions as rules may provide, or

(c)   enabling network transactions to be monitored.

(3)   It shall be a condition of a network access agreement which enables the person granted access to use the network to carry on qualifying transactions that he must comply with any rules for the time being in force under paragraph 5.

(4)   Rules may regulate the terms on which access to a land registry network is authorised.

Termination of access

3.—(1)   The person granted access by a network access agreement may terminate the agreement at any time by notice to the registrar.

(2)   Rules may make provision about the termination of a network access agreement by the registrar and may, in particular, make provision about—

(a)   the grounds of termination,

(b)   the procedure to be followed in relation to termination, and

(c)   the suspension of termination pending appeal.

(3)   Without prejudice to the generality of sub-paragraph (2)(a), rules under that provision may authorise the registrar to terminate a network access agreement if the person granted access—

(a)   fails to comply with the terms of the agreement,

(b)   ceases to be a person with whom the registrar would be required to enter into a network access agreement conferring the authority which the agreement confers, or

(c)   does not meet such conditions as the rules may provide.

Appeals

4.—(1)   A person who is aggrieved by a decision of the registrar with respect to entry into, or termination of, a network access agreement may appeal against the decision to the adjudicator.

(2)   On determining an appeal under this paragraph, the adjudicator may give such directions as he considers appropriate to give effect to his determination.

(3)   Rules may make provision about appeals under this paragraph.

Network transaction rules

5.—(1)   Rules may make provision about how to go about network transactions.

(2) Rules under sub-paragraph (1) may, in particular, make provision about dealings with the land registry, including provision about—

    (a) the procedure to be followed, and

    (b) the supply of information (including information about unregistered interests).

Overriding nature of network access obligations

6. To the extent that an obligation not owed under a network access agreement conflicts with an obligation owed under such an agreement by the person granted access, the obligation not owed under the agreement is discharged.

Do-it-yourself conveyancing

7.—(1) If there is a land registry network, the registrar has a duty to provide such assistance as he thinks appropriate for the purpose of enabling persons engaged in qualifying transactions who wish to do their own conveyancing to do so by means of the network.

    (2) The duty under sub-paragraph (1) does not extend to the provision of legal advice.

Presumption of authority

8. Where—

    (a) a person who is authorised under a network access agreement to do so uses the network for the making of a disposition or contract, and

    (b) the document which purports to effect the disposition or to be the contract—

        (i) purports to be authenticated by him as agent, and

        (ii) contains a statement to the effect that he is acting under the authority of his principal,

he shall be deemed, in favour of any other party, to be so acting.

Management of network transactions

9.—(1) The registrar may use monitoring information for the purpose of managing network transactions and may, in particular, disclose such information to persons authorised to use the network, and authorise the further disclosure of information so disclosed, if he considers it is necessary or desirable to do so.

    (2) The registrar may delegate his functions under sub-paragraph (1), subject to such conditions as he thinks fit.

    (3) In sub-paragraph (1), 'monitoring information' means information provided in pursuance of provision in a network access agreement included under paragraph 2(2)(c).

Supplementary

10. The registrar may provide, or arrange for the provision of, education and training in relation to the use of a land registry network.

11.—(1) Power to make rules under paragraph 1, 2 or 3 is exercisable by the Lord Chancellor.

    (2) Before making such rules, the Lord Chancellor must consult such persons as he considers appropriate.

    (3) In making rules under paragraph 1 or 3(2)(a), the Lord Chancellor must have regard, in particular, to the need to secure—

    (a) the confidentiality of private information kept on the network,

    (b) competence in relation to the use of the network (in particular for the purpose of making changes), and

(c)   the adequate insurance of potential liabilities in connection with use of the network.

12.   In this Schedule—

'land registry network' means a network provided under section 92(1);

'network access agreement' has the meaning given by paragraph 1(2);

'network transaction' means a transaction carried on by means of a land registry network;

'qualifying transaction' means a transaction which—

(a)   involves registration, and

(b)   is capable of being effected electronically.

Section 97   SCHEDULE 6

REGISTRATION OF ADVERSE POSSESSOR

Right to apply for registration

1.—(1)   A person may apply to the registrar to be registered as the proprietor of a registered estate in land if he has been in adverse possession of the estate for the period of ten years ending on the date of the application.

(2)   A person may also apply to the registrar to be registered as the proprietor of a registered estate in land if—

(a)   he has in the period of six months ending on the date of the application ceased to be in adverse possession of the estate because of eviction by the registered proprietor, or a person claiming under the registered proprietor,

(b)   on the day before his eviction he was entitled to make an application under sub-paragraph (1), and

(c)   the eviction was not pursuant to a judgment for possession.

(3)   However, a person may not make an application under this paragraph if—

(a)   he is a defendant in proceedings which involve asserting a right to possession of the land, or

(b)   judgment for possession of the land has been given against him in the last two years.

(4)   For the purposes of sub-paragraph (1), the estate need not have been registered throughout the period of adverse possession.

Notification of application

2.—(1)   The registrar must give notice of an application under paragraph 1 to—

(a)   the proprietor of the estate to which the application relates,

(b)   the proprietor of any registered charge on the estate,

(c)   where the estate is leasehold, the proprietor of any superior registered estate,

(d)   any person who is registered in accordance with rules as a person to be notified under this paragraph, and

(e)   such other persons as rules may provide.

(2)   Notice under this paragraph shall include notice of the effect of paragraph 4.

Treatment of application

3.—(1)   A person given notice under paragraph 2 may require that the application to which the notice relates be dealt with under paragraph 5.

(2)   The right under this paragraph is exercisable by notice to the registrar given before the end of such period as rules may provide.

4.   If an application under paragraph 1 is not required to be dealt with under paragraph 5, the applicant is entitled to be entered in the register as the new proprietor of the estate.

5.—(1)   If an application under paragraph 1 is required to be dealt with under this paragraph, the applicant is only entitled to be registered as the new proprietor of the estate if any of the following conditions is met.

(2)   The first condition is that—

(a)   it would be unconscionable because of an equity by estoppel for the registered proprietor to seek to dispossess the applicant, and

(b)   the circumstances are such that the applicant ought to be registered as the proprietor.

(3)   The second condition is that the applicant is for some other reason entitled to be registered as the proprietor of the estate.

(4)   The third condition is that—

(a)   the land to which the application relates is adjacent to land belonging to the applicant,

(b)   the exact line of the boundary between the two has not been determined under rules under section 60,

(c)   for at least ten years of the period of adverse possession ending on the date of the application, the applicant (or any predecessor in title) reasonably believed that the land to which the application relates belonged to him, and

(d)   the estate to which the application relates was registered more than one year prior to the date of the application.

(5)   In relation to an application under paragraph 1(2), this paragraph has effect as if the reference in sub-paragraph (4)(c) to the date of the application were to the day before the date of the applicant's eviction.

Right to make further application for registration

6.—(1)   Where a person's application under paragraph 1 is rejected, he may make a further application to be registered as the proprietor of the estate if he is in adverse possession of the estate from the date of the application until the last day of the period of two years beginning with the date of its rejection.

(2)   However, a person may not make an application under this paragraph if—

(a)   he is a defendant in proceedings which involve asserting a right to possession of the land,

(b)   judgment for possession of the land has been given against him in the last two years, or

(c)   he has been evicted from the land pursuant to a judgment for possession.

7.   If a person makes an application under paragraph 6, he is entitled to be entered in the register as the new proprietor of the estate.

Restriction on applications

8.—(1)   No one may apply under this Schedule to be registered as the proprietor of an estate in land during, or before the end of twelve months after the end of, any period in which the existing registered proprietor is for the purposes of the Limitation (Enemies and War Prisoners) Act 1945 (8 & 9 Geo. 6 c. 16)—

(a)   an enemy, or

(b)   detained in enemy territory.

(2)   No one may apply under this Schedule to be registered as the proprietor of an estate in land during any period in which the existing registered proprietor is—

    (a)   unable because of mental disability to make decisions about issues of the kind to which such an application would give rise, or

    (b)   unable to communicate such decisions because of mental disability or physical impairment.

(3)   For the purposes of sub-paragraph (2), 'mental disability' means a disability or disorder of the mind or brain, whether permanent or temporary, which results in an impairment or disturbance of mental functioning.

(4)   Where it appears to the registrar that sub-paragraph (1) or (2) applies in relation to an estate in land, he may include a note to that effect in the register.

Effect of registration

9.—(1)   Where a person is registered as the proprietor of an estate in land in pursuance of an application under this Schedule, the title by virtue of adverse possession which he had at the time of the application is extinguished.

(2)   Subject to sub-paragraph (3), the registration of a person under this Schedule as the proprietor of an estate in land does not affect the priority of any interest affecting the estate.

(3)   Subject to sub-paragraph (4), where a person is registered under this Schedule as the proprietor of an estate, the estate is vested in him free of any registered charge affecting the estate immediately before his registration.

(4)   Sub-paragraph (3) does not apply where registration as proprietor is in pursuance of an application determined by reference to whether any of the conditions in paragraph 5 applies.

Apportionment and discharge of charges

10.—(1)   Where—

    (a)   a registered estate continues to be subject to a charge notwithstanding the registration of a person under this Schedule as the proprietor, and

    (b)   the charge affects property other than the estate,

the proprietor of the estate may require the chargee to apportion the amount secured by the charge at that time between the estate and the other property on the basis of their respective values.

(2)   The person requiring the apportionment is entitled to a discharge of his estate from the charge on payment of—

    (a)   the amount apportioned to the estate, and

    (b)   the costs incurred by the chargee as a result of the apportionment.

(3)   On a discharge under this paragraph, the liability of the chargor to the chargee is reduced by the amount apportioned to the estate.

(4)   Rules may make provision about apportionment under this paragraph, in particular, provision about—

    (a)   procedure,

    (b)   valuation,

    (c)   calculation of costs payable under sub-paragraph (2)(b), and

    (d)   payment of the costs of the chargor.

Meaning of 'adverse possession'

11.—(1)   A person is in adverse possession of an estate in land for the purposes of this Schedule if, but for section 96, a period of limitation under section 15 of the Limitation Act 1980 (c. 58) would run in his favour in relation to the estate.

(2) A person is also to be regarded for those purposes as having been in adverse possession of an estate in land—

    (a)   where he is the successor in title to an estate in the land, during any period of adverse possession by a predecessor in title to that estate, or

    (b)   during any period of adverse possession by another person which comes between, and is continuous with, periods of adverse possession of his own.

(3) In determining whether for the purposes of this paragraph a period of limitation would run under section 15 of the Limitation Act 1980, there are to be disregarded—

    (a)   the commencement of any legal proceedings, and

    (b)   paragraph 6 of Schedule 1 to that Act.

Trusts

12. A person is not to be regarded as being in adverse possession of an estate for the purposes of this Schedule at any time when the estate is subject to a trust, unless the interest of each of the beneficiaries in the estate is an interest in possession.

Crown foreshore

13.—(1) Where—

    (a)   a person is in adverse possession of an estate in land,

    (b)   the estate belongs to Her Majesty in right of the Crown or the Duchy of Lancaster or to the Duchy of Cornwall, and

    (c)   the land consists of foreshore,

paragraph 1(1) is to have effect as if the reference to ten years were to sixty years.

(2) For the purposes of sub-paragraph (1), land is to be treated as foreshore if it has been foreshore at any time in the previous ten years.

(3) In this paragraph, 'foreshore' means the shore and bed of the sea and of any tidal water, below the line of the medium high tide between the spring and neap tides.

Rentcharges

14. Rules must make provision to apply the preceding provisions of this Schedule to registered rentcharges, subject to such modifications and exceptions as the rules may provide.

Procedure

15. Rules may make provision about the procedure to be followed pursuant to an application under this Schedule.

Section 99   SCHEDULE 7
                             THE LAND REGISTRY

Holding of office by Chief Land Registrar

1.—(1) The registrar may at any time resign his office by written notice to the Lord Chancellor.

(2) The Lord Chancellor may remove the registrar from office if he is unable or unfit to discharge the functions of office.

(3) Subject to the above, a person appointed to be the registrar is to hold and vacate office in accordance with the terms of his appointment and, on ceasing to hold office, is eligible for reappointment.

Remuneration etc. of Chief Land Registrar

2.—(1) The Lord Chancellor shall pay the registrar such remuneration, and such travelling and other allowances, as the Lord Chancellor may determine.

(2) The Lord Chancellor shall—

    (a) pay such pension, allowances or gratuities as he may determine to or in respect of a person who is or has been the registrar, or

    (b) make such payments as he may determine towards provision for the payment of a pension, allowances or gratuities to or in respect of such a person.

(3) If, when a person ceases to be the registrar, the Lord Chancellor determines that there are special circumstances which make it right that the person should receive compensation, the Lord Chancellor may pay to the person by way of compensation a sum of such amount as he may determine.

Staff

3.—(1) The registrar may appoint such staff as he thinks fit.

(2) The terms and conditions of appointments under this paragraph shall be such as the registrar, with the approval of the Minister for the Civil Service, thinks fit.

Indemnity for members

4. No member of the land registry is to be liable in damages for anything done or omitted in the discharge or purported discharge of any function relating to land registration, unless it is shown that the act or omission was in bad faith.

Seal

5. The land registry is to continue to have a seal and any document purporting to be sealed with it is to be admissible in evidence without any further or other proof.

Documentary evidence

6. The Documentary Evidence Act 1868 (c. 37) has effect as if—

    (a) the registrar were included in the first column of the Schedule to that Act,

    (b) the registrar and any person authorised to act on his behalf were mentioned in the second column of that Schedule, and

    (c) the regulations referred to in that Act included any form or direction issued by the registrar or by any such person.

Parliamentary disqualification

7. In Part 3 of Schedule 1 to the House of Commons Disqualification Act 1975 (c. 24) (other disqualifying offices), there is inserted at the appropriate place—

'Chief Land Registrar.';

and a corresponding amendment is made in Part 3 of Schedule 1 to the Northern Ireland Assembly Disqualification Act 1975 (c. 25).

Section 103   SCHEDULE 8
                      INDEMNITIES

Entitlement

1.—(1) A person is entitled to be indemnified by the registrar if he suffers loss by reason of—

    (a) rectification of the register,

(b) a mistake whose correction would involve rectification of the register,

(c) a mistake in an official search,

(d) a mistake in an official copy,

(e) a mistake in a document kept by the registrar which is not an original and is referred to in the register,

(f) the loss or destruction of a document lodged at the registry for inspection or safe custody,

(g) a mistake in the cautions register, or

(h) failure by the registrar to perform his duty under section 50.

(2) For the purposes of sub-paragraph (1)(a)—

(a) any person who suffers loss by reason of the change of title under section 62 is to be regarded as having suffered loss by reason of rectification of the register, and

(b) the proprietor of a registered estate or charge claiming in good faith under a forged disposition is, where the register is rectified, to be regarded as having suffered loss by reason of such rectification as if the disposition had not been forged.

(3) No indemnity under sub-paragraph (1)(b) is payable until a decision has been made about whether to alter the register for the purpose of correcting the mistake; and the loss suffered by reason of the mistake is to be determined in the light of that decision.

Mines and minerals

2. No indemnity is payable under this Schedule on account of—

(a) any mines or minerals, or

(b) the existence of any right to work or get mines or minerals,

unless it is noted in the register that the title to the registered estate concerned includes the mines or minerals.

Costs

3.—(1) In respect of loss consisting of costs or expenses incurred by the claimant in relation to the matter, an indemnity under this Schedule is payable only on account of costs or expenses reasonably incurred by the claimant with the consent of the registrar.

(2) The requirement of consent does not apply where—

(a) the costs or expenses must be incurred by the claimant urgently, and

(b) it is not reasonably practicable to apply for the registrar's consent.

(3) If the registrar approves the incurring of costs or expenses after they have been incurred, they shall be treated for the purposes of this paragraph as having been incurred with his consent.

4.—(1) If no indemnity is payable to a claimant under this Schedule, the registrar may pay such amount as he thinks fit in respect of any costs or expenses reasonably incurred by the claimant in connection with the claim which have been incurred with the consent of the registrar.

(2) The registrar may make a payment under sub-paragraph (1) notwithstanding the absence of consent if—

(a) it appears to him—

(i) that the costs or expenses had to be incurred urgently, and

(ii) that it was not reasonably practicable to apply for his consent, or

(b) he has subsequently approved the incurring of the costs or expenses.

Claimant's fraud or lack of care

5.—(1)   No indemnity is payable under this Schedule on account of any loss suffered by a claimant—

(a)   wholly or partly as a result of his own fraud, or

(b)   wholly as a result of his own lack of proper care.

(2)   Where any loss is suffered by a claimant partly as a result of his own lack of proper care, any indemnity payable to him is to be reduced to such extent as is fair having regard to his share in the responsibility for the loss.

(3)   For the purposes of this paragraph any fraud or lack of care on the part of a person from whom the claimant derives title (otherwise than under a disposition for valuable consideration which is registered or protected by an entry in the register) is to be treated as if it were fraud or lack of care on the part of the claimant.

Valuation of estates etc.

6.   Where an indemnity is payable in respect of the loss of an estate, interest or charge, the value of the estate, interest or charge for the purposes of the indemnity is to be regarded as not exceeding—

(a)   in the case of an indemnity under paragraph 1(1)(a), its value immediately before rectification of the register (but as if there were to be no rectification), and

(b)   in the case of an indemnity under paragraph 1(1)(b), its value at the time when the mistake which caused the loss was made.

Determination of indemnity by court

7.—(1)   A person may apply to the court for the determination of any question as to—

(a)   whether he is entitled to an indemnity under this Schedule, or

(b)   the amount of such an indemnity.

(2)   Paragraph 3(1) does not apply to the costs of an application to the court under this paragraph or of any legal proceedings arising out of such an application.

Time limits

8.   For the purposes of the Limitation Act 1980 (c. 58)—

(a)   a liability to pay an indemnity under this Schedule is a simple contract debt, and

(b)   the cause of action arises at the time when the claimant knows, or but for his own default might have known, of the existence of his claim.

Interest

9.   Rules may make provision about the payment of interest on an indemnity under this Schedule, including—

(a)   the circumstances in which interest is payable, and

(b)   the periods for and rates at which it is payable.

Recovery of indemnity by registrar

10.—(1)   Where an indemnity under this Schedule is paid to a claimant in respect of any loss, the registrar is entitled (without prejudice to any other rights he may have)—

(a)   to recover the amount paid from any person who caused or substantially contributed to the loss by his fraud, or

(b)   for the purpose of recovering the amount paid, to enforce the rights of action referred to in sub-paragraph (2).

(2)   Those rights of action are—
    (a)   any right of action (of whatever nature and however arising) which the claimant
would have been entitled to enforce had the indemnity not been paid, and
    (b)   where the register has been rectified, any right of action (of whatever nature and
however arising) which the person in whose favour the register has been rectified
would have been entitled to enforce had it not been rectified.

(3)   References in this paragraph to an indemnity include interest paid on an indemnity
under rules under paragraph 9.

Interpretation

11.—(1)   For the purposes of this Schedule, references to a mistake in something include
anything mistakenly omitted from it as well as anything mistakenly included in it.

(2)   In this Schedule, references to rectification of the register are to alteration of the
register which—
    (a)   involves the correction of a mistake, and
    (b)   prejudicially affects the title of a registered proprietor.

Section 107   SCHEDULE 9
                                       THE ADJUDICATOR

Holding of office

1.—(1)   The adjudicator may at any time resign his office by written notice to the Lord
Chancellor.

(2)   The Lord Chancellor may remove the adjudicator from office on the ground of
incapacity or misbehaviour.

(3)   Section 26 of the Judicial Pensions and Retirement Act 1993 (c. 8) (compulsory
retirement at 70, subject to the possibility of annual extension up to 75) applies to the
adjudicator.

(4)   Subject to the above, a person appointed to be the adjudicator is to hold and vacate
office in accordance with the terms of his appointment and, on ceasing to hold office, is
eligible for reappointment.

Remuneration

2.—(1)   The Lord Chancellor shall pay the adjudicator such remuneration, and such other
allowances, as the Lord Chancellor may determine.

(2)   The Lord Chancellor shall—
    (a)   pay such pension, allowances or gratuities as he may determine to or in respect
of a person who is or has been the adjudicator, or
    (b)   make such payments as he may determine towards provision for the payment of
a pension, allowances or gratuities to or in respect of such a person.

(3)   Sub-paragraph (2) does not apply if the office of adjudicator is a qualifying judicial
office within the meaning of the Judicial Pensions and Retirement Act 1993.

(4)   If, when a person ceases to be the adjudicator, the Lord Chancellor determines that
there are special circumstances which make it right that the person should receive
compensation, the Lord Chancellor may pay to the person by way of compensation a sum
of such amount as he may determine.

Staff

3.—(1)   The adjudicator may appoint such staff as he thinks fit.

(2)   The terms and conditions of appointments under this paragraph shall be such as the adjudicator, with the approval of the Minister for the Civil Service, thinks fit.

Conduct of business

4.—(1)   Subject to sub-paragraph (2), any function of the adjudicator may be carried out by any member of his staff who is authorised by him for the purpose.

(2)   In the case of functions which are not of an administrative character, sub-paragraph (1) only applies if the member of staff has a 10 year general qualification (within the meaning of section 71 of the Courts and Legal Services Act 1990 (c. 41)).

5.   The Lord Chancellor may by regulations make provision about the carrying out of functions during any vacancy in the office of adjudicator.

Finances

6.   The Lord Chancellor shall be liable to reimburse expenditure incurred by the adjudicator in the discharge of his functions.

7.   The Lord Chancellor may require the registrar to make payments towards expenses of the Lord Chancellor under this Schedule.

Application of Tribunals and Inquiries Act 1992

8.   In Schedule 1 to the Tribunal and Inquiries Act 1992 (c. 53) (tribunals under the supervision of the Council on Tribunals), after paragraph 27 there is inserted—
'Land Registration — 27B. The Adjudicator to Her Majesty's Land Registry.'

Parliamentary disqualification

9.   In Part 1 of Schedule 1 to the House of Commons Disqualification Act 1975 (c. 24) (judicial offices), there is inserted at the end—
'Adjudicator to Her Majesty's Land Registry.';
and a corresponding amendment is made in Part 1 of Schedule 1 to the Northern Ireland Assembly Disqualification Act 1975 (c. 25).

Section 126   SCHEDULE 10
MISCELLANEOUS AND GENERAL POWERS

PART 1
MISCELLANEOUS

Dealings with estates subject to compulsory first registration

1.—(1)   Rules may make provision—
  (a)   applying this Act to a pre-registration dealing with a registrable legal estate as if the dealing had taken place after the date of first registration of the estate, and
  (b)   about the date on which registration of the dealing is effective.

(2)   For the purposes of sub-paragraph (1)—
  (a)   a legal estate is registrable if a person is subject to a duty under section 6 to make an application to be registered as the proprietor of it, and
  (b)   a pre-registration dealing is one which takes place before the making of such an application.

Regulation of title matters between sellers and buyers

2.—(1)   Rules may make provision about the obligations with respect to—

    (a)   proof of title, or

    (b)   perfection of title,

of the seller under a contract for the transfer, or other disposition, for valuable consideration of a registered estate or charge.

    (2)   Rules under this paragraph may be expressed to have effect notwithstanding any stipulation to the contrary.

Implied covenants

3.   Rules may—

    (a)   make provision about the form of provisions extending or limiting any covenant implied by virtue of Part 1 of the Law of Property (Miscellaneous Provisions) Act 1994 (c. 36) (implied covenants for title) on a registrable disposition;

    (b)   make provision about the application of section 77 of the Law of Property Act 1925 (c. 20) (implied covenants in conveyance subject to rents) to transfers of registered estates;

    (c)   make provision about reference in the register to implied covenants, including provision for the state of the register to be conclusive in relation to whether covenants have been implied.

Land certificates

4.   Rules may make provision about—

    (a)   when a certificate of registration of title to a legal estate may be issued,

    (b)   the form and content of such a certificate, and

    (c)   when such a certificate must be produced or surrendered to the registrar.

PART 2
GENERAL

Notice

5.—(1)   Rules may make provision about the form, content and service of notice under this Act.

    (2)   Rules under this paragraph about the service of notice may, in particular—

    (a)   make provision requiring the supply of an address for service and about the entry of addresses for service in the register;

    (b)   make provision about—

       (i)   the time for service,

      (ii)   the mode of service, and

     (iii)   when service is to be regarded as having taken place.

Applications

6.   Rules may—

    (a)   make provision about the form and content of applications under this Act;

    (b)   make provision requiring applications under this Act to be supported by such evidence as the rules may provide;

    (c)   make provision about when an application under this Act is to be taken as made;

    (d)   make provision about the order in which competing applications are to be taken to rank;

    (e)   make provision for an alteration made by the registrar for the purpose of correcting a mistake in an application or accompanying document to have effect in such circumstances as the rules may provide as if made by the applicant or other interested party or parties.

Statutory statements

7.   Rules may make provision about the form of any statement required under an enactment to be included in an instrument effecting a registrable disposition or a disposition which triggers the requirement of registration.

Residual power

8.   Rules may make any other provision which it is expedient to make for the purposes of carrying this Act into effect, whether similar or not to any provision which may be made under the other powers to make land registration rules.

Section 133

SCHEDULE 11
MINOR AND CONSEQUENTIAL AMENDMENTS

Settled Land Act 1925 (c. 18)

1.   Section 119(3) of the Settled Land Act 1925 ceases to have effect.

Law of Property Act 1925 (c. 20)

2.—(1)   The Law of Property Act 1925 is amended as follows.

(2)   In section 44, after subsection (4) there is inserted—

'(4A)   Subsections (2) and (4) of this section do not apply to a contract to grant a term of years if the grant will be an event within section 4(1) of the Land Registration Act 2002 (events which trigger compulsory first registration of title).'

(3)   In that section, in subsection (5), for 'the last three preceding subsections' there is substituted 'subsections (2) to (4) of this section'.

(4)   In that section, at the end there is inserted—

'(12)   Nothing in this section applies in relation to registered land or to a term of years to be derived out of registered land.'

(5)   In section 84(8), the words from ', but' to the end are omitted.

(6)   In section 85(3), for the words from the beginning to the second 'or' there is substituted 'Subsection (2) does not apply to registered land, but, subject to that, this section applies whether or not the land is registered land and whether or not'.

(7)   In section 86(3), for the words from the beginning to the second 'or' there is substituted 'Subsection (2) does not apply to registered land, but, subject to that, this section applies whether or not the land is registered land and whether or not'.

(8)   In section 87, at the end there is inserted—

'(4)   Subsection (1) of this section shall not be taken to be affected by section 23(1)(a) of the Land Registration Act 2002 (under which owner's powers in relation to a registered estate do not include power to mortgage by demise or sub-demise).'

(9)   In section 94(4), for the words from 'registered' to the end there is substituted 'on registered land'.

(10)   In section 97, for 'Land Registration Act 1925' there is substituted 'Land Registration Act 2002'.

(11)   In section 115(10), for the words from 'charge' to the end there is substituted 'registered charge (within the meaning of the Land Registration Act 2002)'.

(12)   In section 125(2), for the words from '(not being' to '1925)' there is substituted '(not being registered land)'.

(13)   In section 205(1)(xxii)—
  (a)   for 'Land Registration Act 1925' there is substituted 'Land Registration Act 2002;', and
  (b)   the words from ', and' to the end are omitted.

Administration of Estates Act 1925 (c. 23)

3.   In section 43(2) of the Administration of Estates Act 1925, for 'Land Registration Act 1925' there is substituted 'Land Registration Act 2002'.

Requisitioned Land and War Works Act 1945 (c. 43)

4.—(1)   Section 37 of the Requisitioned Land and War Works Act 1945 is amended as follows.

(2)   In subsection (2), for 'Land Registration Act 1925' there is substituted 'Land Registration Act 2002'.

(3)   Subsection (3) ceases to have effect.

Law of Property (Joint Tenants) Act 1964 (c. 63)

5.   In section 3 of the Law of Property (Joint Tenants) Act 1964, for the words from 'any land' to the end there is substituted 'registered land'.

Gas Act 1965 (c. 36)

6.—(1)   The Gas Act 1965 is amended as follows.

(2)   In section 12(3), for 'Land Registration Act 1925' there is substituted 'Land Registration Act 2002'.

(3)   In sections 12(4) and 13(6), for the words from 'be deemed' to the end there is substituted—
  '(a)   for the purposes of the Land Charges Act 1925, be deemed to be a charge affecting land falling within Class D(iii), and
  (b)   for the purposes of the Land Registration Act 2002, be deemed to be an equitable easement.'

Commons Registration Act 1965 (c. 64)

7.—(1)   The Commons Registration Act 1965 is amended as follows.

(2)   In sections 1(1), (2) and (3), 4(3) and 8(1), for 'under the Land Registration Acts 1925 and 1936' there is substituted 'in the register of title'.

(3)   In section 9, for 'the Land Registration Acts 1925 and 1936' there is substituted 'in the register of title'.

(4)   In section 12 (in both places), for 'under the Land Registration Acts 1925 and 1936' there is substituted 'in the register of title'.

(5)   In section 22, in subsection (1), there is inserted at the appropriate place—
  '"register of title" means the register kept under section 1 of the Land Registration Act 2002;'.

(6)   In that section, in subsection (2), for 'under the Land Registration Acts 1925 and 1936' there is substituted 'in the register of title'.

Leasehold Reform Act 1967 (c. 88)

8.—(1)   The Leasehold Reform Act 1967 is amended as follows.

(2)   In section 5(5)—

(a) for 'an overriding interest within the meaning of the Land Registration Act 1925' there is substituted 'regarded for the purposes of the Land Registration Act 2002 as an interest falling within any of the paragraphs of Schedule 1 or 3 to that Act', and

(b) for 'or caution under the Land Registration Act 1925' there is substituted 'under the Land Registration Act 2002'.

(3) In Schedule 4, in paragraph 1(3)—

(a) for paragraph (a) there is substituted—

'(a) the covenant may be the subject of a notice in the register of title kept under the Land Registration Act 2002, if apart from this subsection it would not be capable of being the subject of such a notice; and', and

(b) in paragraph (b), for 'notice of the covenant has been so registered, the covenant' there is substituted 'a notice in respect of the covenant has been entered in that register, it'.

Law of Property Act 1969 (c. 59)

9. In section 24(1) of the Law of Property Act 1969, for 'Land Registration Act 1925' there is substituted 'Land Registration Act 2002'.

Land Charges Act 1972 (c. 61)

10.—(1) The Land Charges Act 1972 is amended as follows.

(2) In section 14(1), for the words from 'Land Registration' to the end there is substituted 'Land Registration Act 2002'.

(3) In section 14(3)—

(a) for the words from 'section 123A' to 'register)' there is substituted 'section 7 of the Land Registration Act 2002 (effect of failure to comply with requirement of registration)', and

(b) for 'that section' there is substituted 'section 6 of that Act'.

(4) In section 17(1), in the definition of 'registered land', for 'Land Registration Act 1925' there is substituted 'Land Registration Act 2002'.

Consumer Credit Act 1974 (c. 39)

11. In section 177(1) and (6) of the Consumer Credit Act 1974, for 'Land Registration Act 1925' there is substituted 'Land Registration Act 2002'.

Solicitors Act 1974 (c. 47)

12.—(1) The Solicitors Act 1974 is amended as follows.

(2) In sections 22(1) and 56(1)(f), for 'Land Registration Act 1925' there is substituted 'Land Registration Act 2002'.

(3) Section 75(b) ceases to have effect.

Local Land Charges Act 1975 (c. 76)

13. In section 10(3)(b)(ii) of the Local Land Charges Act 1975, for 'under the Land Registration Act 1925' there is substituted 'in the register of title kept under the Land Registration Act 2002'.

Rent Act 1977 (c. 42)

14. In section 136(b) of the Rent Act 1977, for the words from 'charge' to the end there is substituted 'registered charge (within the meaning of the Land Registration Act 2002)'.

Charging Orders Act 1979 (c. 53)

15. In section 3(2) and (6) of the Charging Orders Act 1979, for 'Land Registration Act 1925' there is substituted 'Land Registration Act 2002'.

Highways Act 1980 (c. 66)

16. Section 251(5) of the Highways Act 1980 ceases to have effect.

Inheritance Tax Act 1984 (c. 51)

17. In section 238(3) of the Inheritance Tax Act 1984, for paragraph (a) there is substituted—
    '(a) in relation to registered land—
        (i) if the disposition is required to be completed by registration, the time of registration, and
        (ii) otherwise, the time of completion,'.

Housing Act 1985 (c. 68)

18.—(1) The Housing Act 1985 is amended as follows.
    (2) In section 37(5), for the words from 'and' to the end there is substituted—
    '(5A) Where the Chief Land Registrar approves an application for registration of—
        (a) a disposition of registered land, or
        (b) the disponee's title under a disposition of unregistered land,
and the instrument effecting the disposition contains a covenant of the kind mentioned in subsection (1), he must enter in the register a restriction reflecting the limitation imposed by the covenant'.
    (3) In section 154(5), for 'Land Registration Acts 1925 to 1971' there is substituted 'Land Registration Act 2002'.
    (4) In section 157(7), for the words from 'the appropriate' to the end there is substituted 'a restriction in the register of title reflecting the limitation'.
    (5) In section 165(6), for 'section 83 of the Land Registration Act 1925' there is substituted 'Schedule 8 to the Land Registration Act 2002'.
    (6) In Schedule 9A, in paragraph 2(2), for the words from the beginning to 'the disponor' there is substituted 'Where on a qualifying disposal the disponor's title to the dwelling-house is not registered, the disponor'.
    (7) In that Schedule, for paragraph 4 there is substituted—
    '4.—(1) This paragraph applies where the Chief Land Registrar approves an application for registration of—
        (a) a disposition of registered land, or
        (b) the disponee's title under a disposition of unregistered land,
        and the instrument effecting the disposition contains the statement required by paragraph 1.
    (2) The Chief Land Registrar must enter in the register—
        (a) a notice in respect of the rights of qualifying persons under this Part in relation to dwelling-houses comprised in the disposal, and
        (b) a restriction reflecting the limitation under section 171D(2) on subsequent disposal.'
    (8) In that Schedule, for paragraph 5(2) there is substituted—
    '(2) If the landlord's title is registered, the landlord shall apply for the entry in the register of—

    (a)   a notice in respect of the rights of the qualifying person or persons under the provisions of this Part, and

    (b)   a restriction reflecting the limitation under section 171D(2) on subsequent disposal.'

(9)   In that Schedule, paragraph 5(3) ceases to have effect.

(10)   In that Schedule, in paragraph 6, for sub-paragraph (1) there is substituted—

    '(1)   The rights of a qualifying person under this Part in relation to the qualifying dwelling house shall not be regarded as falling within Schedule 3 to the Land Registration Act 2002 (and so are liable to be postponed under section 29 of that Act, unless protected by means of a notice in the register).'

(11)   In that Schedule, in paragraph 9(2), for 'Land Registration Acts 1925 to 1986' there is substituted 'Land Registration Act 2002'.

(12)   In Schedule 17, in paragraph 2(2), for 'Land Registration Acts 1925 to 1971' there is substituted 'Land Registration Act 2002'.

(13)   In Schedule 20, in paragraph 17(2), for 'Land Registration Acts 1925 to 1986' there is substituted 'Land Registration Act 2002'.

Building Societies Act 1986 (c. 53)

19.—(1)   In Schedule 2A to the Building Societies Act 1986, paragraph 1 is amended as follows.

(2)   In sub-paragraph (2), for 'charge or incumbrance registered under the Land Registration Act 1925' there is substituted 'registered charge (within the meaning of the Land Registration Act 2002)'.

(3)   Sub-paragraph (4) ceases to have effect.

(4)   In sub-paragraph (5), the definition of 'registered land' and the preceding 'and' cease to have effect.

Landlord and Tenant Act 1987 (c. 31)

20.   In sections 24(8) and (9), 28(5), 30(6) and 34(9) of the Landlord and Tenant Act 1987, for 'Land Registration Act 1925' there is substituted 'Land Registration Act 2002'.

Diplomatic and Consular Premises Act 1987 (c. 46)

21.—(1)   The Diplomatic and Consular Premises Act 1987 is amended as follows.

(2)   In section 5, after the definition of the expression 'diplomatic premises' there is inserted—

    '"land" includes buildings and other structures, land covered with water and any estate, interest, easement, servitude or right in or over land,'.

(3)   In Schedule 1, in paragraph 1—

    (a)   before the definition of the expression 'the registrar' there is inserted—

       '"registered land" has the same meaning as in the Land Registration Act 2002;', and

    (b)   the words from 'and expressions' to the end are omitted.

Criminal Justice Act 1988 (c. 33)

22.—(1)   The Criminal Justice Act 1988 is amended as follows.

(2)   In section 77(12)—

    (a)   for 'Land Registration Act 1925' there is substituted 'Land Registration Act 2002', and

(b) in paragraph (a), at the end there is inserted ', except that no notice may be entered in the register of title under the Land Registration Act 2002 in respect of such orders'.

(3) In section 79(1) and (4), for 'Land Registration Act 1925' there is substituted 'Land Registration Act 2002'.

Housing Act 1988 (c. 50)

23.—(1) The Housing Act 1988 is amended as follows.

(2) In section 81, in subsection (9)(c), for 'Land Registration Acts 1925 to 1986' there is substituted 'Land Registration Act 2002'.

(3) In that section, for subsection (10) there is substituted—

'(10) Where the Chief Land Registrar approves an application for registration of—

(a) a disposition of registered land, or

(b) the approved person's title under a disposition of unregistered land,

and the instrument effecting the disposition contains the statement required by subsection (1) above, he shall enter in the register a restriction reflecting the limitation under this section on subsequent disposal.'

(4) In section 90(4), for 'Land Registration Act 1925' there is substituted 'Land Registration Act 2002'.

(5) In section 133, in subsection (8)—

(a) for the words 'conveyance, grant or assignment' there is substituted 'transfer or grant',

(b) for the words 'section 123 of the Land Registration Act 1925' there is substituted 'section 4 of the Land Registration Act 2002', and

(c) in paragraph (c), for 'Land Registration Acts 1925 to 1986' there is substituted 'Land Registration Act 2002'.

(6) In that section, for subsection (9) there is substituted—

'(9) Where the Chief Land Registrar approves an application for registration of—

(a) a disposition of registered land, or

(b) a person's title under a disposition of unregistered land,

and the instrument effecting the original disposal contains the statement required by subsection (3)(d) above, he shall enter in the register a restriction reflecting the limitation under this section on subsequent disposal.'

Local Government and Housing Act 1989 (c. 42)

24.—(1) Section 173 of the Local Government and Housing Act 1989 is amended as follows.

(2) In subsection (8)—

(a) for the words 'conveyance, grant or assignment' there is substituted 'transfer or grant',

(b) for the words 'section 123 of the Land Registration Act 1925' there is substituted 'section 4 of the Land Registration Act 2002', and

(c) in paragraph (c), for 'Land Registration Acts 1925 to 1986' there is substituted 'Land Registration Act 2002'.

(3) For subsection (9) there is substituted—

'(9) Where the Chief Land Registrar approves an application for registration of—

(a) a disposition of registered land, or

(b)   a person's title under a disposition of unregistered land,

and the instrument effecting the initial transfer contains the statement required by subsection (3) above, he shall enter in the register a restriction reflecting the limitation under this section on subsequent disposal.'

Water Resources Act 1991 (c. 57)

25.—(1)   Section 158 of the Water Resources Act 1991 is amended as follows.

(2)   In subsection (5)—

(a)   for paragraphs (a) and (b) there is substituted—

'(a)   the agreement may be the subject of a notice in the register of title under the Land Registration Act 2002 as if it were an interest affecting the registered land;

(b)   the provisions of sections 28 to 30 of that Act (effect of dispositions of registered land on priority of adverse interests) shall apply as if the agreement were such an interest;', and

(b)   in paragraph (c), for 'where notice of the agreement has been so registered,' there is substituted 'subject to the provisions of those sections,'.

(3)   In subsection (6), for 'Land Registration Act 1925' there is substituted 'Land Registration Act 2002'.

Access to Neighbouring Land Act 1992 (c. 4)

26.—(1)   The Access to Neighbouring Land Act 1992 is amended as follows.

(2)   In section 4(1), for 'Land Registration Act 1925' there is substituted 'Land Registration Act 2002'.

(3)   In section 5, in subsection (4)—

(a)   in paragraph (b), for 'notice or caution under the Land Registration Act 1925' there is substituted 'notice under the Land Registration Act 2002', and

(b)   for 'entry, notice or caution' there is substituted 'entry or notice'.

(4)   In that section, for subsection (5) there is substituted—

'(5)   The rights conferred on a person by or under an access order shall not be capable of falling within paragraph 2 of Schedule 1 or 3 to the Land Registration Act 2002 (overriding status of interest of person in actual occupation).'

(5)   In that section, in subsection (6), for 'Land Registration Act 1925' there is substituted 'Land Registration Act 2002'.

Further and Higher Education Act 1992 (c. 13)

27.   In Schedule 5 to the Further and Higher Education Act 1992, in paragraph 6(1)—

(a)   for 'Land Registration Acts 1925 to 1986' there is substituted 'Land Registration Act 2002', and

(b)   for 'those Acts' there is substituted 'that Act'.

Judicial Pensions and Retirement Act 1993 (c. 8)

28.   In Schedule 5 to the Judicial Pensions and Retirement Act 1993, there is inserted at the end—

'Adjudicator to Her Majesty's Land Registry'

Charities Act 1993 (c. 10)

29.—(1)   The Charities Act 1993 is amended as follows.

(2)   In section 37, for subsections (7) and (8) there is substituted—

'(7)   Where the disposition to be effected by any such instrument as is mentioned in subsection (1)(b) or (5)(b) above will be—

(a)   a registrable disposition, or

(b)   a disposition which triggers the requirement of registration,

the statement which, by virtue of subsection (1) or (5) above, is to be contained in the instrument shall be in such form as may be prescribed by land registration rules.

(8)   Where the registrar approves an application for registration of—

(a)   a disposition of registered land, or

(b)   a person's title under a disposition of unregistered land,

and the instrument effecting the disposition contains a statement complying with subsections (5) and (7) above, he shall enter in the register a restriction reflecting the limitation under section 36 above on subsequent disposal.'

(3)   In that section, in subsection (9)—

(a)   for 'the restriction to be withdrawn' there is substituted 'the removal of the entry', and

(b)   for 'withdraw the restriction' there is substituted 'remove the entry'.

(4)   In that section, in subsection (11), for 'Land Registration Act 1925' there is substituted 'Land Registration Act 2002'.

(5)   In section 39, in subsection (1), at the end there is inserted 'by land registration rules'.

(6)   In that section, for subsections (1A) and (1B) there is substituted—

'(1A)   Where any such mortgage will be one to which section 4(1)(g) of the Land Registration Act 2002 applies—

(a)   the statement required by subsection (1) above shall be in such form as may be prescribed by land registration rules; and

(b)   if the charity is not an exempt charity, the mortgage shall also contain a statement, in such form as may be prescribed by land registration rules, that the restrictions on disposition imposed by section 36 above apply to the land (subject to subsection (9) of that section).

(1B)   Where—

(a)   the registrar approves an application for registration of a person's title to land in connection with such a mortgage as is mentioned in subsection (1A) above,

(b)   the mortgage contains statements complying with subsections (1) and (1A) above, and

(c)   the charity is not an exempt charity,

the registrar shall enter in the register a restriction reflecting the limitation under section 36 above on subsequent disposal.

(1C)   Section 37(9) above shall apply in relation to any restriction entered under subsection (1B) as it applies in relation to any restriction entered under section 37(8).'

(7)   In that section, in subsection (6), for the words from 'and subsections' to the end there is substituted 'and subsections (1) to (1B) above shall be construed as one with the Land Registration Act 2002'.

Leasehold Reform, Housing and Urban Development Act 1993 (c. 28)

30.—(1)   The Leasehold Reform, Housing and Urban Development Act 1993 is amended as follows.

(2) In sections 34(10) and 57(11), for the words from 'rules' to the end there is substituted 'land registration rules under the Land Registration Act 2002'.

(3) In section 97, in subsection (1)—

  (a) for 'an overriding interest within the meaning of the Land Registration Act 1925' there is substituted 'capable of falling within paragraph 2 of Schedule 1 or 3 to the Land Registration Act 2002', and

  (b) for 'or caution under the Land Registration Act 1925' there is substituted 'under the Land Registration Act 2002'.

(4) In that section, in subsection (2), for 'Land Registration Act 1925' there is substituted 'Land Registration Act 2002'.

Law of Property (Miscellaneous Provisions) Act 1994 (c. 36)

31.—(1) The Law of Property (Miscellaneous Provisions) Act 1994 is amended as follows.

(2) In section 6 (cases in which there is no liability under covenants implied by virtue of Part 1 of that Act), at the end there is inserted—

  '(4) Moreover, where the disposition is of an interest the title to which is registered under the Land Registration Act 2002, that person is not liable under any of those covenants for anything (not falling within subsection (1) or (2)) which at the time of the disposition was entered in relation to that interest in the register of title under that Act.'

(3) In section 17(3)—

  (a) in paragraph (c), for the words from 'any' to the end there is substituted 'the Adjudicator to Her Majesty's Land Registry', and

  (b) for 'section 144 of the Land Registration Act 1925' there is substituted 'the Land Registration Act 2002'.

Drug Trafficking Act 1994 (c. 37)

32.—(1) The Drug Trafficking Act 1994 is amended as follows.

(2) In section 26(12)—

  (a) for 'Land Registration Act 1925' there is substituted 'Land Registration Act 2002', and

  (b) in paragraph (a), at the end there is inserted ', except that no notice may be entered in the register of title under the Land Registration Act 2002 in respect of such orders'.

(3) In section 28(1) and (4), for 'Land Registration Act 1925' there is substituted 'Land Registration Act 2002'.

Landlord and Tenant (Covenants) Act 1995 (c. 30)

33.—(1) The Landlord and Tenant (Covenants) Act 1995 is amended as follows.

(2) In sections 3(6) and 15(5)(b), for 'Land Registration Act 1925' there is substituted 'Land Registration Act 2002'.

(3) In section 20, in subsection (2), for the words from 'rules' to the end there is substituted 'land registration rules under the Land Registration Act 2002'.

(4) In that section, in subsection (6)—

  (a) for 'an overriding interest within the meaning of the Land Registration Act 1925' there is substituted 'capable of falling within paragraph 2 of Schedule 1 or 3 to the Land Registration Act 2002', and

  (b) for 'or caution under the Land Registration Act 1925' there is substituted 'under the Land Registration Act 2002'.

Family Law Act 1996 (c. 27)

34.—(1) The Family Law Act 1996 is amended as follows.

(2) In section 31(10)—

(a) for 'Land Registration Act 1925' there is substituted 'Land Registration Act 2002', and

(b) for paragraph (b) there is substituted—

'(b) a spouse's matrimonial home rights are not to be capable of falling within paragraph 2 of Schedule 1 or 3 to that Act.'

(3) In Schedule 4, in paragraph 4(6), for 'section 144 of the Land Registration Act 1925' there is substituted 'by land registration rules under the Land Registration Act 2002'.

Housing Act 1996 (c. 52)

35. In section 13(5) of the Housing Act 1996, for the words from 'if' to the end there is substituted 'if the first disposal involves registration under the Land Registration Act 2002, the Chief Land Registrar shall enter in the register of title a restriction reflecting the limitation'.

Education Act 1996 (c. 56)

36. In Schedule 7 to the Education Act 1996, in paragraph 11—

(a) in sub-paragraph (a), for 'Land Registration Acts 1925 to 1986' there is substituted 'Land Registration Act 2002', and

(b) in sub-paragraphs (b) and (c), for 'those Acts' there is substituted 'that Act'.

School Standards and Framework Act 1998 (c. 31)

37. In Schedule 22 to the School Standards and Framework Act 1998, in paragraph 9(1)—

(a) in paragraph (a), for 'Land Registration Acts 1925 to 1986' there is substituted 'Land Registration Act 2002', and

(b) in paragraphs (b) and (c), for 'those Acts' there is substituted 'that Act'.

Terrorism Act 2000 (c. 11)

38. In Schedule 4 to the Terrorism Act 2000, in paragraph 8(1)—

(a) for 'Land Registration Act 1925' there is substituted 'Land Registration Act 2002', and

(b) in paragraph (a), at the end there is inserted ', except that no notice may be entered in the register of title under the Land Registration Act 2002 in respect of such orders'.

Finance Act 2000 (c. 17)

39. In section 128 of the Finance Act 2000—

(a) in subsection (2), for the words from 'rule' to the end there is substituted 'land registration rules under the Land Registration Act 2002', and

(b) in subsection (8)(a), for 'Land Registration Act 1925' there is substituted 'Land Registration Act 2002'.

International Criminal Court Act 2001 (c. 17)

40. In Schedule 6 to the International Criminal Court Act 2001, in paragraph 7(1)—

(a) for 'Land Registration Act 1925' there is substituted 'Land Registration Act 2002', and

(b) in paragraph (a), at the end there is inserted ', except that no notice may be entered in the register of title under the Land Registration Act 2002 in respect of such orders'.

Section 134   SCHEDULE 12
                                        TRANSITION

Existing entries in the register

1. Nothing in the repeals made by this Act affects the validity of any entry in the register.

2.—(1) This Act applies to notices entered under the Land Registration Act 1925 (c. 21) as it applies to notices entered in pursuance of an application under section 34(2)(a).

(2) This Act applies to restrictions and inhibitions entered under the Land Registration Act 1925 as it applies to restrictions entered under this Act.

(3) Notwithstanding their repeal by this Act, sections 55 and 56 of the Land Registration Act 1925 shall continue to have effect so far as relating to cautions against dealings lodged under that Act.

(4) Rules may make provision about cautions against dealings entered under the Land Registration Act 1925.

(5) In this paragraph, references to the Land Registration Act 1925 include a reference to any enactment replaced (directly or indirectly) by that Act.

3. An entry in the register which, immediately before the repeal of section 144(1)(xi) of the Land Registration Act 1925, operated by virtue of rule 239 of the Land Registration Rules (S.I. 1925/1093) as a caution under section 54 of that Act shall continue to operate as such a caution.

Existing cautions against first registration

4. Notwithstanding the repeal of section 56(3) of the Land Registration Act 1925, that provision shall continue to have effect in relation to cautions against first registration lodged under that Act, or any enactment replaced (directly or indirectly) by that Act.

Pending applications

5. Notwithstanding the repeal of the Land Registration Act 1925, that Act shall continue to have effect in relation to an application for the entry in the register of a notice, restriction, inhibition or caution against dealings which is pending immediately before the repeal of the provision under which the application is made.

6. Notwithstanding the repeal of section 53 of the Land Registration Act 1925, subsections (1) and (2) of that section shall continue to have effect in relation to an application to lodge a caution against first registration which is pending immediately before the repeal of those provisions.

Former overriding interests

7. For the period of three years beginning with the day on which Schedule 1 comes into force, it has effect with the insertion after paragraph 14 of—

'15. A right acquired under the Limitation Act 1980 before the coming into force of this Schedule.'

8. Schedule 3 has effect with the insertion after paragraph 2 of—

'2A.—(1) An interest which, immediately before the coming into force of this Schedule, was an overriding interest under section 70(1)(g) of the Land Registration Act 1925 by virtue of a person's receipt of rents and profits, except for an interest of a person of whom inquiry was made before the disposition and who failed to disclose the right when he could reasonably have been expected to do so.

(2) Sub-paragraph (1) does not apply to an interest if at any time since the coming into force of this Schedule it has been an interest which, had the Land Registration Act 1925 (c. 21) continued in force, would not have been an overriding interest under section 70(1)(g) of that Act by virtue of a person's receipt of rents and profits.'

9.—(1) This paragraph applies to an easement or profit a prendre which was an overriding interest in relation to a registered estate immediately before the coming into force of Schedule 3, but which would not fall within paragraph 3 of that Schedule if created after the coming into force of that Schedule.

(2) In relation to an interest to which this paragraph applies, Schedule 3 has effect as if the interest were not excluded from paragraph 3.

10. For the period of three years beginning with the day on which Schedule 3 comes into force, paragraph 3 of the Schedule has effect with the omission of the exception.

11. For the period of three years beginning with the day on which Schedule 3 comes into force, it has effect with the insertion after paragraph 14 of—

'15. A right under paragraph 18(1) of Schedule 12.'

12. Paragraph 1 of each of Schedules 1 and 3 shall be taken to include an interest which immediately before the coming into force of the Schedule was an overriding interest under section 70(1)(k) of the Land Registration Act 1925.

13. Paragraph 6 of each of Schedules 1 and 3 shall be taken to include an interest which immediately before the coming into force of the Schedule was an overriding interest under section 70(1)(i) of the Land Registration Act 1925 and whose status as such was preserved by section 19(3) of the Local Land Charges Act 1975 (c. 76) (transitional provision in relation to change in definition of 'local land charge').

Cautions against first registration

14.—(1) For the period of two years beginning with the day on which section 15 comes into force, it has effect with the following omissions—

(a) in subsection (1), the words 'Subject to subsection (3),', and

(b) subsection (3).

(2) Any caution lodged by virtue of sub-paragraph (1) which is in force immediately before the end of the period mentioned in that sub-paragraph shall cease to have effect at the end of that period, except in relation to applications for registration made before the end of that period.

(3) This paragraph does not apply to section 15 as applied by section 81.

15.—(1) As applied by section 81, section 15 has effect for the period of ten years beginning with the day on which it comes into force, or such longer period as rules may provide, with the omission of subsection (3)(a)(i).

(2) Any caution lodged by virtue of sub-paragraph (1) which is in force immediately before the end of the period mentioned in that sub-paragraph shall cease to have effect at

the end of that period, except in relation to applications for registration made before the end of that period.

16.   This Act shall apply as if the definition of 'caution against first registration' in section 132 included cautions lodged under section 53 of the Land Registration Act 1925 (c. 21).

Applications under section 34 or 43 by cautioners

17.   Where a caution under section 54 of the Land Registration Act 1925 is lodged in respect of a person's estate, right, interest or claim, he may only make an application under section 34 or 43 above in respect of that estate, right, interest or claim if he also applies to the registrar for the withdrawal of the caution.

Adverse possession

18.—(1)   Where a registered estate in land is held in trust for a person by virtue of section 75(1) of the Land Registration Act 1925 immediately before the coming into force of section 97, he is entitled to be registered as the proprietor of the estate.

(2)   A person has a defence to any action for the possession of land (in addition to any other defence he may have) if he is entitled under this paragraph to be registered as the proprietor of an estate in the land.

(3)   Where in an action for possession of land a court determines that a person is entitled to a defence under this paragraph, the court must order the registrar to register him as the proprietor of the estate in relation to which he is entitled under this paragraph to be registered.

(4)   Entitlement under this paragraph shall be disregarded for the purposes of section 131(1).

(5)   Rules may make transitional provision for cases where a rentcharge is held in trust under section 75(1) of the Land Registration Act 1925 immediately before the coming into force of section 97.

Indemnities

19.—(1)   Schedule 8 applies in relation to claims made before the commencement of that Schedule which have not been settled by agreement or finally determined by that time (as well as to claims for indemnity made after the commencement of that Schedule).

(2)   But paragraph 3(1) of that Schedule does not apply in relation to costs and expenses incurred in respect of proceedings, negotiations or other matters begun before 27 April 1997.

Implied indemnity covenants on transfers of pre-1996 leases

20.—(1)   On a disposition of a registered leasehold estate by way of transfer, the following covenants are implied in the instrument effecting the disposition, unless the contrary intention is expressed—

(a)   in the case of a transfer of the whole of the land comprised in the registered lease, the covenant in sub-paragraph (2), and

(b)   in the case of a transfer of part of the land comprised in the lease—

    (i)   the covenant in sub-paragraph (3), and

    (ii)   where the transferor continues to hold land under the lease, the covenant in sub-paragraph (4).

(2)   The transferee covenants with the transferor that during the residue of the term granted by the registered lease the transferee and the persons deriving title under him will—

(a)   pay the rent reserved by the lease,

(b) comply with the covenants and conditions contained in the lease, and

(c) keep the transferor and the persons deriving title under him indemnified against all actions, expenses and claims on account of any failure to comply with paragraphs (a) and (b).

(3) The transferee covenants with the transferor that during the residue of the term granted by the registered lease the transferee and the persons deriving title under him will—

(a) where the rent reserved by the lease is apportioned, pay the rent apportioned to the part transferred,

(b) comply with the covenants and conditions contained in the lease so far as affecting the part transferred, and

(c) keep the transferor and the persons deriving title under him indemnified against all actions, expenses and claims on account of any failure to comply with paragraphs (a) and (b).

(4) The transferor covenants with the transferee that during the residue of the term granted by the registered lease the transferor and the persons deriving title under him will—

(a) where the rent reserved by the lease is apportioned, pay the rent apportioned to the part retained,

(b) comply with the covenants and conditions contained in the lease so far as affecting the part retained, and

(c) keep the transferee and the persons deriving title under him indemnified against all actions, expenses and claims on account of any failure to comply with paragraphs (a) and (b).

(5) This paragraph does not apply to a lease which is a new tenancy for the purposes of section 1 of the Landlord and Tenant (Covenants) Act 1995 (c. 30).

Section 135   SCHEDULE 13
                                     REPEALS

Short title and chapter	Extent of repeal
Land Registry Act 1862 (c. 53).	The whole Act.
Settled Land Act 1925 (c. 18).	Section 119(3).
Law of Property Act 1925 (c. 20).	In section 84(8), the words from ', but' to the end. In section 205(1)(xxii), the words from ', and' to the end.
Land Registration Act 1925 (c. 21).	The whole Act.
Law of Property (Amendment) Act 1926 (c. 11).	Section 5.
Land Registration Act 1936 (c. 26).	The whole Act.
Requisitioned Land and War Works Act 1945 (c. 43).	Section 37(3).
Mental Health Act 1959 (c. 72).	In Schedule 7, the entry relating to the Land Registration Act 1925.
Charities Act 1960 (c. 58).	In Schedule 6, the entry relating to the Land Registration Act 1925.

Short title and chapter	Extent of repeal
Civil Evidence Act 1968 (c. 64).	In the Schedule, the entry relating to the Land Registration Act 1925.
Post Office Act 1969 (c. 48).	In Schedule 4, paragraph 27.
Law of Property Act 1969 (c. 59).	Section 28(7).
Land Registration and Land Charges Act 1971 (c. 54).	The whole Act.
Superannuation Act 1972 (c. 11).	In Schedule 6, paragraph 16.
Local Government Act 1972 (c. 70).	In Schedule 29, paragraph 26.
Solicitors Act 1974 (c. 47).	Section 75(b).
Finance Act 1975 (c. 7).	In Schedule 12, paragraph 5.
Local Land Charges Act 1975 (c. 76).	Section 19(3). In Schedule 1, the entry relating to the Land Registration Act 1925.
Endowments and Glebe Measure 1976 (No. 4).	In Schedule 5, paragraph 1.
Administration of Justice Act 1977 (c. 38).	Sections 24 and 26.
Charging Orders Act 1979 (c. 53).	Section 3(3). Section 7(4).
Limitation Act 1980 (c. 58).	In section 17, paragraph (b) and the preceding 'and'.
Highways Act 1980 (c. 66).	Section 251(5).
Matrimonial Homes and Property Act 1981 (c. 24).	Section 4.
Administration of Justice Act 1982 (c. 53).	Sections 66 and 67 and Schedule 5.
Mental Health Act 1983 (c. 20).	In Schedule 4, paragraph 6.
Capital Transfer Tax Act 1984 (c. 51).	In Schedule 8, paragraph 1.
Administration of Justice Act 1985 (c. 61).	In section 34, in subsection (1), paragraph (b) and the preceding 'and' and, in subsection (2), paragraph (b). In Schedule 2, paragraph 37(b).
Insolvency Act 1985 (c. 65).	In Schedule 8, paragraph 5.
Housing Act 1985 (c. 68).	Section 36(3). Section 154(1), (6) and (7). Section 156(3). Section 168(5). In Schedule 9A, paragraphs 2(1), 3 and 5(3).

Short title and chapter	Extent of repeal
Land Registration Act 1986 (c. 26).	Sections 1 to 4.
Insolvency Act 1986 (c. 45).	In Schedule 14, the entry relating to the Land Registration Act 1925.
Building Societies Act 1986 (c. 53).	In Schedule 2A, in paragraph 1, sub-paragraph (4) and, in sub-paragraph (5), the definition of 'registered land' and the preceding 'and'. In Schedule 18, paragraph 2. In Schedule 21, paragraph 9(b).
Patronage (Benefices) Measure 1986 (No. 3).	Section 6.
Landlord and Tenant Act 1987 (c. 31).	Section 28(6). In Schedule 4, paragraphs 1 and 2.
Diplomatic and Consular Premises Act 1987 (c. 46).	In Schedule 1, in paragraph 1, the words from 'and expressions' to the end.
Land Registration Act 1988 (c. 3).	The whole Act.
Criminal Justice Act 1988 (c. 33).	Section 77(13). In Schedule 15, paragraphs 6 and 7.
Housing Act 1988 (c. 50).	In Schedule 11, paragraph 2(3).
Finance Act 1989 (c. 26).	Sections 178(2)(e) and 179(1)(a)(iv).
Courts and Legal Services Act 1990 (c. 41).	In Schedule 10, paragraph 3. In Schedule 17, paragraph 2.
Access to Neighbouring Land Act 1992 (c. 23).	Section 5(2) and (3).
Leasehold Reform, Housing and Urban Development Act 1993 (c. 28).	Section 97(3). In Schedule 21, paragraph 1.
Coal Industry Act 1994 (c. 21).	In Schedule 9, paragraph 1.
Law of Property (Miscellaneous Provisions) Act 1994 (c. 36).	In Schedule 1, paragraph 2.
Drug Trafficking Act 1994 (c. 37).	Section 26(13). In Schedule 1, paragraph 1.
Family Law Act 1996 (c. 27).	Section 31(11). In Schedule 8, paragraph 45.
Trusts of Land and Appointment of Trustees Act 1996 (c. 47).	In Schedule 3, paragraph 5.
Housing Act 1996 (c. 52).	Section 11(4).

Short title and chapter	Extent of repeal
Housing Grants, Construction and Regeneration Act 1996 (c. 53).	Section 138(3).
Land Registration Act 1997 (c. 2).	Sections 1 to 3 and 5(4) and (5). In Schedule 1, paragraphs 1 to 6.
Greater London Authority Act 1999 (c. 29).	Section 219.
Terrorism Act 2000 (c. 11).	In Schedule 4, paragraph 8(2) and (3).
Trustee Act 2000 (c. 29).	In Schedule 2, paragraph 26.
International Criminal Court Act 2001 (c. 17).	In Schedule 6, paragraph 7(2).

Index